W9-BMN-762

Frommer's®

MEMORABLE WALKS IN
NEW YORK

6th Edition

Ethan Wolff

WILEY

Wiley Publishing, Inc.

Published by:

WILEY PUBLISHING, INC.

111 River St.
Hoboken, NJ 07030-5774

ISBN-13: 978-0-471-77339-9
ISBN-10: 0-471-77339-5

Editor: Chris Summers
Production Editor: Katie Robinson
Photo Editor: Richard Fox
Cartographer: Andy Dolan
Production by Wiley Indianapolis Composition Services
Front cover photo: Sidewalk with Café Restaurant, Greenwich Village

For information on our other products and services or to obtain technical support, please contact our Customer Care Department within the
U.S. at 800/762-2974, outside the U.S. at 317/572-3993 or fax
317/572-4002.

Wiley also publishes its books in a variety of electronic formats. Some
content that appears in print may not be available in electronic formats.

Contents

LIST OF MAPS

The Walking Tours

• • • • • • • • • • • • • • • • •

About the Author

Ethan Wolff is a native New Yorker (born and raised in Virginia, but that was a geographic anomaly). When not walking around Manhattan, Ethan enjoys being cheap and irreverent. His other Frommer's guides are *NYC Free & Dirt Cheap* and the *Irreverent Guide to Manhattan*.

Acknowledgments

Special thanks to John Vorwald for sharing the load. Thanks also to Abby Lindenberg, Anna Sandler, Evelyn Grollman, Jenny Bauer, and Roy Wolff for helping to walk.

An Invitation to the Reader

In researching this book, we discovered many wonderful places—hotels, restaurants, shops, and more. We're sure you'll find others. Please tell us about them, so we can share the information with your fellow travelers in upcoming editions. If you were disappointed with a recommendation, we'd love to know that, too. Please write to:

Frommer's Memorable Walks in New York, 6th Edition
Wiley Publishing, Inc.
111 River St. • Hoboken, NJ 07030-5774

An Additional Note

Please be advised that travel information is subject to change at any time—and this is especially true of prices. We therefore suggest that you write or call ahead for confirmation when making your travel plans. The authors, editors, and publisher cannot be held responsible for the experiences of readers while traveling. Your safety is important to us, however, so we encourage you to stay alert and be aware of your surroundings. Keep a close eye on cameras, purses, and wallets, all favorite targets of thieves and pickpockets.

Frommers.com

Now that you have the guidebook to a great trip, visit our website at **www.frommers.com** for travel information on more than 3,000 destinations. With features updated regularly, we give you instant access to the most current trip-planning information available. At Frommers.com, you'll also find the best prices on airfares, accommodations, and car rentals—and you can even book travel online through our travel booking partners. At Frommers.com, you'll also find the following:

- Online updates to our most popular guidebooks
- Vacation sweepstakes and contest giveaways
- Newsletter highlighting the hottest travel trends
- Online travel message boards with featured travel discussions

Introducing
New York

Grasping the big picture of New York all at once is next to impossible. The best way to get to know this amazingly complex city is to do as New Yorkers do: Concentrate on small nooks and crannies rather than the whole. Define the city through its neighborhoods and pay close attention to every detail of architecture, image, and life.

As you explore, you'll run across tiny, funky flower gardens that have sprung up around sidewalk trees, a shop specializing in light bulbs, and a cafe concentrating on peanut butter. You'll find plaques identifying historic buildings, hidden-away public art installations, and ethnic food carts. Once you get a little distance from the major museums and sights, you'll discover the Manhattan in which the rocks in Central Park acquire names, businessmen *schvitz* (Yiddish for sweat) in a Russian bathhouse, and Zabar's grocery store tracks down an unknown cheese in the Pyrenees to introduce to Upper West Siders.

Walking is by far the superior way to see this city. Large-scale New York can seem chaotic, dirty, expensive, and frightening. But on the small scale, in the details, New York gives up its secrets. A focused stroll brings the city back to its constituent parts, to the small communities from which it was formed, and which today maintain their own distinct identities within the seemingly endless metropolis.

MIXED NUTS & MICHELANGELOS

Quentin Crisp once said, "Everyone in Manhattan is a star or a star manqué, and every flat surface in the island is a stage." Street performers run the gamut from a tuxedoed gent who does Fred-and-Ginger ballroom dances with a life-size rag doll (usually in front of the Metropolitan Museum) to the circus-caliber acrobats and stand-up comics who attract large audiences in Washington Square Park. Street musicians range from steel-drum bands and Ecuadorian flute players to the pianist with his candelabra-adorned baby grand perched atop a truck.

Street art abounds. Here and there, especially in the East Village, little mosaic-tile designs pop up to adorn the sidewalk and streetlight pedestals. An area artist created them from cracked plates and crockery picked from people's trash. Today Gotham's walls and street signs are impromptu art galleries featuring posters, stencils, paintings, and even sticker clothes and accessories for the stylized pedestrians on walk/don't walk signs. In New York, nothing can remain small-time for long. By the '80s graffiti was an established art form, and the more highbrow street doodlers such as Keith Haring and Kenny Schraf became international stars.

TENEMENTS & TOWN HOUSES

New York is a city of extraordinarily diverse architecture. The Financial District's neoclassic "temples"—embellished with allegorical statuary, massive colonnades, vaulted domes, and vast marble lobbies—stand side by side with the soaring skyscrapers that make up the world's most famous skyline.

The history of immigrant groups is manifest in the ramshackle tenements of Chinatown and the Lower East Side. SoHo's cast-iron facades hearken back to the ideals of the industrial era, when architectural design first encountered the principles of mass production and became accessible to everyone.

In Greenwich Village, you'll see the stately Greek Revival town houses where Henry James and Edith Wharton lived. Uptown, magnificent private mansions built for the Vanderbilts and the Whitneys, and gargantuan, tony apartment houses overlook Central Park, itself one of the world's most impressive urban greenbelts.

No wonder quintessential New Yorker Woody Allen was inspired to pay tribute to the city's architectural diversity by

The Tours at a Glance

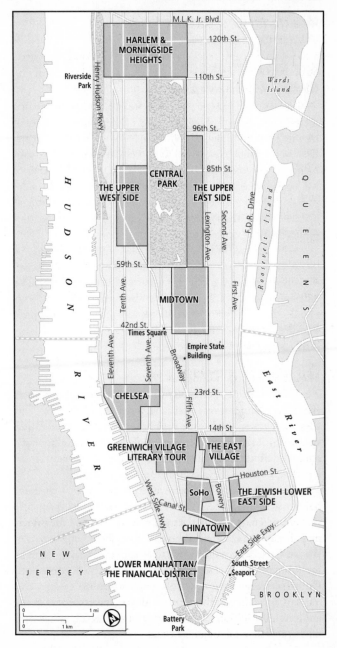

- M.L.K. Jr. Blvd.
- 120th St.
- 110th St.
- 96th St.
- 85th St.
- 59th St.
- 42nd St.
- 23rd St.
- 14th St.

HARLEM & MORNINGSIDE HEIGHTS

THE UPPER WEST SIDE

CENTRAL PARK

THE UPPER EAST SIDE

MIDTOWN

CHELSEA

GREENWICH VILLAGE LITERARY TOUR

THE EAST VILLAGE

SoHo

THE JEWISH LOWER EAST SIDE

CHINATOWN

LOWER MANHATTAN/ THE FINANCIAL DISTRICT

Riverside Park

Henry Hudson Pkwy.

H U D S O N   R I V E R

Tenth Ave.

Eleventh Ave.

Seventh Ave.

Broadway

Fifth Ave.

West Side Hwy.

Canal St.

Bowery

Times Square

Empire State Building

Houston St.

South Street Seaport

Battery Park

Lexington Ave.

Second Ave.

First Ave.

F.D.R. Drive

Wards Island

Roosevelt Island

East Side Expy.

East River

Q U E E N S

NEW JERSEY

BROOKLYN

0   1 mi
0   1 km

including an otherwise gratuitous tour of his favorite buildings in the movie *Hannah and Her Sisters.*

THE NEIGHBORHOODS: BOK CHOY, BEADS & BOHEMIANS

Though the city has been called more of a boiling pot than a melting pot, New Yorkers are proud of the ethnic diversity of the city's neighborhoods. From the days of the early Dutch settlers, immigrants have striven to re-create their native environments in selected neighborhoods. Hence, the restaurants of Mulberry Street, with convivial cafes spilling onto the sidewalks, evoke the streets of Palermo, and Orthodox Jews still operate shops that evolved from turn-of-the-20th-century pushcarts along cobblestoned Orchard Street.

Chinatown, home to more than 160,000 Chinese, is probably New York's most extensive ethnic area, and it's continually expanding, gobbling up parts of the old Lower East Side and Little Italy. Its narrow, winding streets are lined with noodle shops, Chinese vegetable vendors, small curio stores, Buddhist temples, Chinese movie theaters, and several hundred restaurants. New Yorkers don't talk about going out for Chinese food; they specify Sichuan, Hunan, Cantonese, Mandarin, Fukien, or dim sum.

The remnants of the East Village's Ukrainian population can be seen in holdover restaurants serving borscht, blini, and pierogi. Ukrainian folk arts, such as intricately painted Easter eggs, beautifully embroidered peasant blouses, and illuminated manuscripts, are displayed in local shops and even warrant a museum.

There are Hispanic, Czech, German, Greek, Hungarian, Indian, Russian, Arab, and West Indian parts of town as well. But ethnic groups are not the only factor defining New York neighborhoods; commerce also delineates areas. On the streets around Broadway from Macy's to about 39th Street, you're in the heart of the Garment District, where artists race through the streets carrying large portfolios of next season's designs, trying not to collide with workers pushing racks of this year's fashions. Also distinct are the city's bead, book, feather, fur, flower, toy, diamond, and, of course, theater districts.

Different neighborhoods attract different residents. The Upper East Side is where old money lives; rumpled intellectuals prefer the Upper West Side. Young trendies and aging hippies live in the East Village; old bohemians live in the West Village. The West Village and Chelsea are home to sizable gay populations, and the streets they've beautified have proved a magnet for yuppies. These are largely generalizations, of course, but each area does have its own flavor. You probably won't find designer clothing on St. Marks Place. On the other hand, a Madison Avenue boutique is unlikely to carry S&M leather wear. Midtown is the city's main shopping area, the site of ever-diminishing grand department stores. Broadway dissects the town diagonally; though it's most famous for the glitz and glitter of the Great White Way, it spans Manhattan from Battery Park to the Bronx.

IF YOU CAN MAKE IT HERE . . .

New York is, and always has been, a mecca for the ambitious. And though only a small percentage of the ardently aspiring become famous—or even manage to eke out a living—the effort keeps New Yorkers keen-witted, intense, and on the cutting edge.

New York is America's business and financial center, where major deals have gone down over power lunches since the days when Thomas Jefferson and Alexander Hamilton chose the site for the nation's capital over a meal at a Manhattan restaurant. Every major book and magazine publisher is based here. It's an international media and fashion center as well. New York galleries set worldwide art trends. And a lead in a play in Galveston, Texas, is less impressive than a bit part on Broadway. (At least New Yorkers think so.)

For that reason, it seems that almost every famous artist, writer, musician, and actor has, at one time or another, resided in Gotham. This town thrives on the accessibility of its public space, and you'll probably rub elbows with, or at least catch a glimpse of, a celebrity or two. If not, there's always the thrill of downing a drink or two in bars that Dylan Thomas or Jackson Pollock frequented, visiting the Greenwich Village haunts of the Beat Generation, peering up at what was once Edgar Allan Poe's bedroom window, or dining at the Algonquin Hotel where Round Table wits Dorothy Parker, Alexander Woollcott, and George S. Kaufman traded barbs in the 1920s.

The presence of so many movers and shakers gives New York vitality and sophistication. When you study film at the New School or NYU or Columbia, your lecturers are Martin Scorsese, Sydney Pollack, Barry Levinson, and Spike Lee. Robert Wilson and James Levine are at one Met (the Metropolitan Opera), and everyone from Raphael to Rembrandt is at the other (the Metropolitan Museum of Art). Few bookstores are as great as the Strand, no food shop is as alluring as Zabar's (except perhaps Dean & Deluca), no department store is a match for Bloomie's or Macy's, and no mall is comparable to Orchard Street. Where else can you easily satisfy a craving for Thai noodles at 3am? Or have your choice of dozens of art-house and foreign movies on the big screen nightly, many of which will never play in most American towns?

Visitors often question how New Yorkers stand the constant noise, the rudeness, the filth, the outrageous rents and prices, the crime, the crazies, or even one another. But though New Yorkers frequently talk about leaving the city, most find countless reasons to stay. They've created a unique frame of reference, and it doesn't travel well. The constant stimulation feeds Gothamites' creativity. To quote theatrical impresario Joseph Papp, "Creative people get inspiration from their immediate environment, and New York has the most immediate environment in the world."

Lower Manhattan/The Financial District

Start: Battery Park/U.S. Customs House.

Subway: Take the 4 or 5 to Bowling Green, the 1 to South Ferry, or the R or W to Whitehall Street.

Finish: African Burial Ground.

Time: Approximately 3 hours.

Best Time: Any weekday, when the wheels of finance are spinning and lower Manhattan is a maelstrom of activity.

Worst Time: Weekends, when most buildings and all the financial markets are closed.

The narrow, winding streets of the Financial District occupy the earliest-settled area of

Manhattan, where Dutch settlers established the colony of Nieuw Amsterdam in the early 17th century. Before their arrival, downtown was part of a vast forest, a lush hunting ground for Native Americans that was inhabited by mountain lions, bobcats, beavers, white-tailed deer, and wild turkeys. Hunters followed the Wiechquaekeck Trail, a path through the center that today is more often referred to as Broadway.

This section of the city still centers on commerce, much as Nieuw Amsterdam did. Wall Street is America's strongest symbol of money and power; bulls and bears have replaced the wild beasts of the forest, and conservatively attired lawyers, stockbrokers, bankers, and businesspeople have supplanted the Native Americans and Dutch who once traded otter skins and beaver pelts on these very streets.

A highlight of this tour is the Financial District's architecture, in which the neighborhood's modern edifices and grand historical structures are dramatically juxtaposed: Colonial, 18th-century Georgian/Federal, and 19th-century neoclassical buildings stand in the shadow of colossal modern skyscrapers.

Much changed on September 11, 2001, when Lower Manhattan lost its greatest landmark, New York lost a familiar chunk of its skyline, America lost a share of its innocence, and more than 2,700 people lost their lives as a pair of planes commandeered by Osama bin Laden's Al Qaeda terrorists plowed into the Twin Towers of the World Trade Center. Those horrific events have etched themselves into all our memories. Nothing that can be said here can do justice to the heroism of the firefighters and other emergency workers who rushed into the burning buildings to help, only to perish when the towers collapsed. Paying respects at Ground Zero, amid the communal spirit that at times prevails there, may be the best way to acknowledge the incredible sacrifices so many people made that day. The surrounding neighborhood has been remarkably resilient, but it is still in varying stages of recovery. There is a subtle feel of besiegement here, with security an often-visible presence. Expect to pass through metal detectors to access many of the buildings.

●●●●●●●●●●●●●●●●●

The subways mentioned above all exit in or near **Battery Park,** an expanse of green at Manhattan's tip resting

Lower Manhattan/The Financial District

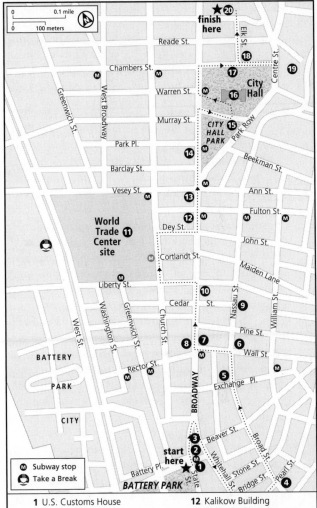

1 U.S. Customs House	12 Kalikow Building
2 Bowling Green Park	13 St. Paul's Chapel
3 Cunard Building	14 Woolworth Building
4 Fraunces Tavern Museum	15 City Hall Park
5 New York Stock Exchange	16 City Hall
6 Federal Hall National Memorial	17 Tweed Courthouse
7 Wall Street	18 Surrogate's Court
8 Trinity Church	(The Hall of Records)
9 Jean Dubuffet's *Group of Four Trees*	19 The Municipal Building
10 Isamu Noguchi's 1967 *The Red Cube*	20 African Burial Ground
11 Ground Zero	

entirely upon a landfill—an old strategy of the Dutch to expand their settlement farther into the bay. The original tip of Manhattan ran along Battery Place, which borders the north side of the park. State Street flanks the park's east side, and stretched along it, filling the space below Bowling Green, is the Beaux Arts bulk of the old:

1. **U.S. Customs House,** home to the Smithsonian's National Museum of the American Indian (© 212/514-3700; www.si.edu/nmai) since 1994. The giant statues lining the front of this granite 1907 structure personify Asia (pondering philosophically), America (bright-eyed and bushy-tailed), Europe (decadent, whose time has passed), and Africa (sleeping) and were carved by Daniel Chester French of Lincoln Memorial fame. The most interesting, if unintentional, sculptural statement—keeping in mind the building's new purpose—is the giant seated woman to the left of the entrance, representing America. The young, upstart America is surrounded by references to Native America: Mayan pictographs on her throne, Quetzalcoatl (an Aztec god symbolized by a feathered serpent) under her foot, a shock of corn in her lap, and a Plains Indian scout over her shoulder.

   The airy oval rotunda inside was frescoed by Reginald Marsh to glorify the shipping industry (and, by extension, the customs office once here). Housing Native American treasures in a former arm of the federal government seems a bit of a cruel irony, but the well-curated exhibits here convey a sense of reverence. Native American art, culture, history, and contemporary issues are presented in sophisticated and thought-provoking ways. The museum is free and highly recommended, open daily 10am to 5pm (to 8pm Thurs).

Kid-Friendly Experiences

- Visiting the National Museum of the American Indian in the old U.S. Customs House (stop 1)
- Riding the Bronze Bull on Broadway (stop 3)

As you exit the building, directly in front of you sits the pretty little oasis of:

2. **Bowling Green Park.** In 1626, Dutchman Peter Minuit stood at this spot (or somewhere close to it) and gave glass beads and other trinkets worth about 60 guilders ($24) to a group of Indians, and claimed that he had thereby bought Manhattan. However, the local Indians didn't consider that they owned this island in the first place because Manhattan ("land of many hills" is the most likely translation from the native tongue) was a communal hunting ground. (The idea that the Indians didn't believe in property is a colonial myth; the Indians had their own territories nearby.) It isn't clear what the Indians thought the trinkets meant. Either (a) they just thought the exchange was a formal way, one to which they were accustomed, of closing an agreement to extend the shared hunting use of the island to this funny-looking group of pale people with yellow beards, or (b) they were knowingly selling land that they didn't own in the first place and thus performing the first of many thousands of such deals in the Financial District. They may have also tried to sell Minuit a bridge just up the river a ways, but he was too busy fortifying his little town of Nieuw Amsterdam to listen. There's evidence that the "sellers" of Manhattan were of the Canarsie tribe from what is today Brooklyn.

Although Bowling Green Park today is just another lunch spot for stockbrokers, when King George III repealed the hated Stamp Act in 1770, New Yorkers magnanimously raised a statue of him here. The statue lasted 5 years, until the day the Declaration of Independence was read to the public in front of City Hall (now Federal Hall) up the street and a crowd rushed down Broadway to topple the statue, chop it up, melt it down, and transform it into 42,000 bullets with which to shoot the British.

The park also marks the start of Broadway—which, if you follow it far enough, leads to Albany. Walk up the left side of Broadway, past the Cunard Building at no. 25. In 1921, this was the ticketing room for Cunard, one of the world's most glamorous shipping and cruise lines and the proprietor of the *QEII*. The deteriorating churchlike ceiling sheltered the local post office until 2005.

Cross to the traffic island to pat the enormous:

3. **Bronze bull,** reared back and ready to charge up Broadway. This symbol of an up stock market began as a practical joke by Italian sculptor Arturo DiModica, who originally stuck it in front of the New York Stock Exchange building in the middle of the night in 1989. The unamused brokers had it promptly removed, and it was eventually placed here.

Turn right to head south on Broadway, on the left side of the U.S. Customs House on Whitehall Street. Take a left onto Pearl Street; just past Broad Street stretches a historic block lined with (partially rebuilt) 18th- and 19th-century buildings. The two upper stories of 54 Pearl St. house the:

4. **Fraunces Tavern Museum** (✆ 212/425-1778; www. frauncestavernmuseum.org), where you can view the room in which Washington's historic farewell to his officers took place on December 4, 1783 (today, it's set up to represent a typical 18th-century tavern room), among other American history exhibits. A moderate admission fee is charged. Hours are Tuesday through Friday from noon to 5pm, and Saturday from 10am to 5pm. The restaurant in the posh, oak-paneled dining room and adjacent pub emerged from several years of extensive renovations in the fall of 2001, which inexplicably did away with much of the wonderful old clubby feel of the place, leaving it rather staid and uninspired. The food's good, but pricey.

From Fraunces Tavern, head straight up Broad Street past the lunch spots that cater to harried brokers. At no. 20, on the left, is the main entrance to the:

5. **New York Stock Exchange** (✆ 212/656-3000; www. nyse.com), which is near the buttonwood tree where merchants met as long ago as 1792 to try and pass off to each other the U.S. bonds that had been sold to fund the Revolutionary War. By 1903, they were trading stocks of publicly held companies in this Corinthian-columned,

Beaux Arts "temple" designed by George Post. Close to 2,800 companies are listed on the exchange, where 1.46 billion shares with a value of $46 billion are traded on an average day.

Sadly, the new security measures have put a stop to tours, which used to allow visitors to peer out at the trading floor from an observation deck where Abbie Hoffman and Jerry Rubin once created chaos by tossing dollar bills in the 1960s. The clunky metal fencing outside the building has the look of a cattle stockade, which may be somewhat appropriate given the recent performance of the market.

Continue north (left) up Broad Street. At the end of the block, you'll see the Parthenon-inspired:

6. **Federal Hall National Memorial,** 26 Wall St. at Nassau Street (*©* **212/825-6990;** www.nps.gov/feha). Fronted by 32-foot fluted marble Doric columns, this imposing 1842 neoclassical temple is built on the site of the British City Hall building, later called Federal Hall. Peter Zenger, publisher of the outspoken *Weekly Journal,* stood trial in 1735 for "seditious libel" against Royal Gov. William Cosby. Defended brilliantly by Alexander Hamilton, Zenger was eventually acquitted (based on the grounds that anything that is printed that is true, even if it isn't very nice, can't be construed as libel), and his acquittal set the precedent for freedom of the press, later guaranteed in the Bill of Rights, which was drafted and signed inside the original structure here.

New York's first major rebellion against British authority occurred here when the Stamp Act Congress met in 1765 to protest King George III's policy of "taxation without representation." J. Q. A. Ward's 1883 statue of George Washington on the steps commemorates the spot of the first presidential inauguration in 1789. Congress met here after the revolution, when New York was briefly the nation's capital.

The majority of historically significant events that occurred on this spot predated the construction of the current building, which began as a customs house and then became a treasury. The foundation was damaged in the 9/11 attacks and the Park Service has closed the museum for repairs, with a gala reopening scheduled for September 2006.

Facing Federal Hall, turn left up the road that has become the symbol of high finance the world over:

7. **Wall Street.** This narrow street, which is just a few short blocks long, started out as a service road that ran along the fortified wall that the Dutch erected in 1653 to defend against Indian attack. (Gov. Peter Stuyvesant's settlers had at first played off tribes against each other in order to trick them into ceding more and more land, but the native groups quickly realized that their real enemies were the Dutch.) Today's fortifications come in the form of security checkpoints, which may force slight detours as you work your way back to Broadway, across the street from:

8. **Trinity Church** (© 212/602-0800; www.trinitywallstreet. org). Serving God and mammon, this Wall Street house of worship—with neo-Gothic flying buttresses, beautiful stained-glass windows, and vaulted ceilings—was designed by Richard Upjohn and consecrated in 1846. At that time, its 280-foot spire dominated the skyline. Its main doors, embellished with biblical scenes, were inspired in part by Ghiberti's famed doors on Florence's Baptistery. The first church on this site was built in 1697 and burned down in 1776.

The church runs a brief tour daily at 2pm, with an additional tour Sunday morning following the 11:15am service. A small museum at the end of the left aisle displays documents (including the 1697 church charter from King William III), photographs, replicas of the Hamilton-Burr duel pistols, and other items. Capt. James Lawrence, whose famous last words were, "Don't give up the ship," and Alexander Hamilton are buried in the churchyard (against the south fence, next to steamboat inventor Robert Fulton), where the oldest grave dates from 1681. The newest item in the churchyard is a red, spider-like cast of the roots of one of the church's sycamore trees, felled by debris on 9/11. The sculpture, *Trinity Root,* by Steve Tobin, makes an eerie organic intrusion into an otherwise marble and stone environment.

Thursdays at 1pm, Trinity holds its Concerts at One series of chamber music and orchestral concerts. Call © **212/602-0747** for details.

Take a left out of the church and head back up Broadway. At your feet you will see enigmatic captions, embedded in the sidewalks of lower Broadway. The dates and events recorded in granite correspond to the ticker-tape parades that have passed along this stretch of Broadway, sometimes referred to as the Canyon of Heroes. The canyon appellation is easy to understand as you look up at the looming buildings. Across Broadway, the Equitable Tower, at no. 120, is a monolith that maximizes its available lot at the expense of light and air for everyone else. After its 1915 construction, New York was inspired to pass its first zoning laws. As you pass Cedar Street, look (don't walk) to your right, across Broadway, and down Cedar Street. At the end of the street, you'll see:

9. **Jean Dubuffet's Group of Four Trees.** Installed in 1972, these amorphous mushroomlike white shapes traced with undulating black lines are representative of the artist's patented style. Dubuffet considered these installations as drawings in three dimensions "which extend and expand into space."

Closer at hand, in front of the tall, black Marine Midlank Bank building on Broadway between Cedar and Liberty streets, is:

10. **Isamu Noguchi's 1967 The Red Cube,** another famed outdoor sculpture of downtown Manhattan. Noguchi fancied that this rhomboid "cube" balancing on its corner and shot through with a cylinder of empty space represented chance, like the "rolling of the dice." This sculpture is appropriately located in the gilt-edged gambling den that is the Financial District.

As you're looking at *The Red Cube* across Broadway, turn around to walk down Liberty Plaza/Liberty Street toward the gaping rent in the fabric of Manhattan:

11. **Ground Zero,** the somber hole in the ground where the World Trade Center once stood. Opened in 1970 under the auspices of the Port Authority, this immense complex

covered 12 million square feet of rentable office space, with 50,000 permanent workers and some 70,000 others (tourists and businesspeople) visiting each day. In the first few months after 9/11, Ground Zero was a dramatic sight. Twisted World Trade Center wreckage rose out of a steaming hole and no matter how many times you went by, it still came as a punch in the stomach. With the rubble long cleared, however, the initial raw horror of the scene is gone. Ground Zero today is indistinguishable from a run-of-the-mill construction pit if you don't know that it's also a final resting place. The ad hoc memorials that originally surrounded the site have been replaced by a uniform series of placards along the fence at Church Street, just south of the newly reopened PATH train station.

Take a Break For a view of Ground Zero with a little perspective, head west toward the World Financial Center's Winter Garden (© **212/945-2600;** open 24 hours), in the center of the enclosed mall complex. The Winter Garden was all but destroyed by the collapsing towers, but you'd never guess it to look at the towering Washingtonia robusta palm trees and gleaming marble inside the atrium. Beneath the stairs you'll find a temporary exhibit outlining the plans for the site, which will hopefully someday include a worthy memorial in addition to the inevitable corporate skyscraper. Walk up the stairs to the panoramic windows and you'll have an elevated view of Ground Zero.

Varied dining choices—everything from pub fare to gourmet pizzas—are scattered throughout the World Financial Center. The lower, west side overlooks a yacht harbor and a pleasant cement park with outdoor tables, weather permitting.

Continue north on Church Street to turn right down Dey Street back to Broadway. Take a left, and on your left is the:

12. **Kalikow Building,** 195 Broadway. This neoclassical tower that dates from 1915 to 1922 is the former headquarters of AT&T and has more exterior columns than any other building in the world. The 25-story structure

rests on a Doric colonnade, with Ionic colonnades above. The lobby evokes a Greek temple with a forest of massive fluted columns. The building's tower crown is modeled on the Mausoleum of Halicarnassus, a great Greek monument of antiquity. The bronze panels over the entranceway by Paul Manship (sculptor of Rockefeller Center's Prometheus) symbolize wind, air, fire, and earth.

Continue north on Broadway. The next block, between Vesey and Fulton streets, contains the small:

13. **St. Paul's Chapel** (✆ 212/233-4164; www.saint paulschapel.org), dating from 1764, is New York's only surviving pre-Revolutionary church. During the 2 years that New York was the nation's capital, George Washington worshipped at this Georgian chapel belonging to Trinity Church; his pew is on the right side of the church, beneath a 1795 painting of the Great Seal, in one of its earliest renditions. Built by Thomas McBean, with a templelike portico and fluted Ionic columns supporting a massive pediment, the chapel resembles London's St. Martin's-in-the-Fields. In the months following the September 11, 2001, terrorist attacks, the chapel became a center for the workers and volunteers to wash up, get something to eat or drink, nap on the pews or on cots, and receive relief in the form of free chiropractic care, massages, and, of course, spiritual counseling. Explore the small graveyard in back, where the ancient headstones restore human scale to a chaotic corner, and provide additional context for the eerie prairie that is Ground Zero. Trinity's Concerts at One series is held here each Monday, featuring a variety of musical performances, from Japanese koto players to brass quartets.

Continue up Broadway, crossing Vesey and Barclay streets, and at 233 Broadway is the:

14. **Woolworth Building.** This soaring "cathedral of commerce" cost Frank W. Woolworth $13.5 million worth of nickels and dimes in 1913. Designed by Cass Gilbert, it was the world's tallest edifice until 1930, when 40 Wall Street and the Chrysler Building surpassed it. The neo-Gothic architecture is rife with spires, gargoyles, flying

buttresses, vaulted ceilings, 16th-century–style stone-as-lace traceries, castlelike turrets, and a churchlike interior.

To get an overview of the Woolworth Building's architecture, cross Broadway. On this side of the street, you'll find scurrying city officials and growing greenery that together make up:

15. **City Hall Park,** a 250-year-old green surrounded by landmark buildings. A Frederick MacMonnies statue near the southwest corner of the park depicts Nathan Hale at age 21, having just uttered his famous words before execution: "I only regret that I have but one life to lose for my country." Northeast of City Hall in the park is a statue of *New York Tribune* founding editor Horace Greeley (seated with newspaper in hand) by J. Q. A. Ward. This small park has been a burial ground for paupers and the site of public executions, parades, and protests.

It now provides the setting for:

16. **City Hall,** the seat of the municipal government, housing the offices of the mayor and his staff, the city council, and other city agencies. City Hall combines Georgian and French Renaissance styles and was designed by Joseph F. Mangin and John McComb Jr. Later additions include the clock and 6,000-pound bell in the cupola tower. The cupola itself is crowned with a stately, white-painted copper statue of Justice. At its opening in 1812, City Hall marked the northern terminus of New York. Since the back of the building was just facing the hills, the city finished that side in cheap sandstone, as opposed to the marble and granite employed in front. (During a later renovation, the city re-clad the back to make the entire exterior uniform.)

City Hall contains quite an impressive collection of American art, including works by George Caitlin, Thomas Sully, Samuel B. Morse, and Rembrandt Peale. The elegant Governor's Room upstairs, where Lafayette was received in 1824, houses Washington's writing desk, his inaugural flag, and artwork by well-known American artists. The building may be visited via a guided tour (call ✆ **212/788-2170** for information and reservations), which is conducted in tandem with a tour of the:

17. **Tweed Courthouse** (52 Chambers St., at the north end
    of City Hall Park). This 1872 Italianate courthouse was
    built during the tenure of William Marcy "Boss" Tweed,
    who, in his post on the board of supervisors, stole millions
    in construction funds. Originally budgeted as a $250,000
    job in 1861, the courthouse project escalated to the stag-
    gering sum of $14 million. Bills were padded to an
    unprecedented extent—Andrew Garvey, who was to
    become known as the "Prince of Plasterers," was paid
    $45,967 for a single day's work! The ensuing scandal
    (Tweed and his cronies were discovered to have pocketed
    at least $10 million) wrecked Tweed's career; he died pen-
    niless in jail after being convicted at trial in, of all places,
    the Tweed Courthouse. The building was meticulously
    restored in 1999 and is now the headquarters for the
    Department of Education.

    Across Chambers Street and to the right, at the corner
    of Elk Street, lies the turn-of-the-20th-century:

18. **Surrogate's Court (The Hall of Records),** 31
    Chambers St. Housed in this sumptuous Beaux Arts
    structure are all the legal records relating to Manhattan
    real estate deeds and court cases, some dating from the
    mid-1600s. Heroic statues of distinguished New Yorkers
    (Peter Stuyvesant, De Witt Clinton, and others) front the
    mansard roof. The doorways, surmounted by arched ped-
    iments, are flanked by Philip Martiny's sculptural groups
    portraying New York in Revolutionary Times (to your
    left) and New York in Its Infancy (to your right). Above
    the entrance is a three-story Corinthian colonnade.

    Step inside to see the vestibule's beautiful barrel-vault-
    ed mosaic ceiling, embellished with astrological symbols,
    Egyptian and Greek motifs, and figures representing ret-
    ribution, justice, sorrow, and labor. Continue back to the
    two-story sky-lit neoclassical atrium, clad in honey-
    colored marble with a colonnaded second-floor loggia and
    an ornate staircase adapted from the foyer of the Grand
    Opera House in Paris.

    Exiting the Surrogate's Court from the front door,
    you'll see to your left, at the end of the block, that
    Chambers Street disappears under:

19. **The Municipal Building,** a grand civic edifice built between 1909 and 1914 to augment City Hall's government office space. The famed architectural firm of McKim, Mead, and White (as in Stanford White) used Greek and Roman design elements such as a massive Corinthian colonnade, ornately embellished vaults and cornices, and allegorical statuary in their design for this building. A triumphal arch, its barrel-vaulted ceiling adorned with relief panels, forms a magnificent arcade over Chambers Street; this arch has been called the "gate of the city." Sculptor Adolph Weinman created many of the building's bas-reliefs, medallions, and allegorical groupings of human figures (they symbolize civic pride, progress, guidance, prudence, and executive power). Weinman also designed the heroic hammered-copper statue of Civic Fame that tops the Municipal Building 582 feet above the street. This statue, which is the largest one in Manhattan, holds a crown with five turrets that represent New York's five boroughs.

See lots of lovey-dovey couples walking in and out? The city's marriage license bureau is on the second floor, and a wedding takes place about every 20 minutes.

Turn around on Chambers and take a right on Elk Street. At the second corner, Duane Street, look to your left for the:

20. **African Burial Ground** (© 212/264-2201; www. africanburialground.gov). This small lot was originally intended to be part of a federal building constructed at 290 Broadway. In 1991, during excavation, the remains of over 400 Africans were discovered. The government initially intended to go forward with construction, but community protest led to this section being preserved as a graveyard, with the remains re-interred after extensive study. In September 2005, a groundbreaking ceremony was held for a permanent memorial designed by architect Rodney Leon. Used by Africans from the late 1600s until 1795, this plot is only a tiny portion of a forgotten burial ground that stretches five city blocks. In some ways it serves as a microcosm for the neighborhood, where history layers on top of history, and the present never wholly sheds the context of the past.

Chinatown

Start: The intersection of Broadway and Canal Street.
Subway: Take the 6, N, Q, R, W, J, M, or Z to Canal Street.
Finish: The intersection of East Broadway and Rutgers Street.
Time: 2 to 3 hours, not including restaurant stops.
Best Time: Anytime the weather is good for walking.

T he main draw in China-
town is the food; the neighborhood's 400-odd restaurants have
satisfied New Yorkers' cravings for Cantonese, Hunan, and
Szechuan fare, as well as Thai and Vietnamese cuisines, for
many years. Outside the doors of the restaurants, the swirling,
exotic street life of one of the largest Chinese communities in
the Western Hemisphere awaits. In the shops along Mott,
Canal, and East Broadway, you'll find unusual foodstuffs,
Chinese herbal medicines, and collectibles that you'd think only
a trip to Hong Kong or Shanghai could net. In Chinatown's
narrow streets and aging tenements, you can discover the lega-
cies of the different waves of immigrants—first the English,
then the Germans, Irish, Italians, Jews, and finally, the Chinese.

Although East Indies trading ships brought small groups
of Chinese to New York from about 1840 on, Chinatown did
not really begin to develop until the 1880s. Thousands of

21

Chinese sailed to California in the mid–19th century, hoping to amass fortunes by working in the mines and building railroads, and return to China rich men. By the 1870s, they became the victims of a tide of racism, violence, and legal persecution throughout the West. In 1882, Congress passed the Chinese Exclusion Act, which denied the Chinese the right to citizenship, barred them from most occupations, and suspended immigration. Additionally, the act forbade any laborers already in the country from bringing their wives here. Some Chinese returned home, but tens of thousands remained. From 1880 to 1890, the Chinese population on Mott, Pell, and Doyers streets increased tenfold to 12,000.

By the 1890s, Chinatown had become a large and isolated ghetto, and it remained so for many years. Since World War II, however, the neighborhood has been building bridges to the American mainstream. A large influx of foreign capital from Taiwan and Hong Kong has helped make Chinatown one of New York's strongest local economies, and many Chinese Americans have joined the middle class. But unlike other famous immigrant neighborhoods such as Little Italy or the Lower East Side, Chinatown isn't ready to be relegated to the history books—immigrants from all parts of Asia continue to stream in, adding new energy and color to the neighborhood.

● ● ● ● ● ● ● ● ● ● ● ● ● ● ● ●

Start off walking east along **Canal Street.** You'll probably have to thread your way through a multiethnic swath of pedestrians and street vendors hawking toys, firecrackers, and dumplings—Canal Street during business hours is one of New York's most frenzied, crowded thoroughfares. From Broadway to the Bowery, Canal Street is lined with bustling variety stores, fish markets, greengrocers, banks, and Chinese-owned jewelry shops. Many of the storefronts have been subdivided into minimalls whose stalls purvey everything from ginseng to martial arts paraphernalia. However, when night falls and the shops are shuttered, Canal Street seems like a ghost town in the hills of China.

You'll see plenty of Chinese-language signs on Canal Street as soon as you walk east of Broadway. The landmark that signals your arrival in Chinatown proper is the former:

Chinatown

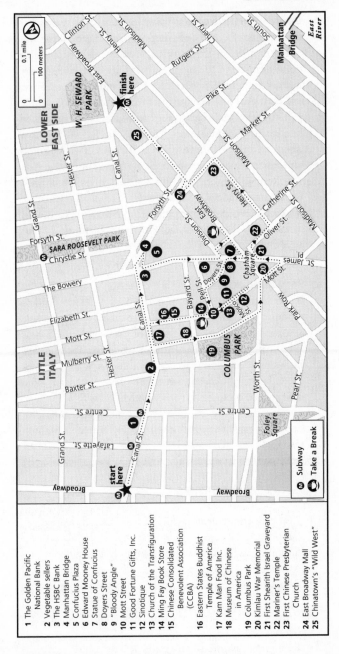

1 The Golden Pacific
   National Bank
2 Vegetable sellers
3 The HSBC Bank
4 Manhattan Bridge
5 Confucius Plaza
6 Edward Mooney House
7 Statue of Confucius
8 Doyers Street
9 "Bloody Angle"
10 Mott Street
11 Good Fortune Gifts, Inc.
12 Sinotique
13 Church of the Transfiguration
14 Ming Fay Book Store
15 Chinese Consolidated
   Benevolent Association
   (CCBA)
16 Eastern States Buddhist
   Temple of America
17 Kam Man Food Inc.
18 Museum of Chinese
   in America
19 Columbus Park
20 Kimlau War Memorial
21 First Shearith Israel Graveyard
22 Mariner's Temple
23 First Chinese Presbyterian
   Church
24 East Broadway Mall
25 Chinatown's "Wild West"

Ⓜ Subway   ☕ Take a Break

23

1. **Golden Pacific National Bank.** Located on the northwest corner of Canal and Centre streets, this building was raised in 1983 as the bank's new home. At first a major point of pride in the neighborhood, the bank failed only 2 years later, and its patrons, largely individual Chinese, lost their uninsured deposits. The colorful building, with a jade-trimmed red pagoda roof and elaborately decorated facade with Oriental phoenix and dragon motifs, has been resurrected as . . . surprise . . . a Starbucks. Walk around on Centre Street to see the building in its entirety.

   Although this one is defunct, Canal Street is still lined with banks; indeed, Chinatown's 161,000 residents are served by several dozen of them, more than most cities of similar size. Many Chinatown residents routinely put away 30% to 50% of their wages.

   Continue east along Canal Street and look for:

2. **Vegetable sellers** plying their trade on a traffic island at Baxter Street. Here you can peruse and purchase Chinese produce: bok choy (delicate Chinese cabbage), small white and red-violet eggplants, taro root, fresh ginger, Chinese squash, big white winter melons, tender bamboo shoots, yard-long green beans, pale golden lily buds, lotus leaves, cucumber-sized okra and sweet snow peas. (There are more stalls just up around the corner on Mulberry St.)

   Cross from the traffic island to the southern side of Canal Street where you'll smell a briny aroma emanating

Kid-Friendly Experiences

- Learning the violent history of the "Bloody Angle" (stop 9)
- Shopping for Chinatown souvenirs at the shops on Mott Street (stop 10)
- Sampling the goodies at Aji Ichiban candy store (see the "Take a Break" box on p. 31)
- Browsing Chinese groceries at Kam Man Food, Inc. (stop 17)
- Exploring Columbus Park (stop 19)

from a fish market (nos. 218 and 214) whose ice-covered offerings spill out onto the sidewalk. The aproned fish sellers keep up a steady patter, extolling the virtues of their shark, squid, snapper, oysters, and live eels, frogs, and snakes. Here and throughout your tour of Chinatown, you'll also pass carts vending Peking duck, chicken feet, roast pork, and lo mein, as well as store windows displaying barbecued chickens, ducks, and squab with heads and beaks fully intact.

Soak up the street scene as you continue up Canal for several more crowded blocks to the southwest corner of Canal Street and the Bowery. Here, at 58 Bowery, you'll find a branch of:

3. **The HSBC Bank.** Built in 1924, and later overhauled and tailored to its Chinese depositors, this dome-roofed bank is one of New York's most distinctive. (It's hard to appreciate from directly underneath; cross Canal for a better view.) Its interior is decorated with tondos (round paintings) extolling Wisdom, Thrift, Success, and Safety.

Across the Bowery to the east is the approach to the:

4. **Manhattan Bridge.** This suspension bridge, built in 1905, may not be as inspirational to poets and artists as the great Brooklyn Bridge, but the recently restored monumental Beaux Arts colonnade and arch that stand at its entrance are quite grand and arresting.

Looming to the right of the bridge, on the east side of the Bowery, is:

5. **Confucius Plaza.** The first major publicly funded housing project built for Chinese use, Confucius Plaza extends from Division Street up to the Bowery, where it rises into a curved 43-story tower.

The activist spirit of the 1960s touched Chinatown in a significant way: Many young people from the neighborhood were involved in a Chinese-American pride movement and created organizations devoted to building community centers, providing social services, and securing Chinatown a voice in city government. Winning the fight to build this plaza and forcing contractors to hire Chinese workers showed that Chinatown was now a political heavy hitter.

Walk south on the Bowery to building no. 18, which sits on the southwest corner of the Bowery and Pell Street and is called the:

6. **Edward Mooney House** (occupied by Summit Mortgage Bankers). This largely Georgian brick row house, painted red with eggshell trim, dates from George Washington's New York days. It was built in 1785 on property abandoned by a Tory during the Revolution and is the oldest Georgian brick row house in the city.

The Bowery ends at Chatham Square, into which nine other streets converge. On a traffic peninsula to your left, extending from the southwest end of Confucius Plaza, you'll see the:

7. **Statue of Confucius.** Raised in 1976, this bronze statue and its green marble base were gifts of the Chinese Consolidated Benevolent Association (CCBA), which has served as Chinatown's unofficial government for more than 100 years. The organization has always represented conservative Chinese who support traditional notions of family loyalty and respect for one's elders and leaders; the statue was built over the strenuous objections of activist groups who felt that the neighborhood should display a more progressive cultural symbol. However, the sage's 2,400-year-old words, inscribed in the monument's base in both Chinese and English, are strikingly descriptive of the strength of Chinatown's tightknit social fabric: Confucius recommends that we look beyond our immediate family and see all elders as our parents and all children as our own.

From the statue of Confucius, follow Catherine Street past the pagoda-roofed bank and turn left onto East Broadway. This thoroughfare is the heart of commercial, workday Chinatown. Very few of its businesses are geared to tourists; instead, they are dedicated to serving the community's needs. These businesses include Chinese video stores, beauty salons, sidewalk shacks purveying grilled meats and dumplings, and bakeries whose wedding cakes are topped with Asian bride-and-groom figurines.

☕ **Take a Break** For lunch, treat yourself to **dim sum** (see box below). Every day from 9am to about 4pm, two huge restaurants—the **Golden Unicorn** at 18 E. Broadway, near Catherine Street (☎ 212/941-0911) and the **Nice Restaurant** at 35 E. Broadway (☎ 212/406-9510)—draw large, hungry crowds. The Golden Unicorn's walkie-talkie–wielding hostess directs incoming diners to the restaurant's second- and third-floor dining rooms; in the Nice Restaurant, the lobby has several tanks full of carp and sea bass. In both restaurants, you'll usually be seated with other parties around a huge banquet table. A distinctly celebratory spirit pervades; the Chinese families dining here often seem to have three or four generations represented. If you're less familiar with dim sum, don't be shy: You can afford to take some risks because everything costs just $2 to $4. (Prices at Nice are a tad lower than those at the Golden Unicorn.) Though servers seldom speak much English, fellow Chinese diners or inveterate dim summers at your table might be able to offer some helpful tips. The Golden Unicorn makes things easier with captions in English on the carts.

Backtrack to Chatham Square. At the Bowery, on the square, a narrow, crooked street bears off to the northwest (in the general direction of Canal St.). This street is:

8. **Doyers Street,** which along with Pell Street and the lower end of Mott Street formed the original Chinatown. Doyers Street was the backdrop for much of the neighborhood's unhappy early history.

   Chinatown's "bachelor society," which existed from 1882 to 1943 (when some provisions of the Exclusion Act were repealed), was a place of grimly limited opportunity and deep poverty. There were 27 men to every woman in the neighborhood. These men were prohibited from competing with whites for work, hemmed into Chinatown by the language barrier, and living under the risk of beatings if they strayed from the 3-block ghetto. Under these harsh conditions, working in the laundry industry was one of the best ways to eke out a living.

Dim Sum

Dim sum is Cantonese for "dot your heart," and a dim sum meal consists of one small gastronomic delight after another. Simply choose what looks appealing from the steaming carts that servers wheel around to your table. Dim sum usually involves more than 100 appetizer-sized items such as steamed leek dumplings, deep-fried minced shrimp rolls wrapped in bacon, sweet doughy buns filled with tangy morsels of barbecued pork, deep-fried shrimp, beef ribs with black pepper sauce, and honey roast pork rolled in steamed noodles. Dessert dim sum may include orange pudding, egg custard rolls covered with shredded coconut, and sweet lotus-seed sesame balls.

Crime compounded the neighborhood's misery. The Chinese moved into the northern end of an area that for 40 years had been a sprawling morass of saloons, gambling dens, and squalid tenements extending from Chatham Square all the way to the waterfront. Prostitution flourished (out of desperation, many Chinese men lived with, or even married, white prostitutes), and opium dens sprang up. The Chinese Consolidated Benevolent Association (CCBA) acted as de facto government, but the real power resided in the *tongs,* "protection societies" (much like the Mafia) involved in racketeering and gambling. There are still tong-controlled gaming dens in Chinatown, still whispers of intimidation, and an occasional outbreak of gang-related violence.

The post office, located a few paces up Doyers Street on your right, occupies the site of the old Chatham Club, one of the uproarious music halls that surrounded Chatham Square a century ago. The clubs boasted singing waiters, accompanied by a tinny piano, who would entertain the clientele with sentimental ballads. Izzy Baline and Asa Yoelson sang at the Chatham and other clubs on Doyers; later, in tonier surroundings, they became better known as Irving Berlin and Al Jolson.

By the 1920s, the sharp bend in Doyers Street had acquired its reputation as the infamous:

9. **"Bloody Angle."** The first two tongs to rise in Chinatown, the On Leong and the Hip Sing, engaged in a fierce turf struggle in Chinatown that dragged on for almost 40 years. Both organizations had large standing armies of henchmen, and the worst of the continual bloodshed occurred here. The crooked street lent itself to ambush, and assassins could usually make a fast escape by ducking through the old Chinese Theatre, which stood at the elbow of the street that Doyers Vietnamese Restaurant now occupies. At the turn of the 20th century, Bloody Angle was the site of more murders than anywhere else in the United States.

At the end of Doyers Street is Pell Street, another short, narrow thoroughfare lined with restaurants. Pell Street has also changed little over the years. At no. 16, next to Happy Sixteen Diner, is the unobtrusive entryway to the headquarters of the organization that has dominated Pell and Doyers streets for 100 years, the Hip Sing tong; the gold lettering above the door symbolizes growth and prosperity.

Leaving the dark side of the neighborhood's history behind, turn left on Pell Street down to its intersection with:

10. **Mott Street,** the heart of old Chinatown. Mott Street is the epicenter of the boisterous Chinese New Year celebrations that begin with the first full moon after January 21. Red and gold streamers festoon every shop window, and the street fills with parades complete with gyrating dragon dancers and the nonstop thunder of firecrackers.

The shops that line Mott Street are a diverse bunch, and their collective stock gives you the chance to bring a piece of Chinatown back home. Just around the corner to your left is one such store:

11. **Good Fortune Gifts, Inc.** at 32 Mott St. For over a century, Quong Yuen Shing & Company (the shop's previous inhabitant) supplied locals with general merchandise, like medicinal herbs, sandalwood fans, tea, mah-jongg sets,

ceramic bowls and vases, and seeds for Chinese vegetables, among other sundries. Opened in 2004, Good Fortune Gifts shares its predecessor's frame and traces of its history remain, like ornate wooden shelves and cabinetry, and an elaborately carved arch decorating the counter. New merchandise fills the shelves: Glass cases that once displayed silk handkerchiefs and brocades are now lined with an odd mix of Barbie-style action figures, from Jackie Chan to Wonder Woman and FDNY firemen. There are also trinkets, like painted ceramic eggs, small crystalline balls enshrining decorative scenes, and ceramic animal figures.

Continue along Mott Street and cross to the:

12. **Sinotique** at 19a Mott St. Inside this refined, decidedly upscale shop you'll find beautiful, high-quality Chinese antiques, crafts, and collectibles. On a recent visit, the offerings included rosewood and teak cabinets with delicate hand-carved ornamentation; pottery ranging from unglazed pieces created in the 2nd millennium B.C. to works from the Ching dynasty (1644–1912); exquisite carved bamboo birdcages from southern China (ask them to explain the traditional bird-keeping hobby common among old Chinese men); Chinese country furniture; Tibetan, Chinese, and Mongolian rugs; hand-wrought mounted bronze gongs; and jewelry.

Backtrack up Mott to cross tiny Mosco Street, and you'll be in front of the:

13. **Church of the Transfiguration** at 25–29 Mott St. This Georgian stone church was built in 1801; the spire was added in the 1860s. Originally consecrated as the English Lutheran First Church of Zion, the church has been a veritable chameleon, always reflecting the changing image of the neighborhood. It was first created as a house of worship for English Lutherans. It then morphed into a church for the newly arrived Irish Catholics, and later, in the 1880s, became a house of worship for Italian Catholics. Nowadays its services are in Cantonese, Mandarin, and English, and the church is the focal point of New York's Chinese Roman Catholic community.

Transfiguration remains true to its long heritage as a mission house, continuing to offer English classes and other services that help its members find their way into the American mainstream.

Take a Break Just beyond Pell Street is the **New Lung Fong Bakery** at 41 Mott St. (© 212/233-7447), offering an array of sweet treats such as red-bean cakes, black-bean doughnuts, lotus seed–moon cake custard tarts, chestnut buns, cream buns, melon cakes, and mixed-nut pies. Sitting in Lung Fong's unadorned cafe section, you can relax with a cup of tea or very good coffee and *yum cha*—that's Chinese for hanging out, talking, and drinking in a cafe.

Next door is the new **Aji Ichiban,** 37 Mott St. (© 212/233-7650; www.ajiichiban-usa.com), a self-proclaimed "munchies paradise" that looks innocuously like any bulk candy store you'd see in the mall—until you start perusing the English translations of what's in each bin: candy-coated chocolates that look like decorative pebbles, shriveled fruits of the sorts you didn't even know could be dried, and dozens of licorices mixed in among bins for snack-sized morsels of such things as dried squid. We dare you to close your eyes and make a selection.

Continue north on Mott. On the right at 42 Mott St. is the:

14. **Ming Fay Book Store.** An eclectic store stocked with everything from art/school supplies and toys to Chinese calendars, newspapers, comics, pinup magazines, and books, Ming Fay also carries a selection of English-language books on Chinese subjects. Here is a sampling of titles: *Chinese Astrology, The Bruce Lee Story, The Book of Tea, The Dictionary of Traditional Chinese Medicine,* and *The Living Buddha.*

A little farther up Mott at no. 62 is the headquarters of the:

15. **Chinese Consolidated Benevolent Association (CCBA).** Until recently, this association functioned as the working government of Chinatown, helping new immigrants find jobs and housing, funneling capital into

neighborhood businesses, offering English classes to children and adults, providing services to the elderly, and
even operating criminal courts. Although its influence has
waned somewhat, it is still a major social and political
force in Chinatown and is the voice of New York's pro-
Taiwan community. Also located in the building is the
Chinese School, which since 1915 has been working to
keep Chinese traditions and language alive, long a primary concern of the CCBA.

Two doors down is the:

16. **Eastern States Buddhist Temple of America.**
Quiet and suffused with incense and the smell of cooking
oil (they use it ritualistically), this storefront shrine has
been here for years and serves as something of a social center; usually a number of elderly ladies are sitting in the
chairs and benches that line the wall. Enter, light a joss
stick, and offer a prayer to Kuan-yin, the Chinese goddess
of mercy. Or perhaps you'd rather supplicate the Four-
Faced Buddha for good luck in business (money will
come from all directions, hence the four faces). You can
also buy a fortune here, in English, for a dollar.

Across the street and up at the corner of Mott and
Canal streets (83–85 Mott), behind a stately facade featuring balconies and a pagoda roof, is the headquarters of
the **Chinese Merchants Association,** better known as the
On Leong tong. Chinatown's oldest tong is still one of its
most prominent neighborhood organizations.

Make a left onto Canal Street, where a steady stream of
shoppers will no doubt be passing in and out of:

17. **Kam Man Food, Inc.** at 200 Canal St. This quintessential Chinese supermarket is a fascinating browse. To your
right as you enter is a selection of elaborately packaged
teas and elixirs laced with ginseng and other mainstays of
Chinese pharmacopoeia. These products include tzepao
sanpien extract (which promises greater potency to men),
heart tonics, smoking cessation and slimming teas, deer-
tail extract, edible bird's nests, tiger liniment, and royal
jelly. Many of these products claim to cure a wide variety
of ailments. *Bu tian su,* for example, is supposedly good
for memory loss, insomnia, an aching back, or lumbago,

among other things. Just beyond this collection is a counter displaying myriad varieties of ginseng. Walk toward the rear of the store, and you'll find packages of pork buns ready for the steamer, quail eggs, dried seafood, exotic mushrooms, sauces ranging from oyster to black-bean garlic, a butcher section, and much more. Downstairs, the kitchenware department offers every-thing from woks to tea sets and a counter for fancy chop-sticks, roasted seaweed, and oodles of noodles. Pick up some essence of *tienchi* flowers, a purported remedy for pimples, dizziness, hot temper, grinding of teeth, and emotional inquietude.

Turn left onto Mulberry Street (another thoroughfare lined with emporia that make for great browsing and win-dow shopping) to visit the:

18. **Museum of Chinese in America,** 70 Mulberry St. (© 212/619-4785; www.moca-nyc.org). In the forward-looking, upwardly mobile climate of today's Chinatown, it's tough to think about the cruel hardships that the first generations of Chinese in New York suffered. This muse-um, founded in 1980, documents the history and culture of Chinese in America from the early 1800s to the pres-ent. An adjoining gallery stages exhibitions of works by Chinese artists and photographers; the museum also includes a gift/bookstore. Hours are noon to 6pm Tuesday through Sunday (until 7pm on Fri). The muse-um charges a small admission, waived on Fridays.

Opening off to the southwest on the other side of Mulberry Street is:

19. **Columbus Park.** Open public spaces are in short supply on the Lower East Side, and lively Columbus Park is pop-ular with Chinatown residents both young and old. The north end of the park underwent extensive renovation in 2005, adding new benches, decorative pavements, and game tables where Chinese women play cards for dimes or have their fortunes told while Chinese men gamble over checkers. The park lies where a huddle of decrepit tene-ments known as Mulberry Bend once stood. In the last quarter of the 19th century, Mulberry Bend was New York's worst slum, as evinced by the frightening nomenclature it

acquired—the filthy tenements went by names such as Bone Alley, Kerosene Row, and Bandits' Roost. Such brawling street gangs as the Dead Rabbits, Plug Uglies, and Whyos were the powers of Mulberry Bend, and police ventured into the area only in platoons of 10 or more.

Mulberry Bend remained New York's disgrace until social reformer Jacob Riis managed to stir up public rage to the point where city officials were obliged to raze the slum between 1892 and 1894. For the last century, Riis's vision of a clean place for neighborhood children to play has been a reality: There's a big playground, and games of basketball, baseball, or hockey are almost always in progress.

At the southern end of the park, make a left turn onto Worth Street, and you'll soon be back at Chatham Square. Up ahead on your right on the traffic island is the:

20. **Kimlau War Memorial,** built in 1962 to honor the Chinese Americans who gave their lives while serving in the U.S. armed forces. Chinatown's extraordinary contribution to the American war effort in World War II—40% of the neighborhood's population served in the military— was a major factor in the annulment of the Chinese Exclusion Act and other anti-Chinese legislation.

St. James Place, which extends south from Chatham Square, is the site of the:

21. **First Shearith Israel Graveyard,** a burial ground for Sephardic Jews who immigrated to New York in the mid–17th century. The 1683 stone of Benjamin Bueno de Mesquita (still legible) is the oldest in the city; the cemetery remained active until 1828 and features the graves of a number of soldiers who died during the American Revolution.

Also buried here, in 1733, is Rachel Rodriguez Marques, an ancestor of New York stockbroker, politico, and college benefactor Bernard Baruch (who paid for the improvement of the site in the 1950s). The gate is usually locked, but you can peer through the fence.

Backtrack on St. James Place, and turn right onto Oliver Street. On the northeast corner of Oliver and Henry streets is the:

22. **Mariner's Temple.** This Greek Revival brownstone church, with a portico entranceway fronted by two massive Ionic columns, was built in 1844. Today a Baptist church serving a mixed Chinese, African American, and Latino congregation, the Mariner's Temple originally catered to the sea captains, dockworkers, and sailors of the sprawling maritime community that dominated the waterfront along the East River in the 19th century.

Turn left onto Henry Street. Two blocks east, on the corner of Henry and Market streets, is the:

23. **First Chinese Presbyterian Church,** which shares a place in neighborhood history with the Mariner's Temple. Built in 1819 on the outskirts of the Cherry Hill section (which after the Revolutionary War was New York's poshest neighborhood and the site of the nation's first presidential mansion), this Georgian-style house of worship was originally named the Northeast Dutch Reformed Church. It was renamed the Church of Sea and Land during the mid–19th century, when the East River waterfront had become rife with cutthroat saloons, dance halls, and "crimps"—lodging houses that often took advantage of their sailor patrons by robbing them or even shanghaiing them aboard outgoing ships. Mission houses such as the Mariner's Temple and the Church of Sea and Land were often the only place to which beleaguered seafarers and immigrants could turn for help. Today, the church continues to assist the immigrants who arrive in Chinatown in droves every year.

Turn left and follow Market Street to East Broadway and turn right. Believe it or not, the dim, noisy area below the Manhattan Bridge is a commercial hot spot of Chinatown. On your left is the modest:

24. **East Broadway Mall.** The stores here cater entirely to Chinese shoppers and include a newsstand at which you'll be lucky to spot a word of English, a Chinese pop music shop, two Chinese-language video stores, several beauty salons and cosmetics shops selling products you won't find in your average beauty store, and Ho's Ginseng Co., where you can get something to cool down your blood (or

warm it up). The mall's centerpiece is a glitzy upstairs restaurant, 88 Palace.

Continue along East Broadway, and you'll soon cross Pike Street. Pike is an unofficial divider between the established area of Chinatown and an expanding area that's been termed:

25. **Chinatown's "Wild West"** by journalist Gwen Kinkead in her book *Chinatown: A Portrait of a Closed Society* (HarperCollins, 1992). Asians have been flooding into New York City ever since U.S. immigration laws were liberalized in 1965. The great majority of them hail from the People's Republic of China, and most of these new immigrants come from Fujian Province, often via Hong Kong or Taiwan. These new arrivals have almost completely replaced the old immigrant residents of the Lower East Side, the Jews. Emblematic of the changing makeup in the neighborhood is the Sons of Israel Kalwarie Synagogue, located on Pike Street to the right of East Broadway—it's now a Buddhist association, with a 99-cent store in the basement.

Walk down East Broadway to Rutgers Street (where you'll find the entrance to the subway's East Broadway F-line stop). The Chinatown you'll pass on your way may not have curio shops or pagoda roofs, but the barber shops, fish markets, and newsstands do a brisk business. Throughout this neighborhood, you'll see hectic commerce, hardworking laborers, and schoolchildren, and you can sense the buzz of a neighborhood where many people are working to leave these gritty tenement streets and make their way into the mainstream, just as people on the Lower East Side have been doing for more than a century.

The Jewish Lower East Side

Start: Gertel's Bakery, 53 Hester St.

Subway: Take the F train to East Broadway.

Finish: Russ and Daughters, 179 Houston St.

Time: 3½ to 4 hours if you do all the tours.

Best Time: Sundays, when Orchard Street is in full form. ***Note:*** Because tours of the highly recommended Lower East Side Tenement Museum sometimes fill up on Sundays, you might want to stop there earlier in the day (it opens at 11am Mon–Fri, 10:45am on the weekends) and pick up tickets; you may also wish to buy tickets in advance online or by phone; see details later (stop 9).

Worst Time: Saturdays and Jewish holidays (when much is closed) and Friday afternoons (when many stores close early).

The Lower East Side (www. lowereastsideny.com) has always been one of New York's most colorful neighborhoods. More than 23 million Europeans immigrated to American shores between 1880 and 1919, seeking escape from famine, poverty, and religious persecution. About 1.5 million Jews, many of them fleeing Russian pogroms, wound up in ramshackle tenements here. They scratched out meager livings peddling wares on Orchard Street or working dawn to dusk in garment-center sweatshops. By 1920, some 500 synagogues and religious schools (Talmud Torahs) dotted the area. The ethnic mix of the Lower East Side has changed, with working-class Chinese and Latinos the dominant populations, joined by an increasing number of young professionals. The area is rich in Jewish history; 80% of today's American Jews are descendants of immigrants who once lived on these streets. Today, more Jews—almost two million—live in New York City than anywhere else in the world outside of Israel. Despite rapid changes on the Lower East Side, the high-rise brick apartment buildings south of Grand Street remain a largely Orthodox Jewish enclave, and many of the local mom-and-pop businesses have retained Jewish proprietors.

Food note: This tour has great noshing (a Yiddish word for snacking) along the way, so you can use it as an eating tour as well as a walking tour.

● ● ● ● ● ● ● ● ● ● ● ● ● ● ● ●

Starting Out Gertel's Bakery, 53 Hester St. between Essex and Ludlow streets (© **212/982-3250**), dates back to 1914, when the area was littered with similar establishments. Gertel's is the last of the originals, still serving up Jewish favorites like hamentaschen, challah, and, of course, rugulah. There are a few seats available. In nice weather you can walk down to Seward Park and enjoy a picnic, which is also a possibility for the following two stops, which don't have seats for eating in.

Another surviving Lower East Side institution is **Kossar's Bialys** (© **877/4-BIALYS**), at 367 Grand St., east of Essex Street. The bialy has a texture similar to a bagel's, but the bread is flatter and lacks an aperture. They've been making them here since the 30s, using a recipe that originated in Bialystok, Poland. More recently Kossar's added bagels to their lineup, cooked fresh on the

The Jewish Lower East Side

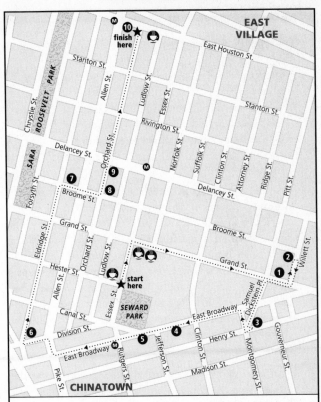

1 Abrons Arts Center/Harry De Jur Playhouse
2 Bialystoker Synagogue
3 The Henry Street Settlement
4 Educational Alliance (the David Sarnoff Building)
5 Forward Building
6 Eldridge Street Synagogue
7 Kehila Kedosha Janina Synagogue and Museum
8 Orchard Street
9 Lower East Side Tenement Museum
10 Russ and Daughters

Ⓜ Subway
☕ Take a Break

| 0 | | 0.1 mile |
| 0 | | 100 meters |

Kid-Friendly Experiences

- Slurping down a pickle at The Pickle Guys (see below)
- Taking the kid-targeted Confino Apartment tour at the Lower East Side Tenement Museum (stop 9)
- Bargain-hunting on Orchard Street (stop 8)

premises—you can't get much more authentic than this. A limited number of schmears can be found in the fridge.

Head a little further east on Grand Street, to no. 379, and you'll find a newcomer that's quickly establishing itself as an institution. **Doughnut Plant** (© 212/505-3700) began in a Lower East Side basement with proprietor Mark Isreal's grandfather's doughnut recipe. This location is both a factory and retail outlet, and the fresh-baked, artisanal doughnuts are spectacular. Valrhona chocolate and seasonal organic fruits glaze insides that are lighter than air.

Start your tour on Essex Street, walking north from the subway stop. Although Chinese shops have spilled over from nearby Chinatown, there are still several old-time Jewish merchants. **Hebrew Religious Articles,** 45 Essex St. (© 212/674-1770), has been here for more than 50 years. Its shelves and display cases are cluttered with Jewish books, ritual phylacteries (leather cases containing Scripture passages, which are worn by Jewish men during weekday-morning prayer) and shawls, sacred scrolls, commentaries on the Torah, menorahs, antique Judaica, electric memorial candles, Seder plates, mezuzahs, yarmulkes, and cantorial and Yiddish recordings.

At 49 Essex St. you'll pass **The Pickle Guys** (© 212/656-9739), with their vats full of sours, half sours, hots, and news. Essex Street was once dotted with pickle sellers, including **Guss',** which gained fame in the film *Crossing Delancey.* After a 2002 schism, Guss' (© 516/569-0909) moved up to 85–87 Orchard St., and some longtime employees stayed on Essex to become The Pickle Guys.

You can't go wrong with either establishment, though in a pinch I'd have to pick The Pickle Guys, whose brine seems to have just a little more flavor. Open 9am to 6pm Sunday through Thursday, closed at 4pm on Fridays and all day Saturday.

Make a right on Grand Street and walk a few blocks up to the:

1. **Abrons Arts Center/Harry De Jur Playhouse,** 466 Grand St. (© **212/598-0400;** www.henrystreet.org). Founded by sisters Alice and Irene Lewisohn in 1915 to stage productions by the Henry Street Settlement's youth dramatic groups, this renowned center went on to present premieres of S. Ansky's *The Dybbuk* (attended by authors Edna Ferber and Willa Cather) and James Joyce's *Exiles,* along with plays by George Bernard Shaw, Havelock Ellis, Anton Chekhov, Sholem Asch, and Eugene O'Neill. It remains a vital performance space and cultural center, offering a comprehensive schedule of dance, theater, music, art exhibits, classes, and workshops. Pick up an events schedule while you're here. The center's original core is a three-story Georgian Revival building. Behind it is a curvilinear brick extension. Walk past that and take a left onto Bialystoker Place/Willett Street. On your left is the:

2. **Bialystoker Synagogue,** 7 Bialystoker Place (Willett St.). Occupying a converted 1826 Federal-style fieldstone church, this beautiful Orthodox landsmanschaft shul (synagogue of countrymen) was purchased in 1905 by an immigrant congregation from Bialystok (home of the bialy, it was then a town in Russia; today, because of changing borders, it's in Poland). The temple's interior walls and ceiling are ornately painted with Moorish motifs, zodiac signs (which are found in Jewish cabala writings), and biblical scenes. To see the interior, you have to arrange a tour in advance (© **212/475-0165;** $10 donation).

Cross Grand and head left down Samuel Dickstein Plaza. After crossing East Broadway, the plaza spills into the intersection of Henry and Montgomery streets. Take a sharp left onto Henry Street, and immediately on your left is:

3. **The Henry Street Settlement,** 263–267 Henry St.
Called to tend a patient on Ludlow Street in 1892, 25-
year-old German-Jewish nurse Lillian Wald was appalled
at the squalor of tenement life. She moved downtown in
order to study the living conditions in the Jewish ghetto
and established a district nursing service on Henry Street
in 1893. Two years later, the service evolved into the
Henry Street Settlement, one of America's first social
agencies. It offered job training, educational facilities,
summer camps for children, concerts, and plays.

Wald dedicated her life to helping the indigent of the
Lower East Side fight disease, malnutrition, and igno-
rance, and the "house on Henry Street" initiated progressive social legislation, including child labor laws. Social
reformer Jacob Riis said of Lillian Wald, "From the very
start, the poor became 'her people.' She took them to her
heart, and they quickly gave her unstinted love and trust."
Years ago, you might have seen Jane Addams, Albert
Einstein, or Eleanor Roosevelt discussing vital social
issues in the dining room. President Bill Clinton visited
during his 1992 campaign. The settlement continues its
good works, operating homeless shelters, and job training
and other programs for neighborhood residents. Its three
original late-Federal/Classic Revival buildings were built
in 1832. Note also the elegant firehouse, built in 1883, at
the end of the block.

Turn around and head back to the corner, where you
make a right back up Montgomery Street (through the
small cement park) toward the high-rise apartments, and
take a left onto East Broadway. The block between
Montgomery and Clinton streets is sometimes referred to
as "Shtiebel Row." *Shtiebel* means room or home, and in
the storefront rooms here dozens of small shuls met.
Several are still functioning. The Federal-style row house
at no. 281 dates back to 1829, when the neighborhood
was upscale and the address would have been fashionable.

A ways down on your left is the:

4. **Educational Alliance (the David Sarnoff Building)**
(*©* **212/780-2300**), 197 E. Broadway. "Uptown"
German-Jewish philanthropists founded The Alliance in
1889 to help fellow immigrants assimilate, Americanize,

and adapt to a baffling alien culture. It offered them training in English, courses in business, cultural and civic programs, legal counsel, music lessons, and athletic facilities, not to mention such hard-to-come-by amenities as hot showers and pasteurized milk for children.

Today, the Educational Alliance's programs operate out of 18 locations and serve not only Jews, but also African-, Chinese-, and Latin-American New Yorkers. A Hall of Fame on the main floor is lined with photos of notable alumni such as Eddie Cantor, David Sarnoff, Jan Peerce, Jacob Epstein, Arthur Murray, and Louise Nevelson.

Continue in the same direction. You'll notice by the signs that, like Essex Street, East Broadway reflects a blend of old Jewish establishments and new, vibrant Chinese entries. At 175 E. Broadway, you'll see the tall, old:

5. **Forward Building.** For 60 years, this building was the home of America's most prominent Yiddish newspaper, the *Forverts* (in English, *The Forward*). Founded in 1897 by a group of Russian Jewish immigrants, the *Forverts* guided thousands of Eastern European Jews through the confusing maze of American society. In the 1920s, its daily circulation reached 250,000 copies.

Lithuanian immigrant Abraham Cahan served as editor of the newspaper from its inception until his death in 1951. Under his guidance, this socialist and zealously pro-labor newspaper examined every facet of Jewish and American life. It explained American customs and social graces to greenhorns—everything from baseball to personal hygiene—and exhorted readers to learn English and educate their children. The paper also presented—along with trashy serialized romance novels—quality fiction by writers like Sholem Asch, Sholom Aleichem, I. J. Singer, and I. B. Singer. The latter Singer worked on the newspaper's staff throughout his adult life, and all of his books, which were written in Yiddish (later translated), were first published in *The Forward.*

The Forward building was constructed in 1912 specifically to house the paper. After years as a Chinese-American community center, with the flaming torches (socialist symbols) and portraits of Marx and Engels on the building's facade obscured by Chinese signage, the building has been painstakingly restored for conversion to luxury condominiums. The male and female figures centered on a sunburst above the door symbolize enlightenment, and *The Forward* continues to inform readers (weekly now, from Midtown) in English and Yiddish.

In the heyday of the *Forverts,* the Chinese restaurant now occupying the corner of Rutgers Street and East Broadway was the Garden Cafeteria, a superb dairy restaurant patronized by members of the Jewish intelligentsia; Leon Trotsky frequently dined here when he was in New York. A 2005 remodeling revealed the original sign, intact, which was promptly stolen by a sharp souvenir hound.

Continue on East Broadway, passing no. 145–147, Mesivtha Tifereth Jerusalem, one of the oldest yeshivas in America (established in 1907). Note also no. 139, with Stars of David among its decorative elements.

Take a right on Pike Street and a left onto Division Street and then a quick right onto Eldridge Street, which angles to the right and reveals the:

6. **Eldridge Street Synagogue** (Congregation K'hal Adath Jeshurun, 12–16 Eldridge St.; ☎ **212/219-0888;** www.eldridgestreet.org). When this synagogue was built in 1886–88 by a congregation of Polish and Russian Jews, it was the most magnificent synagogue on the Lower East Side. It was also the first synagogue built by Eastern European immigrants, who had previously worshipped in converted churches. Designed by the Herter Brothers (interior designers for wealthy New York families like the Vanderbilts), its architectural and interior decor reflects a blend of Gothic, Romanesque, and Moorish styles. The grandiose terra-cotta and brick facade is highly symbolic: Its cluster of five small windows represents the five books of Moses, the 12 roundels of the rose window symbolize the 12 tribes of Israel, and so on. The greatly deteriorated, but once opulent, sanctuary was fitted out under a 70-foot central dome with an ornately carved towering walnut ark from Italy, *trompe l'oeil* murals, stained-glass windows,

scagliola (imitation marble) columns, and Victorian glass-shaded brass chandeliers.

The congregation flourished for several decades, but as wealthy members moved away and quota laws of the 1920s slowed immigration to a trickle, funds became short and by the 1940s the main sanctuary was in such bad repair that it was boarded up. Not until the 1970s did urban preservationists and historians begin taking an interest in the building. The Eldridge Street Project, founded in 1986, is now restoring the building as an active synagogue and Jewish heritage center. The synagogue currently has a small Orthodox congregation.

The synagogue is open for tours between 11am and 4pm on Sundays, Tuesdays, Wednesdays, and Thursdays. Admission is charged (it goes toward the renovation). While you're here, inquire about the synagogue's many programs and lectures.

From the synagogue, continue up Eldridge Street. 87 Eldridge St. is one of dozens of converted synagogues in the neighborhood. Many have become Christian churches and Buddhist temples. This one belonged to the late Milton Resnick, an abstract expressionist painter who came to America via Ellis Island in 1922. Take a right onto Broome Street and at no. 280 you'll find a small synagogue that still fills its original purpose, the:

7. **Kehila Kedosha Janina Synagogue and Museum** (℃ 212/431-1619; www.kkjsm.org). The congregation that built this small synagogue in 1927 is Romaniote, a branch of Judaism with a history that dates back to the destruction of the Second Temple. On a slave ship bound for Rome, the ancestors of this community were freed by a storm, which put them ashore in Greece. A small, free museum in the upstairs gallery is open from 11:00am to 4pm on Sundays.

Continue on Broome, across Allen to:

8. **Orchard Street.** It's hard to imagine, but this nearly tree-less street was once a path to the orchards of an 18th-century farm owned by the de Lancey family, who lent their name to nearby Delancey Street. By the 19th century,

these blocks were part of a vast outdoor marketplace lined with rows of pushcarts.

Today, pushcarts have been replaced by stores, though merchandise is still often displayed outside on tables and racks. Some shop owners will haggle over prices, and bargains can still be found, especially for fabric, luggage, and clothes. However, many of the old retailers have moved or closed shop when faced with rising rents as trendy boutiques increasingly fill the storefronts. On the far side of Delancey, Orchard is closed to traffic on Sundays. This is my backyard and it always feels like a festival to me, with shoppers, browsers, and barkers filling the street.

At the corner of Broome Street you'll see a tattered wall of placards, which were sealed beneath a mural until 2005. The advertising reflects the products of a vanished Lower East Side, including crimson bottles of Hersh's sacramental wine. This corner belongs to Recollections (© 212/387-0341), the antiques and collectibles store operated by the:

9. **Lower East Side Tenement Museum,** whose orientation center is at the end of the block at 108 Orchard St. (© 212/982-8420; www.tenement.org). Conceived as a monument to the experience of "urban pioneers" in America, this unique facility documents the lives of immigrant residents in an 1863 six-story, 22-apartment tenement: 97 Orchard St., halfway up the block on your left. The building is accessible only by guided tour, with tickets sold at the orientation center. To ensure tours aren't sold out, you can get advance tickets for an additional service fee at © 800/965-4827 (www.ticketweb. com). These tickets must be purchased at least 2 days in advance.

The guided tours (there are three to choose from) give a thorough history, but to whet your appetite, here are a few quick facts about the building: 7,000 people from 20 different countries lived at 97 Orchard over a period of 72 years (the landlord sealed the building in 1935 so he wouldn't have to bring it up to code under the new housing laws, inadvertently creating the perfect time capsule). These immigrants probably would have been astonished to hear that their crowded building of cold, cramped, airless apartments would one day be listed on the National Register of Historic Landmarks. It was reopened in 1988.

Residents lived (and often worked, sewing piecework for garment manufacturers or taking in laundry) in three-room apartments with a total area of just 325 square feet. Scant light trickled through windows at distant ends of railroad flats, and the only heat came from the coal- or wood-burning cooking stove. Large families, often supplemented by boarders for extra cash, lived without running water (until the 1890s it had to be fetched from a backyard pump and hauled upstairs). They also had to do without indoor plumbing (chamber pots served as toilets, and slops had to be carried to privies in the backyard; after the turn of the century, there were toilets in the hall) and electricity (which may not have been installed until the 1920s). Bed legs were often placed in cans of kerosene, which, though it created a fire hazard, discouraged bedbugs.

Lucas Glockner, the German immigrant who built the place, was unhampered by building codes; few existed at the time, and the ones that did were not enforced. By 1915, as many as 18 people sometimes occupied one apartment, sleeping in shifts. In such unhealthy conditions, 40% of the babies born here died, and disease was rampant. The museum has re-created five apartments based on records, letters, and the memories of people who once lived here.

The orientation center is open Mondays from 11am to 5:30pm, Tuesdays through Fridays from 11am to 6pm, and on the weekends from 10:45am to 6pm.

Continue north on Orchard Street, turning left on Houston Street. Your last stop is:

10. **Russ and Daughters,** 179 E. Houston St. (© **212/ 475-4880**). Joel and Bella Russ began selling food from a pushcart in 1911. Their operation evolved into one of New York's most famous appetizer stores, which is now run by their grandson, Mark Federman. At this final stop on the tour, you can stock up on Nova lox, creamed or schmaltz herring, whitefish salad, gefilte fish, halvah, and

other Jewish delicacies, and take a little of the Lower East Side home with you.

Winding Down Katz's Delicatessen, 205 E. Houston St. at Ludlow Street (℅ 212/254-2246), is a classic New York deli that's been in business at this location since 1888. The interior is little changed from those days. Even the World War II sign reading "Send a salami to your boy in the Army" is still intact. Katz's was the setting for Meg Ryan's famous faked orgasm scene in the movie *When Harry Met Sally.*

"She didn't really fake it," says owner Fred Austin, "it was the food." Between takes, costar Billy Crystal, a great Katz's fan, wolfed down a dozen corned beef sandwiches, supplemented with hot dogs, cherry peppers, and pickles. Note the photographs of famous patrons; everyone from Jackie Mason to Houdini to Bill Clinton has eaten here. Order a pastrami or corned beef sandwich on rye (it's stuffed with about ¾ pound of meat), a potato knish, and a New York egg cream. Current owner Austin took the place over from the Katz family about a decade ago, but he hasn't changed a thing, not even the archetypal surly Jewish waiter service. "If anyone's nice to a customer, I want to hear about it," he says. There's cafeteria and waiter service. Katz's is open Sunday to Tuesday 8am to 10pm, Wednesday 8am to 11pm, Thursday 8am to midnight, and Friday and Saturday 8am to 3am.

SoHo

Start: Broadway and Prince Street.

Subway: Take the N, R, or W train to Prince Street.

Finish: West Broadway, just below Spring Street.

Time: Between 2 and 3 hours, depending on how long you spend browsing the shops.

Best Time: Start around 10am because most shops are open from 9am to 6pm.

Worst Time: SoHo is congested with shoppers and tourists on the weekends, which may detract from the experience for some.

We all owe Jane Jacobs a debt of gratitude. A community activist and urban theorist, Jacobs became chairman of the Joint Committee to Stop the Lower Manhattan Expressway in 1962. During the '60s she faced off with New York master planner Robert Moses, who intended to connect the Holland Tunnel with the Williamsburg Bridge through SoHo and part of the West Village. The resulting eight-lane superhighway would have wiped out thousands of historic buildings (and displaced their occupants). Instead of considering Lower Manhattan as a logical attachment point for car travel between New Jersey and

Brooklyn, Jane Jacobs and other concerned citizens fought to preserve a fragile urban fabric. SoHo's nearly abandoned industrial lofts had begun to fill with artists seeking light, large spaces and cheap rent. The halting of the Lower Manhattan Expressway project was Moses's first major setback, and the victory of the underdog locals is worth remembering as you tour these streets, which came so close to being lost forever.

Traditional SoHo, incorporating the area south (So) of Houston (Ho) Street and north of Canal Street and bounded by Broadway and West Broadway, is roughly 1 square mile. In the early 19th century, it was a run-down neighborhood lost between lower Manhattan and the mansions of Uptown. Dry-goods merchants and emerging manufacturing companies moved in and filled the area with warehouses that incorporated the latest in cost-cutting building technology: cast-iron facades.

Prefabricated facades of cast iron represented a simple and cheap way to garnish a structure with a face that was ornate, costly looking, and stylish (which at first meant classically inspired Italian Renaissance style and later meant French architectural style). The facades were mass produced in sections, and you could order one to fit your building from a catalog and quickly assemble and bolt it to a building's frame. You could paint it any color you wished, move it to a new building if need be, and even recycle it by melting it down and recasting it when new tastes in architecture arose. The light frames made heavy outer walls unnecessary and allowed the builders to fill up the street frontage with large windows instead, prefacing the skyscraper style.

Beginning in the 1950s, artists began renting unused floors of these warehouses (illegally, because the area wasn't zoned for residential use) and setting up studios with a bed and a hot plate in the corner. By 1973 the area was an official historic district, and as the zoning restrictions changed more artists flooded in. With so much art being produced, it was only natural that new art dealers, in a profession that formerly inhabited only the posh neighborhoods of Uptown, began to open up shops in SoHo. These dealers championed the neighborhood's emerging art stars while turning a nice profit at the same time. Established galleries from Uptown soon followed suit, and SoHo became the mecca of the contemporary

SoHo

1 Singer Building/ Kate's Paperie	**12** Gunther Building
	13 "King of Greene Street"
2 Prada	**14** agnes b. homme
3 Eileen's Special Cheesecake	**15** Richard Haas Mural
	16 Fanelli's Cafe
4 Haughwout Building	**17** Moss
5 101 Spring Street	**18** The DIA Center for the Arts
6 105 Mercer Street	**19** Brooke Alexander Editions
7 Gourmet Garage	**20** The Drawing Center
8 Yohji Yamamoto	**21** Deitch Projects
9 Pearl Paint	**22** *The Broken Kilometer*
10 Greene Street	**23** Vesuvio Bakery
11 91-93 Grand Street	

art world in the late '70s and early '80s. Thrift stores and funky boutiques opened, abandoned shop fronts were filled with inexpensive diners, and, inevitably, the yuppies soon caught wind of it all.

In the 1980s, young professionals living in Manhattan's cramped, expensive apartments and co-ops saw the chance both to be hip and to get a huge pad at a low cost by moving into converted SoHo lofts. They swarmed into the neighborhood, with pricey boutiques trailing along behind. Sandwich shops like Dean & Deluca were transformed into fine-food emporia. These new arrivals quickly drove the rents up into the stratosphere and were almost universally resented by SoHo's artist community, even though some new inhabitants did buy art as decoration for their empty wall space. It wasn't long before artists, even those of the nonstarving persuasion, couldn't afford to move in, and long-established SoHo residents found their own rents escalating.

In the 1990s, tourists quickly followed in the yuppies' wake, and chain stores and other paeans to mass tourism started popping up. Today, a few exhibition spaces remain, and you can find some funky shops and throwback cafes. But the hype has changed SoHo forever: from heavily commercial fine-art "galleries" and chillingly expensive brand-name high-fashion boutiques, to overpriced bistros and converted lofts.

This is probably *not* the SoHo you came to see. Parts of the neighborhood are like a huge outdoor high-end shopping mall that happens to have some lovely cast-iron facades, cobblestone streets, and the ghosts of a few art galleries. Just a few years ago the galleries here provided a collective museum of the best that the international contemporary art world had to offer, but this has changed as galleries close and move out. If you want to see the hottest contemporary art, don't bother with SoHo; head north to Chelsea (see chapter 7) or across the river to Williamsburg in Brooklyn.

Still, there's no denying the neighborhood's architectural charm and (consumer-driven) peripatetic energy. Your walk through SoHo takes you past the weird industrial beauty of the cast-iron age, into some of the more interesting shops and fashion outlets (these things change every few weeks, so except for some long-established ones, I'll limit myself to mentioning the big names in passing as we walk up the block that their outlets currently inhabit) and past the doors of a couple surviving galleries and art spaces.

• • • • • • • • • • • • • • • •

Starting Out **Dean & Deluca** (© 212/226-6800; www.dean-deluca.com), 560 Broadway at the southeast corner of Prince Street, is a New York institution. Although now expanded to multiple branches, and priced a bit out of starving-artist range, Dean & Deluca remains one of Manhattan's older, more beloved fine-food shops. It started as a lunch counter serving superb sandwiches—still for sale, along with a cornucopia of imported, farm-fresh gourmet foods and kitchenware. At the very least, grab a cappuccino and a pastry (or my favorite, a giant spiced ginger cookie) and sit at the bar counter facing the plate-glass window to watch one of SoHo's busiest intersections. The cafe is open daily from 10am to 8pm (Sun to 7pm).

As you exit 560 Broadway, you'll see across the street the terra-cotta facade and long, graceful arches of the:

1. **Little Singer Building,** designed by Ernest Flagg in 1904 as an office and warehouse for the sewing-machine giant. The 12-story facade with large glass windows and a steel frame was an architectural novelty at the time and prefigured the plate-glass walls of later-20th-century skyscrapers.

   The Singer building's ground floor houses **Kate's Paperie** (© 212/941-9816; www.katespaperie.com),

Kid-Friendly Experiences

- Savoring a treat at Eileen's Special Cheesecake (stop 3)
- Exploring the endless art supplies at Pearl Paint (stop 9)
- Taking in the *trompe-l'oeil* Richard Haas mural (stop 15)
- Seeing 140 tons of dirt at *The New York Earth Room* (stop 18)

which sells paper and stationery items of the highest quality and inventiveness, along with housewares in the back. Cross Broadway to at least poke your head in for a glance at the paper geometry of the ceiling. Then cross Prince Street so you're standing on the northwest corner.

Filling the russet 19th-century building at this corner is an emblem of the new SoHo. Once home to the Guggenheim SoHo, it is now occupied by:

2. **Prada** (℃ 212/334-8888; www.prada.com). A few years ago, the Guggenheim, the Alternative Museum, the Museum for African Art, and the New Museum of Contemporary Art were all on this block, but big-time consumption has displaced them. As far as pricey retail spaces go, this store is certainly not without its redeeming artistic qualities. Designed by architect and theorist Rem Koolhaas for a cool $40 million, the space seems as much an art installation as an outlet for designer threads. Opened in late 2001 to much buzz and a fair amount of criticism (it's not the most user-friendly space), it's worth a walk-through even if your wardrobe doesn't need updating.

Turn south down Broadway, passing back by Dean & Deluca. Make a left on Spring Street and continue east to Lafayette Street. If you look to your right at Lafayette, you'll see that the street forks half a block down. Cross to walk down the east side of Lafayette so that you can take the left-hand branch of the fork, called Cleveland Place. At the corner of Cleveland Place and Kenmare Street, you'll find the tiny:

3. **Eileen's Special Cheesecake** (℃ 212/966-5585; www.eileenscheesecake.com). Eileen Avezzano started making cheesecakes for neighbors in the early '70s; now she sends them all over the United States. Cupped in hand-molded graham-cracker crusts, these little pies are held by many (clients have included Robert Redford and Frank Sinatra) to be New York's best cheesecakes. Two dollars and fifty cents will get you a mini-cheesecake in any of about 19 variations, from plain to fruit-topped to chocolate-and-raspberry swirl.

Continue on the short block down Cleveland Place to Broome Street and turn right. Walk a few blocks west to the corner of Broadway; on your right, you'll see the:

4. **Haughwout Building.** This cast-iron building was built in 1857 for E. V. Haughwout's china and glassware company, one-time supplier to the White House. It is a perfect example of how the cast-iron movement brought aesthetic sensibilities of past eras (in this case Renaissance Italy) together with the practicality, technical skill, and replication perfection of the industrial age. The architect used a single element (a window arch) from Jacopo Sansavino's Renaissance Biblioteca on Venice's St. Mark's Square and based this entire cast-iron facade upon it, taking what was once merely a single part of a complex Renaissance structure and repeating it 92 times to make a new, industrial whole. This building was the first to use the steam-driven Otis safety elevator, a contraption that freed buildings from limiting their height to a comfortable walk-up and allowed skyscrapers to soar.

Turn right up Broadway to admire the front of the Haughwout Building as you head back north. Swing left on Spring Street. At the corner of Mercer Street is:

5. **101 Spring St.,** an 1870 cast-iron masterpiece with huge windows that heralded the age of skyscrapers.

Turn right onto Mercer Street and look across the street at one of the oldest houses surviving in SoHo:

6. **105 Mercer St.** Built in 1831, this house was already doing brisk business as a brothel by 1832. In the mid-19th century, SoHo was New York's largest, and most genteel, red-light district. Mercer Street was lined with houses of illicit pleasure, and a full two-thirds of Gotham's ladies of the night trolled the streets looking for likely clients and then plying their trade in rooms on the upper floors of buildings like this one. By the end of the Civil War, the cream of the prostitute crop had moved uptown (arm-in-arm with high society), and SoHo's bordellos declined into houses of truly ill repute, fit only for drunken sailors.

Manhattan businesses began razing these old buildings to put up warehouses on the cheap property, and the cast-iron age was born. This brick house survived and is one of Manhattan's oldest former brothels still standing. (It's now a private home.)

Turn around to walk south down Mercer Street back down to Broome Street. At the far corner, you'll see the:

7. **Gourmet Garage** (© 212/941-5850; www.gourmet garage.com), a specialty foods and sandwich shop similar to Dean & Deluca, but oriented more toward organic, rather than imported, fine foods.

Walk 1 block south. At the southwest corner of Mercer and Grand at no. 103 Grand St. is the chillingly expensive:

8. **Yohji Yamamoto** (© 212/966-9066; www.yohji yamamoto.co.jp), a Japanese designer-clothing boutique with elegantly stylish wares. The fashion here is overwhelmingly basic black, but a Mondrian-print raincoat does make an occasional appearance on the racks.

Trek down the last stretch of Mercer to Canal Street, across which you'll see the unmistakable, dingy white-and-red edifice of:

9. **Pearl Paint** (© 212/431-7932; www.pearlpaint.com) at 308 Canal St. Quite possibly the world's best art-supply store, Pearl Paint (est. 1933) is certainly one of the largest, with more than 45,000 items on six floors, all at a discount. Pearl's narrow aisles are piled high with the raw materials of creativity, and are fun to explore even if you're not an artist (and irresistible if you are).

Cross back to the north side of busy Canal Street and walk 1 block west to turn right on:

10. **Greene Street,** which boasts the highest concentration of cast-iron facades in the world—50 buildings in these 5 SoHo blocks. The first block alone, between Canal and Grand, has the longest continuous row of cast-iron facades left anywhere, a full 13 of them lining the east side of the street (nos. 8–34). Across the street, no. 15–17 is a late example (1895) done in simple Corinthian style. Back on the right, no. 28–30 is known as the "Queen of Greene Street," perhaps the finest cast-iron building ever erected (which, hallelujah, was being cleaned as this edition went to press). It was designed in 1872 by master

Isaac F. Duckworth in an era when French tastes had superseded the original Italian leanings, as evidenced by the Second Empire–style facade with a mansard roof.

At Grand Street, detour right to see:

11. **91–93 Grand St.,** one of the most successfully illusory cast-iron facades. The frontage is made up of iron plates bolted together so seamlessly that the building appears to be made of cut stone blocks.

Turn right back up Greene Street, and continue walking north. As you cross Broome Street, look back over your left shoulder to see the elaborate:

12. **Gunther Building,** with its curved corner windows on the southwest corner of Broome and Greene streets.

A short way up the next block on your right (no. 72–76) rises the:

13. **"King of Greene Street,"** another cast-iron masterpiece designed by that genius of the genre, Isaac Duckworth. The ornate and complex classical facade makes liberal use of Corinthian columns and decorative detail.

Continue north on Greene Street, and across Spring Street, at no. 103, is:

14. **agnes b.** (© 212/925-4649; www.agnesb.fr), SoHo's outlet for women's, men's, and children's fashions from the famed French designer.

At Prince Street, cross to the east side of the street, turn, and look back across Greene Street to see the:

15. **Richard Haas mural.** If cast-iron facades were originally conceived of as illusory imitations of more expensive stone facades, then Richard Haas's *trompe-l'oeil* mural of a cast-iron facade is quite the bit of irony (ha!). Look for the contented cat sitting in a half-open "window" that helps complete the illusion.

Turn right to detour down Prince Street 1 block, past Apple's Station A, Jerry's Restaurant and Bar, and J. Crew, and cross to the southwest corner of Mercer Street, where stands an old Manhattan holdover:

16. **Fanelli's Cafe** (© 212/226-9412). Established in 1847, this bar is the second oldest in New York, though

it's carried the name "Fanelli's" only since 1922 (when it was a speakeasy). Within the turn-of-the-20th-century interior, a clientele of regular-looking folk belly up to the bar or sit at the little tables noshing on bistro and cafe-type dishes.

After a refreshing mug of ale, backtrack along Prince to Greene Street and turn right (north) onto it. At the end of the block on your right at no. 146 sits:

17. **Moss** (℃ 212/204-7100; www.mossonline.com), a housewares design store of exquisite taste, representing the best and most expensive of 20th-century design. It's something between a museum and a shop, showcasing everything that's hot, from the rubber vases of Holland's Droog Design and flexible plastic bookshelves that undulate along the wall to inventive flatware and the collective output from Italy's Alessi firm, including colorful cat-faced bottle openers, Robert Graves's whimsical teakettles, and phallic butane lighters.

Double back down Greene Street to Prince and turn right up Wooster Street, most of whose top galleries became overpriced design boutiques at the turn of this century. Still surviving on your left, at no. 141, is one of the many branches of:

18. **The DIA Center for the Arts** (℃ 212/989-5566; www. diaart.org). Although ostensibly they occasionally change the exhibition at this art, lecture, and symposia center, Walter de Maria's "groundbreaking" work *The New York Earth Room* has filled the space with 250 cubic yards of dirt (22 in. deep) since 1977. Hours are Wednesday through Sunday, noon to 6pm (closed 3–3:30pm). Admission is free.

Turn around to backtrack south on Wooster Street. You have a few blocks of breathing space continuing south on Wooster—passing boutiques for Patagonia, Chanel, and Movado—until just before you reach Broome Street, where on the right (east) side of the street, on the second floor of no. 59, is:

19. **Brooke Alexander Editions** (℃ 212/925-4338; www.baeditions.com), one of the most important

contemporary print galleries in New York. Along with the occasional installation, the American and European artists shown here tend to be well established: Andy Warhol, Joseph Albers, Georg Baselitz, Lucien Freud, Jasper Johns, Donald Judd, Sol Lewit, Robert Mangold, Robert Mapplethorpe, Bruce Nauman, Claes Oldenburg, and Robert Rauschenberg, among many others.

Keep walking south on Wooster Street. In the next block, at no. 35, is:

20. **The Drawing Center** (© 212/219-2166; www.drawing center.org), a prestigious not-for-profit outfit that since 1976 has been instrumental in getting emerging and underrepresented artists' work some SoHo exposure. There are usually three annual experimental shows of new artists and one (held Apr–July) of museum-quality historic drawings (the likes of Rembrandt, Guercino, and architects Gaudi and Inigo Jones). Across the street at no. 40, the Drawing Center has opened **"The Drawing Room"** for even more experimental projects and installations.

Keep walking south; just past Grand Street on the left (no. 18 Wooster) is:

21. **Deitch Projects** (© 212/343-7300; www.deitch.com), showing truly avant-garde (read: often silly) art. The gallery explores the intersection of art, fashion, music, and performance, with a second location just around the corner, at 76 Grand St.

Return up Wooster Street to Grand Street. From there, take a left. At West Broadway—SoHo's restaurant row—take a right to walk up the east (closest) side to:

Take a Break The Cupping Room Cafe (© 212/ 925-2898; www.cuppingroomcafe.com) at 359 Broadway has an eclectic Mediterranean menu, rustic atmosphere (with intimate nooks), and a good selection of wines by the glass. On the $14 to $23 side of the menu, entrees range from pork chops with apple chutney to grilled mahimahi with tomato coulis. Sandwiches, such as burgers and fries or Black Forest ham with Jarlsberg on pumpernickel, run for $10 to $19. For dessert, the white hot chocolate goes well with the range of fresh cakes and pastries made on the premises. On Wednesday and Friday nights, live Mediterranean and jazz music lures a dressed-down 20-something crowd.

Continue north up West Broadway, a street where rising rents brought on by such new tenants as Ralph Lauren and DKNY have forced out most of the funky little shops, old bookstores, and noted galleries. Between Broome and Spring streets, at no. 393, is a second SoHo DIA Center (www.diaart.org), this one showcasing:

22. **The Broken Kilometer,** another semipermanent installation by Walter de Maria. One kilometer's worth of solid brass cylinder segments (500 of them, weighing 18.75 tons in total) lie in five rooms here (working against the optical rules of perspective, the distance between each cylinder increases as they get farther away from you, so they *appear* to be physically equidistant). The companion piece, *The Vertical Kilometer,* is a single, 1,000-meter-long brass rod sticking straight up . . . but sunk almost entirely into the ground near Kassel, Germany. The New York version is open Wednesday to Sunday noon to 6pm (closed 3–3:30pm). Admission is free.

Keep heading north on West Broadway to Prince Street and detour left to no. 160, where you'll find the:

23. **Vesuvio Café and Bakery** (✆ 212/925-8248), a real old-fashioned Italian bakery that's been in the Dapolito family since 1920. The green-edged plate windows, frequently featured in films and photographs, are usually stacked high with bread leaned straight up against them, with a few ring-shaped loafs perched on top for effect.

Greenwich Village Literary Tour

Start: Bleecker Street between La Guardia Place and Thompson Street.

Subway: Take the 6 to Bleecker Street, which lets you out at Bleecker and Lafayette streets. Walk west on Bleecker. Alternatively, you can take the A, B, C, D, E, F, or V to West 4th Street–Washington Square. Walk south on Sixth Avenue. Make a left on Bleecker and head east.

Finish: 14 W. 10th St.

Time: Approximately 4 to 5 hours.

Best Time: If you plan to do the whole tour, start fairly early in the day. (There's a breakfast break near the start.)

The Village has always attracted rebels, radicals, and creative types, from earnest 18th-century revolutionary Thomas Paine, to early-20th-century

Greenwich Village Literary Tour

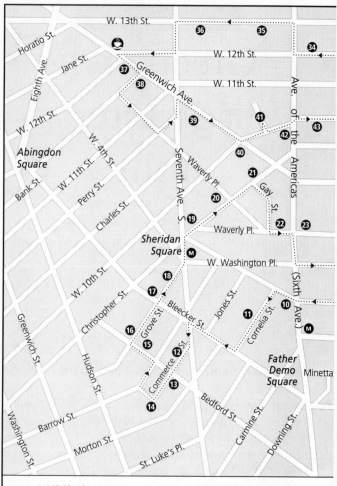

1 145 Bleecker Street
2 The Atrium
3 172 Bleecker Street
4 189 Bleecker Street
5 Minetta Tavern
6 130-132 MacDougal Street
7 85 West 3rd Street
8 The Provincetown Playhouse
9 137 MacDougal Street
10 Sixth Avenue and West 4th Street
11 33 Cornelia Street
12 11 Commerce Street

13 75 1/2 Bedford Street
14 The Cherry Lane Theatre
15 Chumley's
16 17 Grove Street
17 45 Grove Street
18 59 Grove Street
19 The Stonewall
20 The corner of Waverly Place
      & Christopher Street
21 Gay Street
22 139 Waverly Place
23 116 Waverly Place

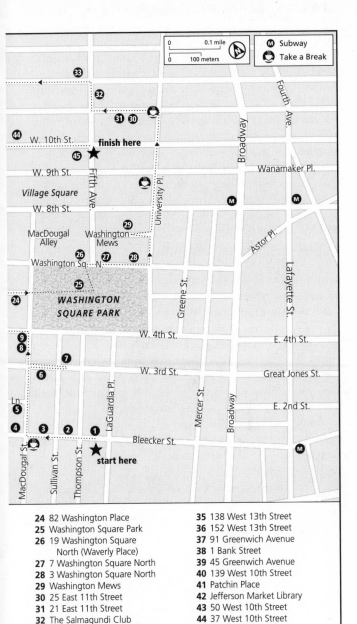

Map labels:

0 0.1 mile
0 100 meters

Ⓜ Subway
☕ Take a Break

㉝

㉜

㉛ ㉚ ☕

㊹ W. 10th St.   **finish here**

㊺ ★

W. 9th St.

Village Square

W. 8th St.

MacDougal Alley   Washington Mews ㉙

㉖ ㉗ ㉘

Washington Sq. N.

☕

Fourth Ave.

Broadway

Wanamaker Pl.

Ⓜ   Ⓜ

Astor Pl.

Fifth Ave.

University Pl.

㉔   WASHINGTON SQUARE PARK

㉕

Greene St.

Lafayette St.

W. 4th St.   E. 4th St.

⑨
⑧

⑦

W. 3rd St.   Great Jones St.

⑥

LaGuardia Pl.

Mercer St.

Broadway

E. 2nd St.

Ln

⑤

④   ③   ②   ①

MacDougal St.   Sullivan St.   Thompson St.

Bleecker St.

★ **start here**

Ⓜ

radicals such as John Reed and Mabel Dodge, to the Stonewall rioters who gave birth to the gay-liberation movement in 1969. A Village protest in 1817 saved the area's colorfully convoluted lanes and byways when the city imposed a geometric grid system on the rest of New York's streets. Much of Village life centers around Washington Square Park, the site of hippie rallies and counterculture demonstrations, and the former stomping ground of Henry James and Edith Wharton.

Many other American writers have at some time made their homes in the Village. As early as the 19th century, it was New York's literary hub and a hot spot for salons and other intellectual gatherings. Both the Metropolitan Museum of Art and the Whitney Museum of American Art came into being here, albeit some 60 years apart.

The 20th century saw Greenwich Village transformed from a bastion of old New York families to a bohemian enclave of struggling writers and artists. Though skyrocketing rents made the Village less accessible to aspiring artists after the late 1920s, it remained a mecca for creative people—so much so that almost every building is a literary landmark. Today, the high cost of housing here means that most modern Villagers are upwardly mobile professionals. There still are, however, plenty of resident throwbacks to the '60s, latter-day bohemians with multiple body piercings, in addition to earnest NYU students, gawking tourists, funky shops, and great cafes that keep this one of the liveliest neighborhoods in town. It also remains one of Manhattan's most downright picturesque neighborhoods.

Though the focus of this tour is the Village's literary history, I think you'll also enjoy strolling along its quaint, tree-shaded streets lined with Federal and Greek Revival buildings. This tour is a long one, and you may want to break it up into two visits.

● ● ● ● ● ● ● ● ● ● ● ● ● ● ● ●

Begin on Bleecker Street, named for a writer, Anthony Bleecker, whose friends included Washington Irving and William Cullen Bryant, at:

1. **145 Bleecker St.** James Fenimore Cooper, author of 32 novels, plus a dozen works of nonfiction, lived here in

Kid-Friendly Experiences

- Visiting 130–132 MacDougal St., if they've read *Little Women* (stop 6)
- Stopping by 11 Commerce St., where Washington Irving wrote "The Legend of Sleepy Hollow" (stop 12)
- Watching the performers in Washington Square Park (stop 25)
- Discovering the eclectic collections at The Forbes Magazine Building (stop 33)
- Having afternoon tea at Tea & Sympathy (see the "Take a Break" box on p. 83)
- Getting a look at 14 W. 10th St., the home of Mark Twain, author of *Tom Sawyer* and *Huckleberry Finn* (stop 45)

1833. Though he is primarily remembered for romantic adventure stories about the American frontier, Cooper also wrote political commentary, naval history, sea stories, and a group of novels about the Middle Ages. His father—judge, congressman, and Federalist Party leader William Cooper—founded Cooperstown, New York, the author's childhood home. This town was the setting for the author's *Leatherstocking Tales,* the epic of frontiersman Natty Bumppo (written over a period of 19 years) that includes *The Pioneers, The Last of the Mohicans, The Prairie, The Pathfinder,* and *The Deerslayer.* The town is more famous today as the home of the Baseball Hall of Fame.

James F. Cooper entered Yale at age 13 (not an uncommon occurrence in the early 19th century), but he was expelled in his junior year for pranks such as putting a donkey in a professor's chair. At 17, his aborted college career was followed by a stint in the merchant marines and the navy. His first novel, *Precaution,* was published in 1820. It created no great stir in the literary world, but a second novel focusing on the American Revolution, *The Spy,* appeared a year later and enjoyed vast success, as did his later books.

Cross the street and continue west (walk right) to:

2. **The Atrium** (no. 160), a 19th-century Beaux Arts building by Ernest Flagg that is today a posh apartment building. Before becoming the sadly defunct Village Gate jazz
club in the late 1950s, this former flophouse was
Theodore Dreiser's first New York residence. (In 1895, he
paid 25¢ a night for a cell-like room.)

Farther west is:

3. **172 Bleecker St.,** where James Agee lived in a top-floor
railroad flat from 1941 to 1951, after he completed *Let Us
Now Praise Famous Men*. Though the book enjoyed great
popularity in the 1960s, it was originally scathingly
reviewed and went out of print in 1948 after selling a
mere 1,025 copies. When it was published, Ralph
Thompson of the *New York Times* called Agee "arrogant,
mannered, precious, gross," and his book "the choicest
recent example of how to write self-inspired, self-con-
scious, and self-indulgent prose." *Time* called it "the most
distinguished failure of the season."

Rallying from critical buffets during his Bleecker Street
tenancy, Agee created the screenplay for *The African
Queen* and worked as a movie critic for both *Time* and
The Nation. He had to move from this walk-up apartment
after he suffered a heart attack.

Nearby, the quintessential Village corner of Bleecker
and MacDougal is a good spot for a breakfast break.

Take a Break Le Figaro Café (℅ 212/677-
1100) at 184–186 Bleecker St. is an old beat-gener-
ation haunt. In 1969, Village residents were disheartened to
see the Figaro close and in its place arise an uninspired and
sterile Blimpie. In 1976, the present owner completely
restored Figaro to its earlier appearance, replastering its
walls once again with shellacked copies of the French newspaper *Le Figaro*. Stop in for pastries and coffee or an omelet
and absorb the atmosphere, or sit at a sidewalk table to
watch the Village parade by. It opens at 10am daily and
serves a full, fixed-price brunch Saturday and Sunday from
10am to 4pm. On Sunday nights, the cafe entertains diners with belly dancing.

On the opposite corner is:

4. **189 Bleecker St.** For several decades, beginning in the late 1920s, the San Remo (today Ciao Café Wine Bar), an Italian restaurant at the corner of Bleecker and MacDougal streets, was a writer's hangout frequented by James Baldwin, William Styron, Jack Kerouac, James Agee, Frank O'Hara, Gregory Corso, Dylan Thomas, William Burroughs, and Allen Ginsberg. John Clellon Holmes wrote about the San Remo in his 1952 novel, *Go,* one of the first published works of the beat generation.

Take a right and head north on MacDougal Street to the:

5. **Minetta Tavern,** 113 MacDougal St. at Minetta Lane (© 212/475-3850), which was a speakeasy called the Black Rabbit during Prohibition. The most unlikely event to take place here in those wild days was the founding of De Witt Wallace's very unbohemian *Reader's Digest* on the premises in 1923; the magazine was published in the basement here in its early days. Since 1937, the Minetta has been a simpatico Italian restaurant and meeting place for writers and other creative folk, including Ezra Pound, e.e. cummings, Louis Bromfield, and Ernest Hemingway.

The Minetta still evokes the old Village. Walls are covered with photographs of famous patrons and caricatures (about 20 of which artist Franz Kline scrawled in exchange for drinks and food), and the rustic pine-paneled back room is adorned with murals of local landmarks. Stop in for a drink or a meal. The Minetta is open daily from noon to midnight and serves traditional Italian fare.

Minetta Lane is named for the Minetta Brook that started on 23rd Street and flowed through here en route to the Hudson. The brook still runs underground.

A little farther up and across the street stands an 1852 house fronted by twin entrances and a wisteria-covered portico.

6. **130–132 MacDougal St.** belonged to Louisa May Alcott's uncle, and after the Civil War, Alcott lived and worked here. Historians believe it was here that she

penned her best-known work, the autobiographical children's classic *Little Women* (Jo, Amy, Meg, and Beth were based on Alcott and her sisters Abbie, Anna, and Lizzie, respectively). Alcott grew up in Concord, Massachusetts, the daughter of transcendentalist Amos Bronson Alcott. Emerson was a close family friend, and Thoreau taught the young Louisa botany. During the Civil War, Alcott briefly served as a Union hospital nurse in Washington, D.C., until a case of typhoid fever nearly killed her. Mercury poisoning from the medication she was given left her in fragile health for the rest of her life. Alcott later published a book of letters documenting her time as a nurse under the title *Hospital Sketches.* Henry James called Alcott "The novelist of children . . . the Thackeray, the Trollope, of the nursery and schoolroom." Die-hard chauvinist G. K. Chesterton found himself admitting in 1907 that "even from a masculine standpoint, the books are very good."

Turn right onto West 3rd Street. Walk 1 block, just beyond Sullivan Street, to:

7. **85 W. 3rd St.,** where Edgar Allan Poe lived, on the third floor, in 1845 (last window on the right). He wrote "Facts in the Case of M. Valdemar" and "The Sphinx" here, and "The Raven" was published during his tenancy. When NYU Law School laid out its plans for the giant structure that subsumed Poe's house, as well as the Judson house on the corner, they intended to entirely demolish the old tenement buildings. A compromise was reached that required the Law School to incorporate the historic structures, which were reconstructed in the perfunctory way you see here. To see the Poe Room and its small collection of Poe artifacts, check with the officer in the lobby of 245 Sullivan St.

Double back down 3rd Street to MacDougal Street and turn right. On your left is:

8. **The Provincetown Playhouse,** 133 MacDougal St. (© 212/998-5867), which was first established in 1915 on a wharf in Provincetown, Massachusetts. Founders George Cram "Jig" Cook and his wife, Susan Glaspell, began by producing their own plays. One day, however,

an intense 27-year-old named Eugene O'Neill arrived in Provincetown with a trunk full of plays, a few of which he brought for Cook and Glaspell to read. They immediately recognized his genius and were inspired to create a theater dedicated to experimental drama. The theater later moved to this converted stable, where O'Neill managed it through 1927. Many of O'Neill's early plays premiered here: *Bound East for Cardiff, The Hairy Ape, The Long Voyage Home, The Emperor Jones,* and *All God's Chillun's Got Wings.* That last play was especially radical for its time because of its portrayal of a racially mixed couple; black star Paul Robeson kissed white actress Mary Blair (literary critic Edmund Wilson's wife) on stage, prompting general outrage and Ku Klux Klan threats. Nevertheless, the play ran for 5 months.

Other seminal figures in the theater's early days were Max Eastman, Djuna Barnes, Edna Ferber, and John Reed. Edna St. Vincent Millay, whose unlikely life plan was to support herself as a poet by earning her living as an actress, snagged both the lead in Fred Dell's *An Angel Intrudes* and Dell himself (their love affair inspired her poems "Weeds" and "Journal"). Millay's own work, *Aria da Capo,* was produced here in 1919. Another notable Provincetown Playhouse production was e.e. cummings's *him,* a play with 21 scenes and 105 characters.

Katharine Cornell, Tallulah Bankhead, Bette Davis (who made her stage debut here), and Eva Le Gallienne appeared on the Provincetown stage in its early years. The theater was a great success, and O'Neill's plays went on to Broadway. But instead of basking in their popularity, Cook and Glaspell disbanded the company and moved to Greece, convinced that acceptance by the establishment signaled their failure as revolutionary artists. Though the Provincetown Players gave their last performance on December 14, 1929, this theater, fully restored in 1997, is now affiliated with NYU and presents plays by and for young people, as well as community playhouse–produced O'Neill works.

Next door is:

9. **137 MacDougal St.** Jack London, Upton Sinclair, Vachel Lindsay, Louis Untermeyer, Max Eastman,

Theodore Dreiser, Lincoln Steffens, and Sinclair Lewis hashed over life theories at the Liberal Club, "A Meeting Place for Those Interested in New Ideas," founded in 1913 on the second floor of the house that once stood here. Margaret Sanger lectured the club on birth control, an on-premises organization called Heterodoxy worked to promote feminist causes, and cubist art was displayed on the walls.

Downstairs were Polly's Restaurant (run by Polly Holladay and Hippolyte Havel) and the radical Washington Square Book Shop, from which Liberal Club members more often borrowed than bought. Holladay, a staunch anarchist, refused to join even the Liberal Club, which, however bohemian, was still an "organization." The apoplectic Havel, who was on the editorial board of *The Masses* (see stop 37), once shouted out at a meeting where fellow members were debating which literary contributions to accept: "Bourgeois pigs! Voting! Voting on poetry! Poetry is something from the soul! You can't vote on poetry!" When Floyd Dell pointed out to Havel that he had once made editorial selections for the radical magazine *Mother Earth,* Havel shot back, "Yes, but we didn't abide by the results!" Hugo Kalmar, a character in O'Neill's *The Iceman Cometh,* is purportedly based on Havel. In a previous incarnation, this building was the home of Nathaniel Currier (of Currier and Ives).

Turn left onto West 4th Street and continue to the corner of:

10. **Sixth Avenue and West 4th Street.** Eugene O'Neill, a heavy drinker, nightly frequented a bar called the Golden Swan (more familiarly known as the "Hell Hole" or "Bucket of Blood"), where the small Golden Swan Park now stands. The bar was patronized by prostitutes, gangsters, longshoremen, anarchists, politicians, artists, and writers. O'Neill later used the bar as a setting for his play *The Iceman Cometh,* a script that was 12 years in the writing. Eccentric owner Tom Wallace, on whom O'Neill modeled saloon proprietor Harry Hope, kept a pig in the basement and seldom ventured off the premises.

Cross Sixth Avenue, angle up the continuation of West 4th Street, and make your first left onto Cornelia Street looking for:

11. **33 Cornelia St.** Throughout the 1940s, film critic/poet/novelist/screenwriter James Agee lived on Bleecker Street and worked in a studio at this address. Here he completed final revisions on *Let Us Now Praise Famous Men,* which portrayed the bleak lives of Alabama sharecroppers. The book originated in 1936 as an article for Henry Luce's *Fortune* magazine, which rejected the piece as too long and too liberal—the book's first pages contain a paraphrase from Marx's *Communist Manifesto:* "Workers of the world, unite and fight. You have nothing to lose but your chains, and a world to win."

Though a Harvard grad from an upper-class background, Agee was extremely sympathetic to the plight of the poor (he once took a hobo into his home); dubious, if not downright cynical, about the very nature of journalism; and ashamed of the intrusive nature of his mission. "It seems to me," he wrote, "obscene and thoroughly terrifying . . . to pry intimately into the lives of an undefended and appallingly damaged group of human beings, an ignorant and helpless rural family, for the purpose of parading the nakedness, disadvantage, and humiliation of these lives before another group of human beings in the name of . . . honest journalism."

Next door, at 31 Cornelia St., **Caffé Cino** once stood. The cafe opened in 1958 and served cappuccino in shaving mugs. In the early 1960s, owner Joe Cino encouraged aspiring playwrights, such as Lanford Wilson, Sam Shepard, and John Guare, to stage readings and performances in his cramped storefront space. Experimentation in this tiny cafe gave birth to New York's Off-Broadway theater scene. Plagued by money troubles, Cino committed suicide in 1967; Caffé Cino closed a year later.

Continue down Cornelia Street to Bleecker Street and turn right. Cross Seventh Avenue, jog a bit left, and angle back down Commerce Street. Near the corner stands:

12. **11 Commerce St.** Washington Irving wrote "The Legend of Sleepy Hollow" while living in this quaint

three-story brick building. Born into a prosperous New York family, he penned biographies of naval heroes as an officer in the War of 1812. In 1819, under the name Geoffrey Crayon, he wrote *The Sketch Book,* which contained the stories "The Legend of Sleepy Hollow," "Westminster Abbey," and "Rip Van Winkle." Irving was one of the elite New Yorkers who served on the planning commission for Central Park and was ambassador to Spain from 1842 to 1846. He coined the phrase "the almighty dollar" and once observed that "A tart temper never mellows with age, and a sharp tongue is the only tool that grows keener with constant use."

Continue walking west on Commerce and turn left at Bedford Street to find:

13. **75½ Bedford St.** The narrowest house in the Village (a mere 9½ ft. across), this unlikely three-story brick residence was built on the site of a former carriage alley in 1873. Pretty, redheaded, feminist poet Edna St. Vincent Millay, who arrived in the Village fresh from Vassar, lived here from 1923 (the year she won a Pulitzer Prize for her poetry) to 1925. Ever a favorite among Village intelligentsia, the vivacious Millay perhaps best expressed her youthful passion for life in the lines:

> *My candle burns at both ends;*
> *It will not last the night;*
> *But ah, my foes, and oh, my friends—*
> *It gives a lovely light!*

Other famous occupants of the narrow house have included a young Cary Grant and John Barrymore.

Return to Commerce Street and turn left, where:

14. **The Cherry Lane Theatre** (© 212/989-2020; www.cherrylanetheatre.com), nestled in a bend at 38 Commerce St., was founded in 1924 by Edna St. Vincent Millay. Famed scenic designer Cleon Throckmorton transformed the Revolutionary-era building (originally a farm silo, and later a brewery and a box factory) into a playhouse that presented works by Edward Albee, Samuel Beckett (*Waiting for Godot* and *Endgame* premiered here), Eugene Ionesco, Jean Genet, and Harold Pinter. In 1951,

Judith Malina and Julian Beck founded the ultra-experimental Living Theatre on its premises. Before rising to megafame, Barbra Streisand worked as a Cherry Lane usher. Today, the theatre produces new American works, with the goal of cultivating a multigenerational audience.

Nearby, in Commerce Street's bend, is **no. 48, a Greek Revival house** fronted by a bona-fide working gas lamp and built in 1844 for malicious merchant maven A. T. Stewart.

Continue around Commerce Street's bend to Barrow Street, where you turn right, and then turn left back onto Bedford Street. A few doors up on the right is:

15. **Chumley's,** 86 Bedford St. (© **212/675-4449**), which opened in 1926 in a former blacksmith's shop. During Prohibition, it was a speakeasy with a casino upstairs. Its convoluted entranceway with four steps up and four down (designed to slow police raiders), the lack of a sign outside, and a back door that opens on an alleyway are remnants of that era.

Original owner Lee Chumley was a radical labor sympathizer who held secret meetings of the IWW (Industrial Workers of the World) on the premises. Chumley's has long been a writer's bar. Its walls are lined with book jackets of works by famous patrons who, over the years, have included Edna St. Vincent Millay (she once lived upstairs), John Steinbeck, Eugene O' Neill, e.e. cummings, Edna Ferber, John Dos Passos, F. Scott Fitzgerald, Theodore Dreiser, William Faulkner, Gregory Corso, Norman Mailer, William Carlos Williams, Allen Ginsberg, Lionel Trilling, Harvey Fierstein, Calvin Trillin, and numerous others. Even the elusive J. D. Salinger hoisted a few at the bar here, and Simone de Beauvoir came by when she was in town.

With its working fireplaces (converted blacksmith forges), wood-plank flooring, amber lighting, and old, carved-up oak tables, Chumley's lacks nothing in the way of mellowed atmosphere. Think about returning for drinks or food. Dinner is served starting at 5:30pm daily. A blackboard menu features fresh pasta and grilled fish. The bar is open nightly from 4pm to midnight (to

1:30am on Fri and Sat), and lunch is served on weekends starting at 2pm.

Continue up Bedford to Grove Street, named in the 19th century for its many gardens and groves, and make a right to:

16. **17 Grove St.** Parts of this picturesque wood-frame house date from the early 1800s. A friend of James Baldwin's lived here in the 1960s, and Baldwin frequently stayed at the house. Baldwin, whose fiery writings coincided with the inception of the civil rights movement, once said, "The most dangerous creation of any society is that man who has nothing to lose."

Farther along this street is:

17. **45 Grove St.** Originally a freestanding two-story building, this was, in the 19th century, one of the Village's most elegant mansions, surrounded by verdant lawns with greenhouses and stables. Built in 1830, it was refurbished with Italianate influences in 1870. In the movie *Reds,* which is based on the life of John Reed, 45 Grove was portrayed (inaccurately) as Eugene O'Neill's house.

Ohio-born poet Hart Crane rented a second-floor room at 45 Grove St. in 1923 and began writing his poetic portrait of America, *The Bridge.* (Hart depicted the Brooklyn Bridge as a symbol of America's westward expansion.) Crane was born in 1899 with "a toe in the 19th century." His parents' marriage was a miserably unhappy one, and his mother, an artistic beauty subject to depression, concentrated her aesthetic energies on her son, giving him music and dancing lessons, taking him to art galleries, and providing him with every kind of children's book and classic. Although constant traveling with his mother kept Crane from finishing school, he was a voracious reader and brilliantly self-educated. By the time he was 17, his poetry had been published in prestigious New York magazines, and Nobel Prize–winning Indian poet Rabindranath Tagore was so impressed that he arranged to meet Crane when visiting Cleveland.

In later years, frustrated by frequent rejection from magazines and other exigencies of his craft, Crane would occasionally toss his typewriter out the window. Often moody and despondent, he was chronically in debt, plagued by guilt over homosexual encounters on the nearby docks, and given to almost nightly alcoholic binges; fellow Villager e.e. cummings once found him passed out on a sidewalk, bundled him into a taxi, and had him driven home. In 1932, returning by ship from Mexico (where, on a Guggenheim fellowship, he had been attempting to write an epic poem about Montezuma), Crane made sexual advances to a crew member, was badly beaten up, and jumped into the waters to his death at the age of 33.

Continue up the street to:

18. **59 Grove St.** English-born American revolutionary/political theorist/writer Thomas Paine died here in 1809. Paine came to America (with the help of Benjamin Franklin) in 1774, and in 1776 he produced his famous pamphlet, *The Crisis,* which was critical in rallying support for American independence, and begins with the words: "These are the times that try men's souls." After fighting in the American Revolution, he returned to England to advocate the overthrow of the British monarchy. Indicted for treason, he escaped to Paris and became a French citizen. While imprisoned in Paris during the Reign of Terror, he wrote *The Age of Reason.* He returned to the United States in 1802, where he was vilified for his atheism. Benjamin Franklin once said to Paine, "Where liberty is, there is my country." To which Paine replied: "Where liberty is not, there is mine."

The downstairs space has always been a restaurant, which today is called **Marie's Crisis Cafe (© 212/243-9323)**. Though the building Paine lived in burned down, some of the interior brickwork is original. Of note is a WPA-era mural behind the bar depicting the French and American revolutions. Up a flight of stairs is another mural (a wood-relief carving) called *La Convention,* depicting Robespierre, Danton, and Thomas Paine. In the 1920s, you might have spotted anyone from Eugene O'Neill to Edward VIII of England here.

At Seventh Avenue, cross to the opposite side of the wide intersection, walk around to the left of the little park, and head half a block up Christopher Street, the hub of New York's gay community, to no. 53:

19. **The Stonewall.** The current bar in this spot shares a name with its more famous predecessor, the Stonewall Inn. This bar was the scene of the Stonewall riots of June 1969, when gay customers decided to resist the police during a routine raid. The event launched the lesbian and gay rights movement and is commemorated throughout the country every year with gay-pride parades. In the tiny Sheridan Square Park you just skirted, several of George Segal's realist sculptures honor the gay community. By portraying same-sex couples enjoying the park just like anybody else would, these sculptures point to the ludicrousness of marginalizing gay members of the community.

Continue up the block to:

20. **The Corner of Waverly Place and Christopher Street.** The wedge-shaped Georgian Northern Dispensary building dates from 1831. Edgar Allan Poe was treated for a head cold here in 1836, the year he came to New York with his 13-year-old bride, for whom he would later compose the pain-filled requiems "Ulalume" and "Annabel Lee":

> *I was a child and she was a child,*
> *In this kingdom by the sea;*
> *But we loved with a love that was more than*
> *love—*
> *I and my Annabel Lee.*

Keep walking up Christopher Street to take a right onto:

21. **Gay Street.** Famous residents of this tiny street (originally a stable alley) have included New York Mayor Jimmy Walker, who owned the 18th-century town house at no. 12. More recently, Frank Paris, creator of Howdy Doody, lived here.

In the 1920s, Ruth McKenney lived in the basement of no. 14 with her sister Eileen, who later married Nathanael West. It was the setting for McKenney's zany *My Sister Eileen* stories, which were first published in the *New Yorker* and then collected into a book. They were then turned into a popular stage comedy that ran on Broadway from 1940 to 1942, followed by a Broadway musical version called *Wonderful Town* and two movie versions, one of them starring Rosalind Russell. The house dates from 1827.

Mary McCarthy, the *Partisan Review's* drama critic and author of *The Stones of Florence* and *The Group,* lived in a studio apartment at no. 18 in the 1940s. During Prohibition, the street held several speakeasies.

At the end of the short street, take a left onto Waverly Place and look for:

22. **139 Waverly Place.** Edna St. Vincent Millay lived here with her sister, Norma, in 1918. Radical playwright Floyd Dell, her lover, who found the apartment for her, commented: "She lived in that gay poverty which is traditional of the Village, and one may find vivid reminiscences of that life in her poetry." An interesting note: Edna St. Vincent Millay's middle name was derived from St. Vincent's Hospital, which had saved the life of her uncle.

    Cross Sixth Avenue to check out:

23. **116 Waverly Place.** Dating from 1891, the building has hosted William Cullen Bryant, Horace Greeley, Margaret Fuller, poet Fitz-Greene Halleck, and Herman Melville. Here Poe read his latest poem, "The Raven," to assembled literati. Waverly Place, by the way, was named in 1833 for Sir Walter Scott's novel, *Waverley.*

    Return to Sixth Avenue and turn left (south) down it. Take another left onto Washington Place to:

24. **82 Washington Place,** residence from 1908 to 1912 of Willa Cather, whose books celebrated pioneer life and the beauty of her native Nebraska landscape. Cather came to New York in 1906 at the age of 31 to work at the prestigious *McClure's* magazine and rose to managing editor before resigning to write full time. As her career advanced, and she found herself besieged with requests for lectures and interviews, Cather became almost reclusive and fiercely protective of her privacy. She complained,

    *In this country, a writer has to hide and lie
    and almost steal in order to get time to work*

> *in—and peace of mind to work with . . . If
> we lecture, we get a little more owlish and self-
> satisfied all the time. We hate it at first, if we
> are decently modest, but in the end we fall in
> love with the sound of our own voice. There is
> something insidious about it, destructive to
> one's finer feelings . . . It's especially destructive
> to writers, ever so much worse than alcohol, it
> takes their edge off.*

Band leader John Philip Sousa owned the beautiful
1839 building next door (**no. 80**).

Washington Place ends at:

25. **Washington Square Park,** the hub of the Village. This
area was once a swamp frequented largely by duck hunters.
Minetta Brook meandered through it. In the 18th and
early 19th centuries, it was a potter's field (more than
10,000 people are buried under the park) and an execution
site (one of the makeshift gallows survives—a towering
English elm in the northwest corner of the park). The park
was dedicated in 1826, and elegant residential dwellings,
some of which have survived NYU's cannibalization of the
neighborhood, went up around the square. At this time, it
was the citadel of stifling patrician gentility so evocatively
depicted in the novels of Edith Wharton. She defined
Washington Square society as "a little set with its private
catch-words, observances, and amusements" indifferent to
"anything outside its charmed circle."

One of the city's most recognizable landmarks, the
Washington Square Arch (1891) at the Fifth Avenue
entrance, underwent a nearly $3 million renovation from
August 2002 to January 2004, removing over a century's
worth of air pollution. Inspired by the larger Arc de
Triomphe in Paris, the arch was designed by Sanford
White to replace a wooden arch, which was erected in
1889 to commemorate the centenary of Washington's
inauguration. From pranks to political protests, the
memorial has been a magnet for public demonstrations.
One night in 1917, a group of Liberal Club pranksters
climbed the Washington Square Arch, fired cap guns, and

proclaimed the "independent republic of Greenwich Village," a utopia dedicated to "socialism, sex, poetry, conversation, dawn-greeting, anything—so long as it is taboo in the Middle West." Today, Washington Square Park would probably surpass any of this group's most cherished anarchist fantasies and might even lead them to question the philosophy altogether.

Along the square's north edge stand many of the surviving old homes, including, just west of Fifth Avenue:

26. **19 Washington Square North** (Waverly Place). Henry James's grandmother, Elizabeth Walsh, lived at this now-defunct address. (The no. 19 that exists today is a different house, the numbering system having changed since James's day.) Young Henry spent much time at her house, which was the inspiration for his novel *Washington Square,* later made into the Olivia de Havilland movie *The Heiress.* In 1875, James moved to Europe, where he became an expert on expatriatism and penned many novels about Americans living abroad.

Farther east, across Fifth Avenue, is:

27. **7 Washington Square North,** where Edith Wharton, age 20, and her mother lived in 1882. A wealthy aristocrat, born Edith Jones, Wharton maintained a close friendship with Henry James and, like him, left New York's stultifying upper-class social scene for Europe (Paris) in 1910, where she wrote the Pulitzer Prize–winning *The Age of Innocence.* Both she and James were immensely popular in Europe and were deluged with invitations. (James once admitted to accepting 107 dinner invitations in a single year.) Wharton wrote almost a book a year her entire adult life, while also finding time to feed French and Belgian refugees during World War I and take charge of 600 Belgian orphans. For these efforts, she was awarded the Legion of Honor by the French government in 1915. No. 7 was also once the home of Alexander Hamilton.

Nearby is:

28. **3 Washington Square North** (today the NYU School of Social Work). Critic Edmund Wilson, managing editor

of the *New Republic,* lived here from 1921 to 1923. Another resident, John Dos Passos, wrote *Manhattan Transfer* here. Dos Passos, a fiery New York radical in the 1920s, became disillusioned with Communism after journeying to Spain with Hemingway during the Spanish Civil War. He was appalled that the Marxist-backed Republicans executed his friend Jose Robles, himself a Republican supporter. The incident, which caused a break between Dos Passos and Hemingway when the latter refused to challenge the integrity of the Republican cause, was the basis of Dos Passos's next novel, *Adventures of a Young Man* (1939). His books thereafter also demonstrated a marked shift to the right. In the 1940s, Dos Passos returned to his native Virginia.

Make a left at University Place and another immediate left into:

29. **Washington Mews.** This picturesque 19th-century cobblestoned street, lined with vine-covered, two-story buildings (converted stables and carriage houses constructed to serve posh Washington Square town houses), has had several famous residents, among them John Dos Passos, artist Edward Hopper (no. 14A), and writer Sherwood Anderson (no. 54). No. 54 dates from 1834.

Double back to University Place and turn left to head north to the southeast corner of 9th Street, where stands the first of two possible places to:

Take a Break The more expensive and formal of the choices is the **Knickerbocker Bar and Grill** (© 212/228-8490) at the southeast corner of 9th Street and University Place. This comfortable wood-paneled restaurant and jazz club attracts an interesting clientele, including writers (Jack Newfield, E. L. Doctorow, Erica Jong, Sidney Zion, Christopher Cerf) and actors (Richard Gere, F. Murray Abraham, Susan Sarandon, Tim Robbins). Harry Connick Jr. got his start playing piano at the Knickerbocker, and Charles Lindbergh signed the contract for his transatlantic flight at the bar here. The restaurant is open daily for lunch/brunch from 11:45am; an eclectic menu offers entrees ranging from pasta dishes to bangers and mash to Southwestern paella.

For smaller appetites, head 2 blocks up to a branch of **Dean & Deluca,** 75 University Place, at 11th Street (*©* **212/869-6890**). It offers superior light fare (pastries, croissants, ham and Brie sandwiches on baguette, pasta salads) in a pristinely charming setting, usually enhanced by recorded classical music. Be sure to look up at the gorgeous plasterwork ceiling. It's open daily from 7am to 10pm.

This address is also a stop on the tour. When Thomas Wolfe graduated from Harvard in 1923, he came to New York to teach at NYU and lived at the Hotel Albert (depicted as the Hotel Leopold in his novel *Of Time and the River*), which stood at this address. Today the Albert Apartments occupy the site.

From University Place, turn left onto 11th Street to:

30. **25 E. 11th St.** The unhappy and sexually confused poet Hart Crane lived here for a short time. His neighbor at:

31. **21 E. 11th St.** was Mary Cadwaller Jones, who was married to Edith Wharton's brother. Her home was the setting of literary salons; Henry Adams, Theodore Roosevelt, Augustus Saint-Gaudens, and John Singer Sargent often came to lunch, and Henry James was a houseguest when he visited America from Europe. Jones's daughter, landscape architect Beatrix Farrand, grew up here before designing such renowned outdoor spaces as the White House's East Garden and the New York Botanical Gardens' Rose Garden.

Continue to Fifth Avenue, and turn right. On your right is:

32. **The Salmagundi Club,** 47 Fifth Ave., which began as an artist's club in 1871 and was originally located at 596 Broadway. The name comes from the *Salmagundi* papers, in which Washington Irving mocked his fellow New Yorkers and first used the term *Gotham* to describe the city. *Salmagundi*, which means "a stew of many ingredients," was thought an appropriate term to describe the club's diverse membership of painters, sculptors, writers, and musicians. The club moved to this mid-19th-century brownstone mansion in 1917. Theodore Dreiser lived at

the Salmagundi in 1897, when it was located across the street where the First Presbyterian Church stands today. It was at the Salmagundi that Dreiser probably wrote *Sister Carrie*, a work based on the experiences of his own sister, Emma.

Cross 12th Street. At the northwest corner is:

33. **The Forbes Magazine Building,** 60–62 Fifth Ave., with a museum (© **212/206-5548**) housing exhibits from the varied collections of the late Malcolm Forbes, who was famous as a financier, magazine magnate, frequent Liz Taylor escort, and father of presidential hopeful Steve Forbes. On display are hundreds of model ships; legions formed from a collection of more than 100,000 military miniatures; signed letters, papers, and other paraphernalia from almost every American president; an exhibit of the evolution of the game Monopoly (natch); and changing exhibits and art shows. Admission is free. The galleries are open Tuesday to Wednesday and Friday to Saturday, from 10am to 4pm.

Make a left on 12th Street and walk about halfway down the block; on your left you'll see:

34. **The New School,** at 66 W. 12th St. Formerly The New School for Social Research, this university was founded in 1919 as a forum for professors too liberal-minded for Columbia University's then stiflingly traditional attitude. In the 1930s, it became a "University in Exile" for intelligentsia fleeing Nazi Germany. Many great writers have taught or lectured in its classrooms over the decades: William Styron, Joseph Heller, Edward Albee, W. H. Auden, Robert Frost, Nadine Gordimer, Max Lerner, Maya Angelou, Joyce Carol Oates, Arthur Miller, I. B. Singer, Susan Sontag, Christopher Hitchens, and numerous others.

Turn right up Sixth Avenue and left onto 13th Street to:

35. **138 W. 13th St.** Max Eastman and other radicals urged revolution in the pages of the *Liberator,* headquartered in this lovely building on a pleasant tree-lined street. The magazine published works by John Reed, Edna St. Vincent Millay, Ernest Hemingway, Elinor Wylie, e.e. cummings (who later became very right-wing and a

passionate supporter of Sen. Joseph McCarthy's Communist witch hunts), John Dos Passos, and William Carlos Williams. The *Liberator*, established in 1919, succeeded *The Masses*, an earlier Eastman publication (see stop 37).

Further west along the block is:

36. **152 W. 13th St.** Offices for the *Dial*, a major avant-garde literary magazine of the 1920s, occupied this beautiful Greek Revival brick town house. The magazine dated from 1840 in Cambridge, Massachusetts, where transcendentalists Margaret Fuller and Ralph Waldo Emerson were its seminal editors. The *Dial* took its name from an Amos Bronson Alcott (stop 6) work. In the '20s, its aim was to offer "the best of European and American art, experimental and conventional." Contributors included Marianne Moore, Hart Crane, Conrad Aiken, Ezra Pound, Theodore Dreiser (who once wrote an article claiming that American literature had to be crude to be truly American), and artist Marc Chagall. T. S. Eliot, who once grumbled of the *Dial*, "there is far too much in it, and it is all second rate and exceedingly solemn," nevertheless published *The Waste Land* in its pages.

Continue west on 13th Street, and make a left on Seventh Avenue, a right on 12th Street, and then another right for some afternoon tea.

☕ **Take a Break** When Londoner Nicky Perry moved to New York, she was disappointed to find no proper British teahouses where she could get a decent cup of tea, so she opened her own in 1990. **Tea & Sympathy** (℅ **212/989-9735**), at 108 Greenwich Ave., is straight out of the English countryside, a hole-in-the-wall crammed with a few tables (always crowded), a friendly British waitstaff, and plenty of old-time charm in the form of Anglo paraphernalia plastered over the walls. Elbow room is at a minimum here, and prices reflect the store's high-rent location: Full afternoon tea for one is $22, but it includes a tiered serving tray stuffed full of finger sandwiches with the crusts cut off (cucumber and mayo or egg salad), cakes, biscuits, scones, jam, and clotted cream, plus, of course, a pot of tea. (Go for the

Typhoo.) There are also cheaper, bona fide British dishes, like shepherd's pie, bangers and mash, and Welsh rarebit, which run from $9 to $13. For dessert, try a treacle pudding or warm ginger cake. Tea & Sympathy is open Monday through Friday from 11:30am to 10:30pm, and Saturday and Sunday from 9:30am to 10:30pm.

From Tea & Sympathy, turn left to walk back down Greenwich Avenue to the corner of 12th Street and:

37. **91 Greenwich Ave.** At the beginning of the 20th century, Max Eastman was editor of a radical left-wing literary magazine called *The Masses*. This magazine published, among others, John Reed, Carl Sandburg, Sherwood Anderson, Upton Sinclair, Edgar Lee Masters, e.e. cummings, and Louis Untermeyer. John Sloan, Stuart Davis, Picasso, and George Bellows provided art for its pages, which a newspaper columnist dismissed thusly:

> *They draw nude women for The Masses,*
> *Thick, fat, ungainly lasses—*
> *How does that help the working classes?*

Reed wrote the magazine's statement of purpose: "To everlastingly attack old systems, old morals, old prejudices." *The Masses* was suppressed by the Justice Department in 1918 because of its opposition to World War I (it called on Woodrow Wilson to repeal the draft and claimed that America's enemy was not Germany but "that 2% of the United States that owns 60% of all the wealth"). Reed, Eastman, political cartoonist Art Young, and writer/literary critic Floyd Dell were put on trial under the Espionage Act and charged with conspiracy to obstruct recruiting and prevent enlistment. Pacifist Edna St. Vincent Millay read poems to the accused to help pass the time while juries were out. The trials all ended in hung juries.

Continue another block down Greenwich Avenue; turn right on Bank Street and look for:

38. **1 Bank St.** In 1913, shortly after the publication of *O Pioneers!*, Willa Cather, at age 40, moved to a seven-room, second-floor apartment in a large brick house here. Here

she lived with her companion, Edith Lewis, and wrote *My Antonia* (the third of a trilogy about immigrants in the United States), *Death Comes to the Archbishop,* and several other novels. In 1920, H. L. Mencken called *My Antonia* "the best piece of fiction ever done by a woman in America . . . I know of no novel that makes the remote folk of the western farmlands more real than *My Antonia* makes them, and know of none that makes them seem better worth knowing."

When she became successful, Cather rented the apartment above hers and kept it empty to ensure perfect quiet. Her Friday-afternoon at-homes here were frequented by D. H. Lawrence, among others. Unlike many Village writers of her day, Cather eschewed the radical scene and took little interest in politics.

From Bank Street, take a left onto Waverly Place, cross 11th Street to take another left on Perry Street, and make a final right back onto Greenwich Avenue to:

39. **45 Greenwich Ave.** In 1947, William Styron came to New York from North Carolina to work as a junior editor at McGraw-Hill. He moved to this address (today a vintage clothing shop) in 1951 after a stint in the marines and the success of his first novel, *Lie Down in Darkness.* Styron originally showed manuscript pages from that novel, begun at age 23, to Hiram Haydn, a Bobbs-Merrill editor whose writing class he was taking at the New School. Haydn told Styron he was too advanced for the class and took an option on the novel.

Continue down Greenwich Avenue to West 10th Street and detour right to:

40. **139 W. 10th St.** Today an Italian restaurant, this was the site, for decades, of a popular Village bar called the Ninth Circle. But it was in 1954 at a former bar at this location that playwright Edward Albee saw graffiti on a mirror reading, "Who's afraid of Virginia Woolf?" and, years later, appropriated it. He recalled the incident in a *Paris Review* interview: "When I started to write the play, it cropped up in my mind again. And, of course, 'Who's afraid of Virginia Woolf' means . . . who's afraid of living life without false illusions."

Double back up West 10th Street, cross Greenwich Avenue, and walk a block where, on your left, you will see the gated entry to:

41. **Patchin Place.** This tranquil, tree-shaded cul-de-sac has sheltered many illustrious residents. From 1923 to 1962, e.e. cummings lived at no. 4, where visitors included T. S. Eliot, Ezra Pound, and Dylan Thomas. The highly acclaimed but little-known Djuna Barnes (literary critics have compared her to James Joyce) lived in a tiny one-room apartment at no. 5. Reclusive and eccentric, she almost never left the premises for 40 years, prompting cummings to occasionally shout from his window, "Are you still alive, Djuna?"

Among other works, Barnes wrote a memoir called *Life Is Painful, Nasty, & Short . . . In My Case It Has Only Been Nasty* (it certainly wasn't short; she lived to the age of 90); an experimental poetic novel called *Nightwood* (for which T. S. Eliot penned an introduction); and a collection of poetry called *The Book of Repulsive Women.* Three of her one-act plays were produced at the Provincetown Playhouse in 1919 and 1920.

Louise Bryant and John Reed maintained a residence at Patchin Place for several years until Reed's death in 1920. During this time, he wrote his eyewitness account of the Russian Revolution, *Ten Days That Shook the World.* To avoid interruptions from callers at Patchin Place, Reed rented a room atop a restaurant at 147 W. 4th St. to do his writing. Theodore Dreiser and John Masefield were also Patchin Place residents, the former in 1895 when he was still an unknown journalist.

Continue down West 10th Street, but look to your right as you cross Sixth Avenue to see the:

42. **Jefferson Market Library** at 425 Sixth Ave., a former produce market. The turreted, redbrick-and-granite, Victorian-Gothic castle was built as a courthouse in 1877 and named for Thomas Jefferson. Topped by a lofty clock/bell tower (originally intended as a fire lookout), with traceried and stained-glass windows, gables, and steeply sloping roofs, the building was inspired by a

Bavarian castle. In the 1880s, architects voted it one of the 10 most beautiful buildings in America.

Head east down 10th Street to:

43. **50 W. 10th St.** After his great success with *Who's Afraid of Virginia Woolf?*, Edward Albee bought this late-19th-century converted carriage house in the early 1960s. It's a gem of a building, with highly polished wooden carriage doors. Albee wrote *Tiny Alice* and *A Delicate Balance* here, the latter being a Pulitzer Prize winner. In 1994, he won a second Pulitzer Prize for *Three Tall Women*.

Now look for:

44. **37 W. 10th St.** Sinclair Lewis, already a famous writer by the mid-1920s, lived in this early-19th-century house with his wife, journalist Dorothy Thompson, from 1928 to 1929. Lewis fell in love with the recently divorced Thompson at first sight in 1927 and immediately proposed to her. Once, when asked to speak at a dinner party, he stood up and said, "Dorothy, will you marry me?" and resumed his seat. Lewis later followed her to Russia and all over Europe until she accepted his proposal. Unfortunately, the marriage didn't last.

Your final stop is:

45. **14 W. 10th St.** When Mark Twain came to New York at the turn of the 20th century (at the age of 65), he lived in this gorgeous 1855 mansion. An extremely successful writer (Twain's first book was a travel book, *The Innocents Abroad*), he entertained lavishly. Born Samuel Langhorne Clemens, Twain was once a riverboat captain, and he took his pseudonym from the singsong calls of the sounding men stationed at the prows of Mississippi paddle boats. ("Mark twain" meant the waters were a safe 2 fathoms deep.) Twain was famous for his witticisms, including a quip on the art of quipping: "How lucky Adam was. He knew when he said a good thing, nobody had said it before."

The East Village

Start: The Strand Bookstore at the intersection of Broadway and 12th Street.

Subway: Take the 4, 5, 6, L, N, Q, R, W to 14th Street/Union Square station; walk south on Broadway.

Finish: Astor Place subway kiosk.

Time: 2 to 4 hours.

Best Time: Weekdays after 9:30am, when the Strand has opened.

Worst Time: Weekends, when some places may be closed; however, even then there's plenty to see.

Like other New York City neighborhoods, the East Village has reinvented itself time and time again in the years since its inception as part of Dutch governor Peter Stuyvesant's farm. Its current incarnation is the funky fringe of the city's arts and nightlife scene. From about 1840, one immigrant enclave after another has filled the neighborhood's town houses and tenements, and all of these people have left their stamp, from the early Irish and German settlers to the still-extant mix of Jews, African Americans, Latin Americans, Japanese, Indians, Eastern Europeans (especially

The East Village

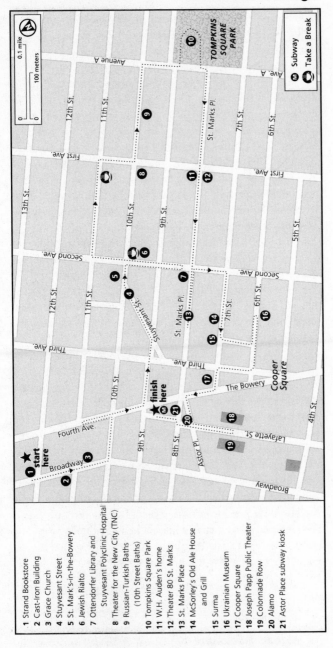

1 Strand Bookstore
2 Cast-Iron Building
3 Grace Church
4 Stuyvesant Street
5 St. Mark's-in-the-Bowery
6 Jewish Rialto
7 Ottendorfer Library and
   Stuyvesant Polyclinic Hospital
8 Theater for the New City (TNC)
9 Russian-Turkish Baths
   (10th Street Baths)
10 Tompkins Square Park
11 W.H. Auden's home
12 Theater 80 St. Marks
13 St. Marks Place
14 McSorley's Old Ale House
   and Grill
15 Surma
16 Ukrainian Museum
17 Cooper Square
18 Joseph Papp Public Theater
19 Colonnade Row
20 Alamo
21 Astor Place subway kiosk

TOMPKINS
SQUARE
PARK

Cooper Square

start here

finish here

Take a Break

Subway

0.1 mile

100 meters

Ukrainians), and Italians. In that melting pot boils an important ingredient: latter-day-bohemian middle-class nonconformists who still arrive here daily from all over the country. This mix is the East Village's defining characteristic.

In the '60s and '70s, this neighborhood was the hub of hippiedom. The action then centered on St. Mark's Place between Second and Third avenues where activist Abbie Hoffman lived. Other major players included Allen Ginsberg, activist Jerry Rubin, Timothy Leary, cartoonist R. Crumb, Paul Krassner (editor of *The Realist*), Andy Warhol, concert promoter Bill Graham, and an assortment of Indian swamis, witches and warlocks, tarot card readers, Hell's Angels, Hare Krishnas, flower children, and political radicals. East Villagers of those decades ate macrobiotic diets, took yoga classes, and lived in $30-a-month railroad flats with bathtubs in the kitchen (barely renovated, these apartments now rent for over $2,000 a month). They thrilled to Janis Joplin and the Grateful Dead at the Fillmore East, danced at Warhol's Electric Circus, listened to jazz at the Five Spot, read the *East Village Other* and the *Bhagavad-Gita,* and took in three-for-a-dollar features at the St. Mark's Cinema.

In the 1980s, the East Village took a stab at becoming the next SoHo, complete with chic galleries and nightclubs, co-op conversions, and escalating rents. A declining economy toward the end of the decade rendered the nascent art scene stillborn, but trendy clubs and upscale restaurants are still thriving today—as are the high rents. The hippies were replaced by spike-haired punks and anarchists, who are now being displaced by youthful yuppie types who, oddly enough, are the ones eating macrobiotic and taking yoga. Old-time residents still find it jarring to see the suit-and-tie set hoisting beers at the local bars. Despite the inroads of gentrification, the East Village remains colorful and vital, a last holdout of bohemianism.

• • • • • • • • • • • • • • • • •

Begin your tour at the northeast corner of Broadway and 12th Street, where you will see a beehive of activity surrounding the:

1. **Strand Bookstore** (℃ 212/473-1452), which is the world's largest used bookstore and one of New York's most

Kid-Friendly Experiences

- Exploring the Ukrainian Museum and purchasing an egg-decorating kit there (stop 16)
- Munching a cannoli at Veniero's Pasticceria (see the "Take a Break" box on p. 98)
- Playing on the playground and in the pool at Tompkins Square Park (stop 10)
- Spinning the *Alamo* sculpture and checking out the action on St. Mark's Place nearby (stops 20 and 13)

cherished institutions. The last survivor of Fourth Avenue's old Book Row, the Strand, named for the famous London street, was founded by Benjamin Bass in 1929. Currently run by his son, Fred Bass, and Fred's daughter Nancy, the Strand continues to be a favorite haunt of the city's rumpled intellectuals. Lee Strasberg, Anaïs Nin, and Andy Warhol were all regular customers, and the late Saul Bellow used to stop by when he was in town. It's a madhouse, a maze of narrow aisles threading past towering stacks of books shelved haphazardly within their categories, but die-hard book lovers enjoy the treasure hunt.

"Every book," says Bass, "eventually turns up here." The store claims "18 miles of books." At any given time, its inventory comprises more than two million tomes, a variety of books on every subject you can imagine at bargain-basement prices, including remainders, reviewer copies (sold at half price), used paperbacks, great art books, and hard-to-find novels. On the third floor is a huge collection of rare books where you might run across a second-folio Shakespeare for $250,000, or a *Gone With the Wind* first edition for $10,000. You can also find signed first editions (some for as little as $15). The Strand is open 9:30am to 10:30pm Monday to Saturday, 11am to 10:30pm Sundays.

Walk downtown on Broadway to 11th Street. On the northwest corner is the:

2. **Cast-Iron Building.** Cast-iron architecture was in vogue in New York throughout the latter half of the 19th century, providing an economical means of embellishing buildings with ornate, often neoclassical facades. This one, constructed in 1868 to house the James McCreery Dry Goods Store, is one of the few buildings left standing from the stretch of Broadway between 23rd and 8th streets that became known after the Civil War as "Ladies' Mile."

Luxury hotels and elegant department stores such as Wanamaker's, B. Altman, and Lord & Taylor opened up in this area; by the 1870s and 1880s, the high society of New York's Gilded Age enjoyed a splendor unrivaled in the New World. As writer Robert Macoy boasted in 1876, Broadway was "the grand promenade and swarm[ed] with the beauty, fashion, and wealth of New York. No avenue or street in London or Paris or Berlin, or any of our cities, can be compared with it." Toward the end of the 19th century, New York's wealthy families moved uptown, creating fashionable neighborhoods along Park, Madison, and Fifth avenues, and Ladies' Mile went into decline.

When McCreery's moved uptown in 1913, the Cast-Iron Building was converted first to office and warehouse space and then in 1971 to apartments. McCreery, an Irish immigrant who became a major New York merchandiser, was a patron of the arts, leaving much of his fortune to the Metropolitan Museum.

Continue downtown on Broadway; immediately on your left is:

3. **Grace Church.** One of the finest examples of Gothic Revival architecture in the United States, Grace Church was built between 1843 and 1847. It was the first masterpiece of 23-year-old architect James Renwick, Jr., who would go on to design St. Patrick's Cathedral and the Smithsonian "castle." Renwick was also a regular parishioner, and his bust graces the west corner of the north transept. The garden in front of the parish house and rectory on Broadway was created by Calvert Vaux, who helped design Central Park.

Despite its stunning architecture and traditional upper-class congregation, the most famous event ever to occur at Grace Church was a less-than-dignified one. P. T. Barnum arranged for the nuptials of two of his "biggest" sideshow stars, the diminutive Gen. Tom Thumb and his like-sized bride, Lavinia Warren, to be celebrated at the church. Though attended by the cream of society, their 1863 wedding exhibited all of the rowdiness and hoopla of a typical Barnum production. A parishioner who challenged sexton Isaac Hull Brown about the propriety of the affair received the response: "Even little people have the right to marry in a big church."

In the middle of the 19th century, this was the most fashionable church in New York, with reserved pew seating costing $1,200 to $1,400. The church was always booked with weddings. Former New York City Mayor Philip Hone wrote in his diary that the stiff price of pews "may have a good effect; for many of them, though rich, know how to calculate, and if they do not go regularly to church, they will not get the worth of their money." He described the aisles of the church as filled with "gay parties of ladies in feathers and mousseline-de-laine dresses and dandies with moustaches and high-heeled boots."

In his inaugural sermon at Grace Church, Dr. Thomas House Taylor exclaimed, "I do not believe that the commonest laborer who has wrought on these stones can ever look back upon his work without a feeling of reverence and awe." The church is laden with stone carvings, the pulpit is of carved oak, and lofty columns rise from the handsome mosaic floors to support the vaulted ceiling. The building is constructed of hewn white marble, and its slender marble spire, atop a 110-foot tower, dramatically marks the horizon. Over the main entrance is a large, circular stained-glass window, and 45 additional interior Gothic windows sparkle with richly hued stained glass. Though all of the windows merit attention, note especially the five pre-Raphaelite windows by Henry Holiday: "Ruth and Naomi" and "Joseph and Benjamin" on the left aisle, "The Raising of Lazarus/The Raising of Jairus' Daughter" and "The Four Marys" on the right aisle.

The church's interior is open from noon to 1am Tuesday through Friday, and on weekend afternoons from 1 to 5pm. For information on church services, organ recitals and chorale evensong, and Sunday tours, call ✆ **212/254-2000,** or check out www.gracechurchnyc.org.

Turn left on 10th Street to follow the perimeter of the church grounds (the intensive construction work is to sink a gym beneath the lawns) around to Fourth Avenue between 10th and 11th streets and see (on the west side of the street) the trio of houses built decades later in a Gothic Revival style faithful to the church itself. The northern house of the trio, the Grace Memorial House, was designed by James Renwick, Jr., himself; the others were designed by his firm.

Turn around to make your way south on Fourth Avenue. At 9th Street, you'll see the former Wanamaker Department Store Annex looming over the southwest corner of Fourth Avenue and Wanamaker Place. Another Italianate cast-iron survivor from Ladies' Mile, the annex is now a Kmart.

Turn left to walk east on 9th Street, cross Third Avenue, and bear left onto the diagonal:

4. **Stuyvesant Street.** This street, one of the most charming in New York, is named for the dour Dutch peg-legged governor of Nieuw Amsterdam, Peter Stuyvesant, who built a large *bouwerie* (farm) for himself here in the mid-1600s. Stuyvesant Street was the entrance to his property, extending all the way to the East River. The governor's descendants continued to reside in the area into the 19th century. When city officials decided in 1811 to impose the street grid that characterizes Manhattan today, the wealthy families here saved the street from being razed; it is one of the few true east-west streets in the city (alluded to by a compass inside the George Hecht Viewing Garden in the triangle along Third Ave. just north of Stuyvesant St.).

The stately edifices along this street are most famous as wealthy private homes from the mid-19th century. However, the early 20th century saw many of them doing a brisk business as brothels (in particular nos. 25, 27, 29, and 31).

No. 21, a wide, Federal-style, three-story brick building known as the Stuyvesant-Fish House, was built in 1804 for the governor's great-great-granddaughter, Elizabeth, and her husband, Nicholas Fish, a Revolutionary War hero who had served at Valley Forge. Nicholas and Elizabeth's son Hamilton went on to become governor of New York, a U.S. senator, and secretary of state under President Grant.

Adjacent to the Stuyvesant-Fish House begins the Renwick Triangle, a group of 16 elegant brick-and-brownstone Anglo-Italianate town houses built in 1861 (nos. 23–35 on Stuyvesant St. and nos. 114–128 on 10th St.) and attributed to James Renwick. Architect Stanford White once lived at 118 E. 10th St. You'll have to walk around the corner to see these 10th Street houses, but before you do, note the earliest house on Stuyvesant Street, no. 44, which was built in 1795 for Nicholas William Stuyvesant, a merchant. Its splayed lintels and Flemish bond brickwork are typical of the period, and the proportions of the doorway are an indication of this residence's original grandeur.

At the end of Stuyvesant Street, at 10th Street, is:

5. **St. Mark's-in-the-Bowery.** This late-Georgian Episcopal stone church, completed in 1799, replaced the 1660 chapel that was part of Peter Stuyvesant's farm. To the left and right of the Italianate cast-iron portico are statues of Native Americans called "Aspiration" and "Inspiration," and busts of Peter Stuyvesant and Daniel Tompkins. The sculptor, Solon Borglum, isn't as well known as his brother Gutzon, who carved the heads at Mount Rushmore.

Tompkins (vice president under President Monroe and a former New York governor) is buried here in the cobblestoned courtyard, along with other prominent 18th- and 19th-century New Yorkers, including Mayor Philip Hone, several British colonial governors, Commodore Matthew Perry (who forced Japan to open diplomatic relations with the United States in the early 1850s), and Peter Stuyvesant himself—along with seven generations of his descendants. According to some accounts, there are more graves beyond the churchyard under Second Avenue.

St. Mark's Greek Revival steeple was added in 1828; its brick Parish Hall was designed by James Renwick in 1861, and its rectory was designed by noted architect Ernest Flagg in 1900. To get a look at the interior, you have to call ahead for an appointment (© **212/674-6377;** www.stmarkschurch-in-the-bowery.com) or attend a service or cultural event here. After a 1978 fire, the top stained-glass windows had to be replaced; the new windows depict life on the Lower East Side. The original bottom windows (including one portraying Peter Stuyvesant) remain intact. If the garden courtyards are open, walk in and browse around. Especially lovely is the west courtyard behind the church, a tranquil oasis with benches shaded by ancient maple and London plane trees.

For many decades, St. Mark's Church has ardently supported the East Village arts community. Along with La Mama and Caffé Cino, it was a major birthplace of Off-Broadway theater, nurturing playwrights such as Sam Shepard (whose first two plays, *Cowboys* and *Rock Garden,* were produced here). Another long-running church program is Danspace (www.danspaceproject.org), a venue for independent experimental choreographers; Isadora Duncan danced here in the 1920s, Martha Graham danced here in the 1930s, and more recently, Merce Cunningham performed here. The Poetry Project has featured readings by Kahlil Gibran, William Carlos Williams, Edna St. Vincent Millay, Carl Sandburg, Amy Lowell, Allen Ginsberg, and W. H. Auden (a member of the parish, Auden sometimes used to come to church in his bathrobe and slippers). St. Mark's was the setting for a wedding in the movie *The Group,* based on Mary McCarthy's bestseller.

Take a Break The East Village offers nothing if not choice, and dining options abound. Diagonally across the street from the church at 156 Second Ave. is the famed **Second Avenue Deli** (© **212/677-0606**), a New York institution for more than 50 years, serving up Jewish soul food nonpareil. Mafia don

John Gotti was a regular before his imprisonment, even sending for takeout during his trial. Comedian Jerry Seinfeld reportedly ate his last bachelor dinner here, the night before his wedding. Stop in for authentic pastrami and corned beef piled high on fresh-baked rye, plus chopped liver, *kasha varnishkes* (egg noodles stuffed with fried cracked wheat), knishes, and other deli favorites.

Nearby **Veselka** (© **212/228-9682;** www.veselka. com) at 144 Second Ave. (on the corner of 9th St.) offers an appealing mix of Eastern European authenticity and hipster cachet. Opened in 1954, the diner once catered mostly to the Village's large Eastern European population. Today, the tables bustle with a mix of students, yuppies, and self-consciously mussed locals. The menu serves up a tasty selection of Eastern European specialties, like blini, pierogi, potato pancakes, and borscht, as well as hearty American diner grub—mac and cheese, sandwiches, and burgers. The restaurant is next door to the **Ukrainian National Home** (140 Second Ave.), which housed the infamous Stuyvesant Casino in the early 20th century. Gangsters would throw parties here, forcing local merchants both to buy tickets and to pay for ads in a souvenir booklet. The ensuing fetes tended to be rowdy and were nicknamed after the racket they raised. The term "racket" would eventually be applied to all illegal gangster revenue-raising activities, and racketeering became the official name for the crime they were committing.

Be sure to stop in front of the Second Avenue Deli, where brass-lined plaques set into the sidewalk (and the interior Molly Picon Room) commemorate Second Avenue's heyday as the:

6. **Jewish Rialto.** New York's Jewish community increased in number and prosperity in the early years of the 20th century, and the new Jewish middle class turned Second Avenue between Houston and 14th streets into a center of Yiddish culture. Dubbed the Yiddish Broadway, it was the site of cafes, bookstores, and a score of Yiddish-language theaters, many of them lasting until the 1950s. Actors such as Jacob Adler (father of noted drama teacher Stella

Adler) and comic actors Menashe Skulnik, Boris and Bessie Thomashevsky, and Maurice Schwartz took the stage every night in "immigrant-makes-good" plays, melodramas, and stock Yiddish comedy situations transposed to an American setting. Jacob Adler spearheaded a more serious dramatic movement, becoming famous for his "improved and enlarged" portrayal of King Lear and his proud version of Shylock. Thomashevsky adapted Shakespeare and Goethe to the Yiddish stage, and such well-known actors as Paul Muni, Edward G. Robinson, and Walter Matthau came up through the Yiddish theater.

Across from Veselka, at 135–137 Second Ave., are the:

7. **Ottendorfer Library and Stuyvesant Polyclinic Hospital.** These two ornately embellished redbrick facilities are the 1884 gift of Anna and Oswald Ottendorfer, publishers of a German-language daily newspaper called *Staats-Zeitung,* to the once-thriving German community of this neighborhood. Their aim was to nurture both the intellect and physical well-being of the immigrant population. The oldest extant branch of the New York City Public Library, the Ottendorfers' late Victorian building is adorned with terra-cotta wisdom symbols: globes, books, scrolls, owls, and torches. Its original name, the Freie Bibliothek und Lesehall, is still chiseled into the facade.

The adjacent clinic, even more elaborately adorned, features portrait busts of Hippocrates, Celsius, Galen, Humboldt, Lavoisier, and other scientists and physicians. The clinic was originally named the German Dispensary, but its administrators attempted to deflect anti-German sentiment during World War I by changing its name to the Stuyvesant Polyclinic Hospital. Architect William Schickel designed both buildings.

Walk back up Second Avenue and take a right on 11th Street.

Take a Break If you've passed on diner and deli food, you may be enticed by pastries. On 11th Street between First and Second avenues is **Veniero's Pasticceria** (© **212/674-7070;** www.venierospastry. com), at no. 342. Opened in 1894, this Italian bakery and cafe is the perfect place for a cannoli and cappuccino. Veniero's is charming, with old-fashioned tile floors, beveled mirrors, an ornate pressed-copper ceiling punctuated by stained-glass skylights, and marble cafe tables. Its vast display cases offer myriad sweet temptations, including velvety cheesecake. Note, too, some marvelous Italian food shops reside here, such as tiny **Russo's Mozzarella and Pasta Corp.** (344 E. 11th St.), in business since 1908 as an emporium for imported and fresh cheeses and fresh pastas and sauce.

Continue east on 11th St. and take a right on First Avenue. Just past the southwest corner of the intersection with 10th Street is the:

8. **Theater for the New City (TNC).** After a quarter of a century of presenting cutting-edge drama, poetry, music, dance, and visual arts, TNC's productions remain eclectic, politically engaged, fearless, multicultural, and creative. Go in and pick up a program or call the box office (✆ **212/254-1109;** www.theaterforthenewcity.net) to find out what's on their current schedule.

Take a right onto 10th Street. On your right, at no. 268, is a venerated New York institution, the:

9. **Russian and Turkish Baths, also known as the 10th Street Baths,** established in 1892 (✆ **212/674-9250;** www.russianturkishbaths.com). There were once numerous Turkish-style bathhouses in New York City; some of them became the hangouts of gangsters and celebrities, and evolved by the 1970s into notorious singles' scenes for gay men. With some bordering on orgy emporiums, most of these gay baths closed their doors in the mid-1980s when AIDS became widespread and widely feared.

The 10th Street Baths have remained staunchly straight and old-fashioned since their 19th-century inception. They are the last of the genre, open daily 11am (7:30am Sat–Sun) to 10pm, with an admission of $25 (more for various special massages and treatments; see box). They are co-ed except on Sunday from 7:30am to 2pm, which is reserved for men only, and Wednesday from 9am to 2pm, which is ladies' day.

The 10th Street Baths

The regular patrons of the 10th Street Baths, who come here for a *schvitz* (Yiddish for sweat), are quite a heterogeneous group. They include Orthodox Jews, Russian wrestlers, fashion models, Wall Street brokers, and even rap stars such as L. L. Cool J. John F. Kennedy Jr. used to schvitz here, as did Frank Sinatra, Mikhail Baryshnikov, and Timothy Leary.

The setting is far from glamorous; the dank interior of the baths evoke a 19th-century dungeon. In the Russian Room, where 11 tons of rocks raise the temperature well above 200°F (93°C), patrons sit and steam, intermittently dumping buckets of ice water over their heads. Occasionally, they ask an attendant (in the old days, a deaf man incapable of following the conversations of mobsters) for a *platza,* a vigorous scrubbing with a brush made of oak leaves. (It opens the pores and lets toxins sweat away.) Afterward, the bathers flop into an ice-cold pool, wrap themselves in robes, and head upstairs for sustenance and conversation over fresh-squeezed juices and a meal of borscht, schmaltz herring, or whitefish salad. The premises also house massage rooms (offering everything from shiatzu to Dead Sea salt rubs), a small gym, tanning, a redwood sauna, cots to lounge on, and a pine-fenced sun deck on the second floor.

Tenth Street next intersects with the first of the "Alphabet City" thoroughfares, Avenue A. Opening up from the southeast corner of the intersection is:

10. **Tompkins Square Park.** This beautiful 16-acre park was created on a salt marsh that was known as Stuyvesant Swamp; the Stuyvesant family gave the land to the city in 1833. It is as much a focus of the East Village as Washington Square Park is of Greenwich Village. Like Washington Square, Tompkins Square was designed to be the hub of an upscale neighborhood, a vision that never materialized due to its out-of-the-way location. Although Washington Square attracts throngs of tourists, Tompkins

Square remains a true neighborhood park. Many of its surrounding buildings date from the mid-19th century.

Head into the park at the 9th Street entrance. About halfway across the 9th Street walkway, through a brick portico, is an eroded monument commemorating a tragedy that was a swan song for the first immigrants to put their stamp on this area, the Germans. In 1904, the passenger ferry *General Slocum* burst into flame, was incinerated in under 15 minutes, and sank in the East River with over 1,200 aboard, most of whom were women and children from the East Village's "Dutchtown" ("Dutch" is a common corruption of *Deutsch,* which is German for "German"). The aging ship hadn't updated its safety equipment in years. The undrilled crew hefted the dried, old canvas fire hoses, but the useless things burst under the water pressure; frightened passengers grabbed rotted life preservers, which crumbled to dust in their hands. Many of the survivors, who lost friends and even entire families, found it emotionally impossible to continue living here after the disaster and moved to other German neighborhoods in the city. As Germans moved uptown, Eastern European Jews moved into the area.

Follow the park's walkways toward the southwest, and just behind the playground, you'll see the Temperance Fountain under a classical stone canopy, built in 1891 in hopes of convincing the thirsty to choose water over alcoholic spirits.

At the southwest corner of the park is a statue of 19th-century Congressman Samuel Cox, the "Postman's Friend," whose efforts to increase salaries and improve working conditions in the U.S. Postal Service made him a sort of patron saint of letter carriers.

Over the years, Tompkins Square has frequently been the site of riots and rebellions. In the 19th and early 20th centuries, it functioned as a venue for socialist and labor rallies. In 1874, one such gathering, resulting from a financial panic, was violently dispersed by city police, an event that became known as the Tompkins Square Massacre. Numerous peace rallies—not to mention some great rock concerts—took place here during the Vietnam War era.

Tensions in recent years, arising from the real estate industry's attempts to gentrify the neighborhood, have focused on the Christadora House (at the northeast corner of 9th St. and Ave. B), which was converted to high-priced condominiums by developers in 1986. It became the target of anti-gentrification forces when, in 1988, police attempted to enforce a curfew in Tompkins Square, and an ugly riot ensued. Officers clubbed and arrested not only protesters, but also innocent bystanders, and vandals did extensive damage to the Christadora. In the 1990s, the park was extensively renovated, and an encampment of homeless people was forced to move elsewhere, although a few still make it their living room by day.

These tumultuous events notwithstanding, the park is essentially a recreational setting: Children entertain themselves in playgrounds, there's fierce hoop action on the basketball courts, swimmers cool off in the pool (open to children only), and people sunbathe on expanses of lawn and picnic under ancient elms. My favorite spot here is the dog run, in the center of the park, where you can stand along the fence and enjoy tangled canine and human politics.

Leave the park on the Avenue A side (west) and stroll west toward First Avenue along St. Marks Place (which, to the numerically minded, should be 8th St.), which is lined with neighborhood cafes, thrift shops, and tattoo parlors. Just across First Avenue on the north side of the street is:

11. **W. H. Auden's home,** at 77 St. Marks Place. Auden lived and worked in a third-floor apartment here, amid a clutter of books and manuscripts, from 1953 to 1972, a year before his death. Although he generally kept a low profile in the neighborhood, he occasionally breakfasted on scotch at the Holiday Cocktail Lounge next door (no. 75) and was a parishioner at St. Mark's-in-the-Bowery. Earlier in the century, the Russian Communist periodical *Novy Mir* was published at no. 77. Leon Trotsky, a contributor, came by when he visited New York in 1917.

Across the street is:

12. **Theatre 80 St. Marks.** Until the advent of VCRs, revival cinema houses flourished in New York. This

160-seat facility was one of the last of the genre. It opened originally as a live theater in 1967; its first show, *You're a Good Man Charlie Brown,* played to sellout audiences for 4½ years. From 1971 on, proprietor Howard Otway, a former stage actor, dreamt up appealing double features and made his theater a shrine to the silver screen, adorned with photographs of the matinee idols of yesteryear. After Otway died in 1993, his son Lawrence decided to use the space for theatrical productions once more.

Today, 80 St. Marks is the home of a classical repertory group called the **Pearl Theatre Company** (© 212/598-9802; www.pearltheatre.org), which for 10 years was located in Chelsea. Unlike many contemporary theater companies, the Pearl does traditional interpretations of classic plays.

Keep following this street west and you will soon reach the center of the East Village counterculture:

13. **St. Marks Place,** between Second and Third avenues. Today populated by would-be punks and anarchists, NYU students, and various street people who defy categorization, this hippie mecca of the 1960s and 1970s is now mostly a tourist trap for Long Island teenagers, covered in a veneer of seediness. Sketchy tattoo parlors and funky shops selling cheap jewelry, alt-rock T-shirts, leather, tapes, and CDs have been augmented by a new crop of generic minimall-type shops. One landmark of days gone by is the **Gem Spa,** at the corner of Second Avenue, ever and always the area's most famous egg cream venue. Stop off for a glass of this New York–invented seltzer water, milk, and chocolate syrup beverage. The store also offers a huge selection of magazines and newspapers.

Make your way back to Second Avenue and turn left, and then turn right onto 7th Street. Toward the end of the block you'll find one of the few vestiges of the days when the East Village had a significant Irish population:

14. **McSorley's Old Ale House and Grill,** 15 E. 7th St. (© 212/473-9148). One of New York's oldest watering holes, established in 1854, McSorley's looks (and smells) every bit its age. The wood floor is strewn with sawdust, and the pressed-tin walls are cluttered with a thicket of

photos and newspaper clippings, all gone yellow with age and a century's worth of tobacco smoke. Over the bar you'll see dust-encrusted wishbones, left by soldiers after turkey dinners here on their last nights before shipping out. The wishbones that remain belong to men who never made it back.

Over the years, luminaries from Peter Cooper (see stop 17) to Brendan Behan have earned the right to a particular chair or bar stool, and the bar's beery charm was captured in Joseph Mitchell's *New Yorker* stories, later collected in a book, *McSorley's Wonderful Saloon*. Artist John Sloan immortalized the saloon's unique atmosphere in a painting called *A Mug of Ale at McSorley's* (1913). Perhaps the only significant change McSorley's has undergone in a century was to open its doors to women in 1971. If you drop in during an afternoon for a mug of sweet McSorley's ale (the food here, deli sandwiches and chili, is not notable), you'll catch a glimpse of the New York Peter Cooper knew.

These days, 7th Street retains traces of a Ukrainian immigrant community that once numbered some 20,000 strong. Representative of this community is:

15. **Surma** (✆ **212/477-0729;** www.surmastore.com), a store-cum-community center at no. 11, selling Ukrainian newspapers and books and Eastern European handicrafts. The latter include embroidered peasant blouses (Karen Allen wore one in the film *Raiders of the Lost Ark*), paintings, traditional porcelain, dolls, and *pysanky* (decorated eggs; see stop 16). Across the street is St. George's Ukrainian Catholic Church, its dome adorned with 16 beautiful stained-glass windows.

On the south side of 7th Street you'll see the short block of Taras Shevchenko Place. Take it to 6th Street and make a left, where you'll see the new:

16. **Ukrainian Museum,** 222 E. 6th St. (✆ **212/228-0110;** www.ukrainianmuseum.org). Recently relocated to this custom-built space, the museum displays Ukrainian folk-art items, including traditional costumes and textiles of intricate embroidery and needlework. You'll find a large

number of gorgeous, exquisitely decorated *pysanky,* wax-resistant-decorated Easter eggs that, according to legend, will conquer evil if enough are painted. In ancient times, these eggs were created only by women and young girls—in secret, lest someone cast an evil spell on the egg—using fertilized eggs of chickens that had laid for the first time.

The museum also displays Ukrainian art, *rushnyky* (woven and embroidered ritual cloths traditionally used as talismans in births, weddings, funerals, and rites associated with the change of seasons), ceramics, and decorative brass and silver jewelry. The museum gift shop offers you the opportunity to buy examples of all of these items, as well as egg-decorating kits—pick some up for Easter (after all, the regular PAAS decorating kit doesn't promise to help you conquer evil). Courses in Ukrainian folk crafts—embroidery, bead-stringing, making Christmas decorations—are also offered. The hours are Wednesday to Sunday 11:30am to 5pm. An $8 admission fee is charged.

Walk west to Third Avenue and make a right. Across from 7th Street you'll find:

17. **Cooper Square.** Situated on this wedge-shaped lot are the chocolate-brown Cooper Union Foundation Building and a small park housing a bronze likeness of Peter Cooper, who was an inventor, industrialist, philanthropist, and one of the great geniuses of his day. He made the bulk of his fortune through an ironworks and a glue factory, built the first steam locomotive in the United States (the Tom Thumb), developed the first rolled-steel railroad rails, and was instrumental in laying the first transatlantic telegraph cable. Cooper, a self-educated man from modest roots, believed that his wealth carried with it a responsibility to improve the working man's situation, so he founded the Cooper Union to provide free education in the practical trades and arts to any man or woman who wished to attend. A sense of Cooper as a benevolent, fatherly figure flows from the statue, and it's only natural: The sculptor, Augustus Saint-Gaudens, was able to attend Cooper Union's art school because of its founder's characteristic generosity.

The Cooper Union Foundation Building was completed in 1859. It was the first building in New York to use wrought-iron beams (another Cooper innovation), the forerunners of the steel I-beams that form the skeletons of present-day skyscrapers. The Italianate brownstone exterior remains much as it was in the 19th century.

The interior, however, underwent extensive renovations in 1975. Downstairs, the Great Hall continues to function as Peter Cooper hoped, supporting free speech and community dialogue through readings, lectures, and debates. The Great Hall's most famous moment occurred in 1860, when Abraham Lincoln's fiery "right makes might" antislavery speech carried public opinion in New York and sped him to the Republican Party's presidential nomination. Many contemporary events are free (check the calendar at www.cooper.edu or ℂ 212/353-4100), as are student art exhibitions.

Walk around Cooper Union, turn left on Astor Place, and then hang another left onto Lafayette Street. A few paces down on your left is the:

18. **Joseph Papp Public Theater** (ℂ 212/260-2400 or 212/539-8500; www.publictheater.org). The Public, one of New York's most vital cultural institutions, is housed in the old Astor Library. This redbrick German Romanesque Revival–style palace, the first public library in the United States, was the lone public bequest of John Jacob Astor, who made millions in the fur trade and was a notoriously tightfisted landowner. In 1911, the library's collection was moved to the New York Public Library on 42nd Street. From 1920 to 1966, the Hebrew Immigrant Aid Society used the building to shelter and feed thousands of Jewish immigrants and help them gain a footing in the United States. When they moved out, city officials and Joseph Papp's New York Shakespeare Festival rescued the Astor Library from a developer who had planned to raze it, and the building was designated a city landmark and became the permanent indoor home of the New York Shakespeare Festival.

The Public Theater opened in 1967 with the original production of *Hair,* which moved on to Broadway; in 1975, *A Chorus Line* followed suit, becoming one of the longest-running shows in Broadway history. Over the years, the New York Shakespeare Festival has utilized the Public's five stages to present new plays by such major playwrights as David Rabe, John Guare, David Mamet, Caryl Churchill, Sam Shepard, and Larry Kramer. Joseph Papp died in 1992, but the theater continues to thrive, with poetry readings, lectures, and workshops. Unsold theater tickets are often available as reduced-price Quiktix (sold half an hour before curtain time) in the main lobby. Joe's Pub (✆ **212/539-8777**), a cabaret space on the north side of the building, brings in big-time acts performing everything from jazz to rock to world music. The dim, luscious interior has excellent acoustics.

Across the street from the Public Theater is:

19. **Colonnade Row,** a group of row houses fronted by a crumbling marble colonnade. Of the nine row houses built by developer Seth Geer in 1831, only four remain; the five on the south end were demolished to make room for the Wanamaker Department Store warehouse. Lafayette Street was once a quiet, posh residential district. John Jacob Astor lived here, as did members of the Vanderbilt and Delano families and writer Washington Irving. President John Tyler married Franklin Delano's daughter, Julia, here in 1844. The fashionable set moved uptown after the Civil War, and these houses have been in decline ever since.

Turn back and walk toward Astor Place. The next and last stop, across 8th Street, is the:

20. **Astor Place subway kiosk.** Earlier in the last century, almost every IRT subway stop in Manhattan had a kiosk much like this one. The Transportation Authority tore them all down in 1911, but restored the Astor Place subway station in 1985. (Down in the station, Milton Glaser's mosaics and the ceramic low-relief tiles depicting beavers—the animal whose pelt made John Jacob Astor's fortune—are worth a look.) Peter Cooper would no doubt have been deeply satisfied to know that the architect of the new kiosk was a Cooper Union graduate.

West Chelsea

Start: 14th Street and Ninth Avenue.

Subway: Take the A, C, or E train to 14th Street, or the L train to Eighth Avenue.

Finish: Pier 63, the Hudson River at 23rd Street.

Time: From 2 to 4 hours, depending on how long you linger in the galleries.

Best Time: Start around 10am; most galleries are open 11am to 5pm. Return in the evening for an opening to experience the art scene at its schmooziest.

Worst Time: Sunday and Monday, when almost all galleries are closed; mid-July to early September, when many galleries are closed or open only by appointment.

Chelsea is a patchwork of taxi-repair shops and elite art galleries, where housing projects tower over priceless town-house blocks, and ultramodern condominiums mingle with neighborhood institutions that have barely changed over a century's time. Through the center of it all runs Eighth Avenue, gay America's main street, connecting the longstanding gay haven of the West Village with the emerging gay center of Clinton. Chelsea's boundaries are roughly

West Chelsea

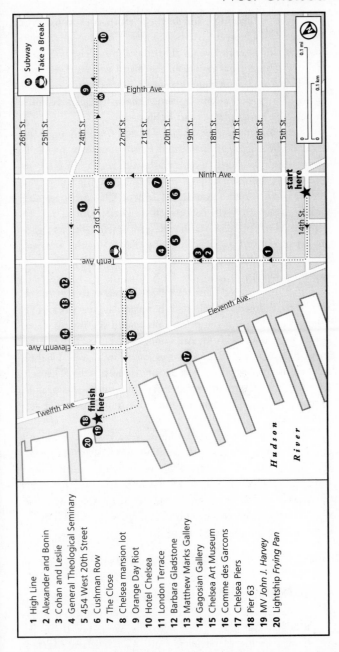

1 High Line
2 Alexander and Bonin
3 Cohan and Leslie
4 General Theological Seminary
5 454 West 20th Street
6 Cushman Row
7 The Close
8 Chelsea mansion lot
9 Orange Day Riot
10 Hotel Chelsea
11 London Terrace
12 Barbara Gladstone
13 Matthew Marks Gallery
14 Gagosian Gallery
15 Chelsea Art Museum
16 Comme des Garcons
17 Chelsea Piers
18 Pier 63
19 MV *John J. Harvey*
20 Lightship *Frying Pan*

14th Street to the high 20s north to south, and from Sixth Avenue to the Hudson River east to west. The Hudson's waters once ran along Tenth Avenue, but the fill produced by industrial development has expanded the island westward. In converted warehouses on these manmade blocks, you'll find the world's densest collection of galleries, many transplanted from SoHo, New York's previous art headquarters.

Retired British army captain Thomas Clarke bought the farmland here in 1750, naming it Chelsea, perhaps as a self-deprecating reference to London's Royal Chelsea Hospital, an old soldiers' home. The land remained agricultural until the 1830s, when Clarke's grandson Clement Clarke Moore and partner James N. Wells subdivided it. Their planned suburb conformed to the 1811 Manhattan grid system, with its right-angled streets and flattened hills. By the 1850s, the area was affluent, with genteel row houses set back behind gardens on tree-lined blocks.

The area west of Tenth Avenue soon began to service the increasing industrial needs of a burgeoning New York. The Hudson piers were a center of activity, and the intermediary streets were filled with factories and warehouses. During the silent-film area, production houses joined in as well. Chelsea reached its greatest population density in those years. The rich left and the neighborhood became the rough-and-tumble domain of longshoremen immortalized in the film *On the Waterfront.*

Those same piers today are home to parks, spas, and high-end restaurants, as the entire neighborhood has shifted with the rising tide of Manhattan's continuing gentrification. Industrial chic is the mode of the moment, and it's West Chelsea's specialty. Marrying the brawny machine age with the sleek computer age, this neighborhood has established itself at the forefront of New York's avant-garde.

• • • • • • • • • • • • • • •

Starting Out It took some vision to imagine this part of the city as anything but an industrial afterthought, but the chance taken by developer Irwin B. Cohen seems to be paying off. The **Chelsea Market** (www.chelseamarket.com) holds down a prime corner between the Meat Packing District to the south, and Chelsea to the north and east. Inside the block-long ground floor you can find an impressive selection of snacks and meals, from lobster to soup to pad Thai. Most retailers have tables and chairs, and there are multiple public areas where you can settle in with a coffee and a treat. **Sarabeth's Kitchen** (© **212/989-2424**) is a New York legend; try the sticky buns, pumpkin muffins, or a slice of the lemon-buttermilk bundt cake. Closer to the Ninth Avenue entrance is **Ruthy's Bakery and Café** (© **212/463-8800**), which offers equally tempting sweets such as red velvet cake and rugelach.

The building itself was the home of the National Biscuit Company, better known as Nabisco. The Oreo was invented here in 1912. The 1998 conversion made no attempt to paper over the building's ramshackle layout (original construction began in 1890 and alterations were ongoing for 40 years), with the original railshed among the infrastructure preserved along the main corridor. Permanent art installations, a waterfall, and rotating exhibitions provide further incentive to explore the space. The merchants keep varying hours; the complex itself is open 8am to 8pm weekdays and 10am to 8pm on weekends.

Exit the Chelsea Market on the Tenth Avenue side. Begin walking north. Overhead you'll see a railroad trestle belonging to the:

1. **High Line.** This railway line was built between 1929 and 1934 to service the factories and warehouses along Manhattan's west side. Between the Depression and the development of the Eisenhower Interstate Highway System, which led to the ascendance of trucking over rails, the $150-million project was soon outmoded. The tracks were abandoned in 1980 and all but 22 blocks through Chelsea were dismantled. A quarter-century's worth of neglect has permitted weeds and wildflowers, and even an apple tree, to colonize the broad double-tracked expanse. Plans are underway to convert the High Line into a promenade and park, although first the rails will have to be wrested from CSX, which for now has decreed that the area be off-limits to the public.

The Art of Gallery Hopping

Even to the initiated, the art world and its gallery scene can seem intimidating. But don't sweat it—treat gallery hopping like a visit to the candy store and give an easygoing once-over to everything on display, and then choose to savor the few that appeal to you the most.

Storefront galleries are the most visible, but the majority of galleries hide on the upper floors of nondescript buildings, often half a dozen or more per address. Most galleries are open to the public, unless they're hanging a new show, from 10 or 11am to 5 or 6pm Tuesday to Saturday. Mid- or late July to early September is the worst time to try to explore the art scene because many galleries shut down around this time.

Galleries present their works in the form of 4- to 6-week-long shows, either solo exhibitions or group shows featuring the work of several artists. The lion's share of people who pop by are just looking, so don't feel shy about sauntering in if you have no intention of buying. Also, don't feel as though you have to spend a certain amount of time in every gallery; galleries are accustomed to people who literally just poke their heads in, glance around, and withdraw quickly. You might zip through 10 shows before you find one that appeals to you. Serendipity is the key to a good art tour, so don't restrict yourself to the galleries suggested below. With more than 230 separate dealers, twice as many as SoHo had even in its heyday, you should also acknowledge that you can't see it all in 1 day—take care not to burn out.

Although you should take this walking tour during the day, the best way to catch a glimpse into the art world is to attend the evening opening of a new show, most of which are open to the public. *The Village Voice* newspaper, the "Weekend" section of Friday's *New York Times,* and *The New Yorker* and *New York* magazines all list upcoming openings, as well as current shows. The website www.westchelseaarts.com keeps a list of every gallery.

Kid-Friendly Experiences

- Sampling the goodies at the Chelsea Market (see above)
- Bowling or hitting a batting cage at Chelsea Piers (stop 17)
- Playing Ping-Pong near the historic boats at Pier 63 (stop 18)

As you tour Chelsea you will see the High Line repeatedly, running north-south just a few doors to the west of Tenth Avenue, two stories above the street. The rails were elevated because their ground-level incarnation was incredibly dangerous, providing Tenth Avenue with the nickname "Death Avenue." To reduce carnage at rail crossings, riders on horseback preceded the trains, waving red lanterns and earning themselves the moniker "West Side Cowboys."

Walking north on Tenth Avenue you will come to, on your right just above 18th Street, the first of the neighborhood's many, many art galleries:

2. **Alexander and Bonin** (℗ 212/367-7474; www.alexanderandbonin.com). This gallery at no. 132 occupies three floors and focuses on international contemporary artists. Solo shows are accompanied by selections from the gallery's stable of artists, which includes painters Matthew Benedict and Stefan Kürten, and sculptor/installation artist Doris Salcedo.

A couple of doors up at no. 138 is:

3. **Cohan and Leslie** (℗ 212/206-8710; www.cohanandleslie.com), a gallery that emphasizes up-and-coming New York artists. The team of Chris Hanson and Hendrika Sonnenberg show their paintings and installations here. Elisa Sighicelli, Judith Eisler, and Simon Aldridge are also on the roster.

Continue up to 20th Street. On the corner looms the:

4. **General Theological Seminary** (℗ 212/243-5150; www.gts.edu), the oldest seminary in the Episcopal

Church. Chelsea Square, the block-long campus that hosts this learning center, was part of Clement Clarke Moore's holdings. Moore (who was a professor of Biblical languages at the seminary from 1823–1850) donated 66 of his Chelsea lots. The first building was completed in 1827. As the seminary grew, the older structures were replaced. Under architect Charles Coolidge Haight, the majority of the campus was constructed between 1883 and 1902, in the English collegiate-Gothic style. In 1960 a clunky and out-of-character structure was installed on the east side of campus. The seminary seems to have learned from that experience, and the new Desmond Tutu Education Center, on the campus's west side, will be integrated into the existing historical structures.

Jack Kerouac and Allen Ginsberg used to stroll through the seminary grounds (which can be accessed from Ninth Ave.; see stop 7 below), which is not surprising given its proximity to:

5. **454 W. 20th St.,** just to your right off Tenth Avenue, which was Kerouac's home at the beginning of 1951. He wrote his third draft of *On the Road* in this town house, typed on a famous continuous scroll of paper. That draft did not become the published version of the book—the 29-year-old author had yet to discover the "spontaneous bop prose" method that would make his name. The town house was recently converted by a brother-and-sister architect team, who named it the "Node House" and installed a lot of glass and steel. The two resulting units were on the market for a combined $5.5 million, which seems pretty steep even for a piece of literary history.

Continuing east on 20th Street toward Ninth Avenue will bring you to more history in the form of:

6. **Cushman Row, no. 406 through 418.** This elegant row of houses was built in 1840 by Don Alonzo Cushman, a developer and friend of Clement Clarke Moore. The architectural style is Greek Revival, which held sway over the American architectural imagination during the first half of the 19th century. These houses are remarkably well-preserved, with simple column-framed doorways and subtle decorative details, like the wreaths

on the porthole attic windows. Cushman's descendents went on to form the real estate firm Cushman & Wakefield, which has some 160 offices in 50 countries.

Directly to the east of Cushman Row is no. 404, which is the oldest house in Chelsea, built in 1830. The brick facade is a little misleading. If you look to the narrow alleyway to the left of the house, you'll see that the majority of the structure is actually made of wood.

Continue to Ninth Avenue and take a left, where halfway up the block you'll see an entrance to:

7. **The Close,** which is the name for the grounds of the General Theological Seminary (see stop 4). The seminary opens the area to the public from 11am to 3pm Monday through Saturday, with shorter hours when school is out of session. The pleasant campus is an oasis in the city, with a leafy quad and anarchic wisteria vines. In addition to fine examples of Gothic Revival architecture, the campus is also home to the **St. Mark's Library** (ℂ **212/ 243-5150**), a theological research institution with nearly a quarter of a million volumes. The rare books collection includes the 1535 Coverdale Bible, the first complete Bible printed in English, and a 1611 King James first edition. The library also once owned a Guttenberg Bible, which was sold when the seminary came under financial stress. St. Mark's Library is closed to the general public; visiting scholars can get in, but a letter of introduction is required.

Continue up Ninth Avenue. On the far corner of 21st Street, at no 183 Ninth Ave., is the **Royer-Wells House,** the second-oldest house in Chelsea. This Federal-style home from 1831 to 1832 now holds a pleasant cafe.

The next block of Ninth, between 22nd and 23rd streets, marks the eastern side of the original:

8. **Chelsea mansion lot.** There were actually two mansions, the latter one standing from 1777 to 1854 (the first had burned) on a low knoll that was eventually tipped into the Hudson. Clement Clarke Moore was born and raised here, later attending Columbia University. Moore composed a *Compendious Lexicon of the Hebrew Language,* published in 1809 and one of the first English study aids

for Hebrew. Moore's lasting fame, however, comes from the credit he took for an anonymously published poem called "A Visit from St. Nicholas," ("'Twas the night before Christmas"). *The Troy Sentinel* ran the poem in 1823, and when Moore published his own collected verse in 1844, he included "A Visit from St. Nicholas." Until 2000 few seriously questioned his authorship. Don Foster, who unmasked Joe Klein as the anonymous writer of *Primary Colors,* makes a very convincing case that Henry Livingston, Jr., of Poughkeepsie, New York, was the real author. In *Author Unknown: On the Trail of Anonymous,* Foster compares the temperaments and styles of Moore and Livingston, and concludes that a foe of frivolity like Moore could never have written the poem.

Continue up Ninth Avenue and take a right onto 23rd Street. The stretch of Eighth Avenue between 23rd and 25th streets was the site of the:

9. **Orange Day Riot,** on July 12, 1871. By the late 1860s, Chelsea had developed a large Irish population, drawn by the availability of waterfront work. And just as back home in Ireland, conflict was inevitable between Protestants and Catholics. Every July, Protestant Irish-Americans celebrated the 1690 victory of Protestant William of Orange over his Catholic father-in-law King James II. In 1871, protected by New York police and militiamen, Protestants formed their parade over the strong objection of the Irish Catholic community, which had been unusually provoked by the previous year's festivities. The Protestants were protected by the authorities, and when general partisanship turned violent, the Catholic protesters bore the brunt. At least 50 Catholics died, while the Orangemen regrouped and finished their parade relatively unscathed. To the Catholic community, the riot was remembered as the "Slaughter on Eighth Avenue."

Cross Eighth Avenue eastward and about halfway down the block at no. 222 you'll reach the:

10. **Hotel Chelsea** (© 212/675-5531; www.hotelchelsea. com). The preponderance of historical plaques at the entrance are an indicator of the depth of history here. Built as an ambitious co-op in 1884, these 12 brick

stories comprised the tallest building in New York until 1902. The co-op went bankrupt in 1903, and in 1905 the building was reborn as the Hotel Chelsea. It proceeded to attract dozens of major artistic figures, from Mark Twain to Sarah Bernhardt to Jimi Hendrix. Thomas Wolfe's *Look Homeward Angel* was assembled while he was living here, as were William S. Burroughs' *Naked Lunch* and Arthur C. Clarke's *2001: A Space Odyssey.* This is also the place where Bob Dylan stayed up for days writing "Sad-Eyed Lady of the Lowlands."

On the ground floor is the Spanish restaurant **El Quijote** (℡ **212/929-1855**), which came by its retro look honestly: It's still furnished with many of the original appointments from its 1930 opening. Janis Joplin hung out here, as did Andy Warhol's entourage while he was upstairs filming *Chelsea Girls.* Warhol himself was a frequent patron. The food, especially the lobster, is actually quite good.

Double back west on 23rd Street. The grand Art Deco apartment building on the southwest corner of Eighth Avenue, no. 300 W. 23rd, was designed by architect Emery Roth, who also designed the **Beresford** and the **San Remo** on Central Park West (p. 158 and 159).

Walk north 1 block to 24th Street, following the massive block-long bulk of:

11. **London Terrace.** This 1931 apartment complex comprises 1,665 units, which break out into 4,000 rooms. Despite the density, the building has always been desirable, with attractive amenities like an indoor pool and rooftop sun deck. Though the brick and terra-cotta architecture owes much to Southern Italy, the building name refers to a previous block of houses on the site. When first opened, the building adhered to the London theme by dressing its doormen as bobbies. Current residents include Annie Leibovitz, Teri Hatcher, Debbie Harry, and Chelsea Clinton.

On the north side of 24th Street, note the stretch of buildings from no. 437 to 459. These buildings were built between 1849 and 1850 and have unusually large garden setbacks.

Continue west and cross Tenth Avenue. This stretch of 24th Street has an embarrassment of art gallery riches, beginning with:

12. **Barbara Gladstone** (𝒞 212/206-9300; www.gladstone gallery.com) at no. 515. Gladstone has an impressive roster of artists, including Vito Acconci, Thomas Hirschhorn, Anish Kapoor, Shirin Neshat, Lari Pittman, Richard Prince, and the artist responsible for the *Cremaster Cycle,* Matthew Barney.

Pay a visit to **Metro Pictures** (no. 519), and then move on to:

13. **Matthew Marks Gallery** (𝒞 212/243-0200; www. matthewmarks.com), which has its main space at no. 523. Marks has a miniempire in West Chelsea, with additional locations on a similar latitude of 21st and 22nd streets. Top-tier painting, photography, and sculpture can be found here, by such superstars as Nan Goldin, Willem de Kooning, Lucian Freud, Ellsworth Kelly, and tabloid idol Weegee.

Further up the block you'll find Andrea Rosen (no. 525), Luhring Augustine (no. 531), and Charles Cowles Gallery (no. 537). Near the end of the block at no. 555 you'll reach the legendary:

14. **Gagosian Gallery** (𝒞 212/741-1111; www.gagosian. com), a space large enough to accommodate Richard Serra. Serra's oversized sheet-metal sculptures have shown here, as have elaborate installations by Anselm Kiefer and Damien Hirst. Much-hyped painter John Currin is the latest big name to have been snatched up by Gagosian. This gallery (which also has locations Uptown, in Beverly Hills, and in London) is as much a major institution as many museums, and the shows here tend to be among the most talked about in New York.

Take a left on Eleventh Avenue and walk south to 22nd Street. On the corner, the three-story redbrick building houses the:

15. **Chelsea Art Museum** (𝒞 212/255-0719; www.chelsea artmuseum.org), a new institution focused on 20th-century and contemporary abstract art. European artists

dominate the permanent collection, although Americans like Robert Motherwell can also be found. Temporary exhibits are mounted regularly in the renovated rooms of this 1850 structure. Beginning in 1915, the building was leased by The Church Temperance Society, who used it as a rest haven for longshoremen, to keep them away from the predominant local institution, the saloon. The museum charges an admission and stays open Tuesday through Saturday, noon to 6pm, with reduced prices and extended hours on Thursday nights until 8pm.

The Chelsea Art Museum is also the temporary home of **The New Museum of Contemporary Art** (© 212/219-1222; www.newmuseum.org), which has decided in the long term to eschew Chelsea for the aesthetic pleasures of the Bowery. Until the New Museum's headquarters are completed Downtown, this ground-floor space will host its rotating exhibits, which show off the work of contemporary artists from around the world. The New Museum's hours and admission policies mirror those of the Chelsea Art Museum.

Across the street and a few doors to the east is **no. 535,** a great building for riding the elevator to the top floor and then working your way down the stairs, popping your head into various galleries along the way. **Yancey Richardson** and **Julie Saul,** two of my favorite photography galleries, are located here. On the ground floor is **Printed Matter,** a bookstore dedicated to artists' publications, often small-edition books. There's an exhibit space there as well.

In addition to other galleries on the block, at no. 520 you can see modern art in the design of the:

16. **Comme des Garçons** (© 212/604-9200) store. The clothing line launched by Japanese fashion designer Rei Kawakubo is outré in its own right, but the retail location here manages to overshadow the threads. Runway lights lead down an aluminum tunnel entryway, seemingly drilled through the old brick warehouse's facade. The modular interior shows off cutting-edge men's and women's fashions, most of which are priced well beyond the budgets (and tastes) of anyone who doesn't wear clothing as a profession.

Take a Break On 22nd Street and Tenth Avenue, the Art Moderne charm of the **Empire Diner** (*©* **212/243-2736**) beckons, open 24 hours a day. Built by the Fodero Dining Car Company in 1946, every detail in this diner has been lovingly preserved, including the chrome replica of the Empire State Building on the roof. The food is upscale diner fare, with omelettes, burgers, rib-eye steak, and a slew of cakes and pies. For more modern palates, the menu also includes salads, quesadillas, and lentilburgers. Prices are higher than they'd be at a real greasy spoon, but then real greasy spoons don't have piano players and cloth napkins.

Other galleries abound between Eleventh and Twelfth avenues, as far south as Fourteenth, and into the higher twenties to the north. If you are arted-out, however, turn west and walk toward the Hudson. A pedestrian crosswalk will get you across the West Side Highway at 22nd Street, where you'll approach the entrance to:

17. **Chelsea Piers** (*©* **212/336-6666;** www.chelseapiers. com), the 30-acre fitness and recreation compound. The piers themselves date to 1910, when they were embarkation and disembarkation points for oceanic travel. The *Titanic* was bound here on its fateful 1912 maiden voyage. Crowds gathered to greet survivors rather than passengers. Cunard's *Carpathia* delivered 675 of the rescued 6 days after the sinking. Three years later, the *Lusitania* departed Chelsea Piers, to be torpedoed by a German U-boat 6 days later. The sinking of a civilian luxury liner, with 1,195 fatalities, played a hand in America's eventual entry into World War I. Photographs in the center of the complex recount these events.

As planes displaced ocean liners and cargo containers changed the mechanics of shipping, the piers were all but abandoned, by the late '60s. In 1995, the surviving piers were converted into a high-end playground, with a massive gym, ball courts, and playing fields. Walk-up visitors can enjoy golf, bowling, ice-skating, and batting cages. Public decks afford river views, though I prefer the more ramshackle space, directly to the north at:

18. **Pier 63** (www.pier63maritime.com). This pier was built in 1946 as a railroad-car barge for the Erie Lackawanna Railroad (then the Delaware, Lackawanna, and Western). The city wants to clear it for a new riverfront parkland, but for now it's a wonderfully overlooked spot. To access it, go north of the Basketball City complex to the narrow ramp at the back of the parking lot. (Pier 63 is at the same latitude as 23rd St.) Several historical boats are docked here. On your left is the:

19. **MV John J. Harvey** (www.fireboat.org), built in 1931 for the New York Fire Department. One of the most powerful fireboats ever constructed, the Harvey can pump 18,000 gallons of water a minute. The NYFD kept the boat in service until 1994. The boat is now in private hands, and makes free trips periodically, in addition to putting on pump demonstrations. On the right, near the Erie Lackawanna Railroad caboose, is the:

20. **Lightship Frying Pan** (© 212/989-6363; www.frying pan.com), 1 of 13 surviving U.S. lightships. The vessel was built in 1929 as a floating lighthouse off Frying Pan Shoals, near Cape Fear, North Carolina. Now it's a party space, with DJs on Friday nights. The barnacle-encrusted interior retains the ambiance of the bottom of the Chesapeake Bay, where the *Frying Pan* spent 3 years before being salvaged by the current owners.

    Pier 63 has terrific views of New Jersey and the Hudson. Kids can take advantage of a free Ping-Pong table near the *Frying Pan,* while adults kick back with a beer from the beachside-style bar of the **Café du Soleil.** The cafe, which is open from May through October, also serves reasonably priced light fare (Sun–Wed noon–midnight, and Thurs–Sat noon–2am). Pier 63 is open daily from dawn to dusk, although you can access the area much later for the cafe or events at the *Frying Pan.* When it comes time to leave, you might consider the liquid route. The **New York Water Taxi** (© 212/742-1969; www.nywatertaxi.com) stops at Pier 63 from May to October, connecting to docks around the city and through New York Harbor to Brooklyn and Queens.

Midtown: The Concrete Jungle

Start: Grand Central Terminal.

Subway: Take the 4, 5, 6, 7, or the shuttle to 42nd Street/Grand Central.

Finish: The St. Regis Hotel.

Time: Approximately 4 hours, not counting time for browsing in shops and galleries.

Best Time: Weekdays, when Midtown is bustling but the attractions aren't as packed as they tend to be on weekends.

Worst Time: Rush hour (weekdays from 8:30–9:30am and 4:30–6pm).

The cosmopolitan clamor and bustle that define New York are pronounced nowhere more than on the streets of Midtown. The sky fills with glass towers and the sidewalks overflow (you only need 6% of the population of Manhattan to fill all available pavement in Midtown). Though at first glance the area seems like a monolithic playground of corporate lobbies and high-end boutiques,

Midtown: The Concrete Jungle

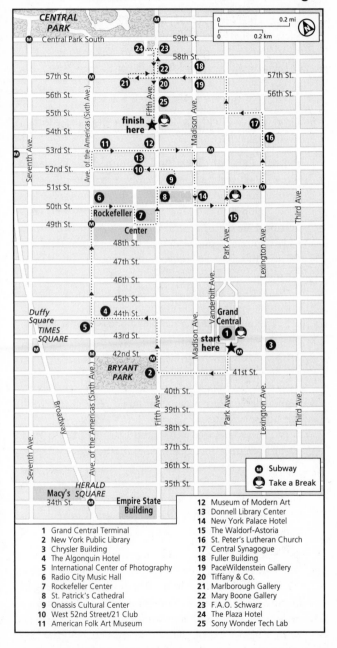

1   Grand Central Terminal
2   New York Public Library
3   Chrysler Building
4   The Algonquin Hotel
5   International Center of Photography
6   Radio City Music Hall
7   Rockefeller Center
8   St. Patrick's Cathedral
9   Onassis Cultural Center
10 West 52nd Street/21 Club
11 American Folk Art Museum
12 Museum of Modern Art
13 Donnell Library Center
14 New York Palace Hotel
15 The Waldorf-Astoria
16 St. Peter's Lutheran Church
17 Central Synagogue
18 Fuller Building
19 PaceWildenstein Gallery
20 Tiffany & Co.
21 Marlborough Gallery
22 Mary Boone Gallery
23 F.A.O. Schwarz
24 The Plaza Hotel
25 Sony Wonder Tech Lab

public spaces from vest-pocket parks to the grand boulevards of Rockefeller Center provide plenty of respite. Museums, art galleries, and houses of worship add depth to the consumer-capital surfaces. The overall result is Manhattan at its most glamorous.

● ● ● ● ● ● ● ● ● ● ● ● ● ● ● ● ●

From the subway platform, follow the Metro North signs to the main concourse of:

1. **Grand Central Terminal.** Commodore Vanderbilt himself named the station "Grand Central" in the 1860s, despite the fact that it was out in the boondocks at that time. The present terminal was built in 1913. This engineering tour de force combines subways, surface streets, pedestrian malls, underground shopping concourses, and 48 pairs of railroad tracks into one smoothly functioning organism.

   Masterfully restored in 1997, the main concourse is breathtaking. It's one of America's most impressive interior spaces, with gleaming marble floors, sweeping staircases, and an aqua vaulted ceiling soaring 125 feet high. Twenty-five hundred pinpricks of electronic stars litter this "sky" with a view of a Mediterranean winter sky's constellations (seemingly backward, the zodiac symbols are supposedly represented as they would be seen from outside our solar system).

   When a developer announced plans to place a huge tower over the concourse in the 1970s, preservationists came to the rescue, with Jackie Onassis leading the charge. The terminal's design survived intact after a series of legal challenges that went all the way to the Supreme Court and resulted in a 1978 decision that upheld New York City's landmarks laws.

   Take a Break   Grand Central has numerous spots where you can pick up coffee, a muffin, or a sandwich to fortify yourself for the tour. The basement **Dining Concourse** is a food court with a "greatest hits" package of local restaurants, including Indian from Café Spice, Cajun-flavored pizzas at Two Boots, and the best cheesecake in the city, which comes from Junior's.

Kid-Friendly Experiences

- Whispering in the "whispering gallery" at Grand Central Station (see the "Take a Break" box above)
- Skating at Rockefeller Center skating rink in winter (stop 7)
- Paying a visit to the original Winnie-the-Pooh (stop 13)
- Investigating F.A.O. Schwarz toy store (stop 23)
- Playing at Sony Wonder Tech Lab (stop 25)

For a more formal experience, head downstairs from the main concourse to the **Oyster Bar,** which dates back to the opening of the station. Passable seafood is served in a first-rate setting beneath a wide-vaulted ceiling Monday through Friday from 11:30am to 9:30pm, and Saturday from noon until 9:30pm. You might take a seat at the counter for an appetizer of fried oysters, New Zealand greenlip mussels in Dijon dressing, or New England clam chowder. Full meals, including the catch of the day, are available in the dining room. The acoustics of the curved ceiling "whispering gallery" outside the restaurant's entrance allow people to stand in opposite corners and hold a whispered conversation.

Leave the main concourse via the 42nd Street exit and walk south on Park Avenue. Turn right at 41st Street, where the sidewalks on either side between Park and Fifth avenues are covered with some 96 plaques. Artfully done, these markers contain literary quotes that make a nice warm-up for the:

2. **New York Public Library** (© 212/930-0830; www.nypl.org), whose triangular facade faces down 41st Street, straight ahead. Officially known as the Humanities and Social Sciences Library, the building sits in splendor, resembling a Greek temple with rows of Corinthian columns. Completed in 1911, this Beaux Arts palace, one of the greatest research libraries in the world, cost $10 million to construct. Everything inside was designed as a

unit, from the marble walls to the chairs, stepladders, and wastebaskets.

Climb up the broad stone steps guarded by twin stone lions, named Patience and Fortitude by mayor Fiorello LaGuardia in the 1930s for the qualities he proclaimed New Yorkers would need to survive the Depression.

The interior of the library contains manuscripts, maps, journals, prints, and more than 38 million volumes occupying 80 miles of bookshelves. You can sign up for tours (offered Mon–Sat at 11am and 2pm) at the information desk just inside the lobby, which is made entirely of unmortared Vermont marble. The staff can also point you to the library's current exhibits, its wonderful **bookstore and gift shop** (© **212/930-0641**), and the third-floor main reading room, a magnificent space extending the entire block-long length of the building. The library is open Tuesday and Wednesday from 11am to 7:30pm, and Thursday through Saturday from 10am to 6pm. The shop is open Tuesday, Wednesday, and Saturday from 11am to 6pm, and Thursday and Friday from 10am to 6pm.

Turn left out of the library to head uptown on the west side of Fifth Avenue. Look up and to your right as you cross 42nd Street to get a wonderful perspective view down the block to the:

3. **Chrysler Building,** one of the most beautiful and distinctive features of the Manhattan skyline. The stainless-steel crown, with its jeweled notches, is perpetually aglow, whether from sunlight or its own internal illumination. The Brooklyn-born architect, William Van Alen, kept the crown's design a secret. A rival building was going up downtown at 40 Wall St., which claimed the title of the world's tallest upon its completion in 1930. Only then did Van Alen hoist up the secret spire he'd been building in his upper stories, topping the Chrysler building off at 1,046 feet, the tallest in the world. Alas, this Art Deco masterpiece didn't reign long—in 1931 the 102 stories of the Empire State Building eclipsed it.

Continue north on Fifth Avenue for 2 blocks to 44th Street, where you'll turn left. On the north side of 44th Street, at no. 27, is the Harvard Club, designed by McKim, Mead, and White in 1894 in an architectural style that mimicked Harvard's (at the time). The "Veritas" coat of arms tops the building. A few doors down at no. 37 is the Yacht Club, with a fanciful and flowing concrete facade of captain's cabin windows. Note the tower of the Sofitel Hotel, completed in 2000, rising incongruously from a narrow slot just west of the Yacht Club.

Continue along 44th Street. Near Sixth Avenue stands one of New York's most famous literary landmarks:

4. **The Algonquin Hotel.** In the 1920s, *Vanity Fair's* editorial staff included literary all-stars Dorothy Parker, Robert Benchley, and Robert Sherwood. Their offices were at 19 W. 44th, and they began hanging out in the nearby Algonquin. Their gatherings grew into the famous "Round Table," which also included Alexander Woollcott (drama critic for the *New York Times*), George S. Kaufman, Franklin Adams (columnist for the *New York World*), and Edna Ferber. The group became famous for its witty, acerbic commentary on theater, literature, and the social scene, though Dorothy Parker herself played down its importance: "The Round Table was just a lot of people telling jokes and telling each other how good they were."

One of the regulars, Harold Ross, took it into his head to start a magazine that would incorporate the group's sophisticated, satirical outlook and rounded up investors to begin publication of *The New Yorker,* with offices set up nearby at 25 W. 45th St. The first few issues were extremely uneven, but within a couple of years E. B. White and James Thurber had been added to the staff and were reshaping the magazine into one of the most prestigious publications in the country.

Even after the Round Table stopped gathering at the hotel, the Algonquin continued to count famous writers among its guests, including Gertrude Stein and her companion, Alice B. Toklas, F. Scott Fitzgerald, and William Faulkner, who wrote the acceptance speech for his 1949 Nobel Prize on Algonquin stationery.

To soak up this hotel's genteel ambience, ensconce yourself with a cocktail on a comfortable sofa in the lobby lounge.

Across the street from the Algonquin, but light-years away in design, is the **Royalton Hotel.** Poke your head inside and take a look; the whimsically futuristic Jetsons-meets-'50s-lounge decor, created by Philippe Starck, has to be seen to be believed.

Cross Sixth Avenue (also known as Ave. of the Americas) and turn left. Before the corner of 43rd Street is the:

5. **International Center of Photography** (℡ 212/857-0000; www.icp.org), massively renovated and expanded in 2000. With two floors of exhibition space, ICP usually has one main show up, in addition to one or two auxiliary shows in the smaller galleries. The bookstore/gift shop can be entered for free, but admission is charged for the museum, which is open Tuesday to Sunday from 10am to 6pm, extended until 8pm on Fridays. (Admission charges are voluntary Fri from 5–8pm.)

Double back north along Sixth Avenue and look to your right along 47th Street. This chaotic block is the **Diamond District,** where millions of dollars' worth of gems are traded every day. Continue up Sixth Avenue, where a building boom in the '60s and '70s transformed the area into a canyon of 50-story glass skyscrapers. Although the buildings aren't of great note individually, together they form an urban environment of considerable grandeur.

On the right side of Sixth Avenue, north of 50th Street, stands:

6. **Radio City Music Hall,** which was built in 1932 and has been restored to its original Art Deco elegance. Its original owner, Samuel "Roxy" Rothafel of Roxy Theater fame, ran it as a vaudeville house, but the enterprise was a flop, and Rothafel, in poor health, sold out to the Rockefellers. Eventually it became basically a glorified movie theater with Rockettes, but economic considerations and a 1979 overhaul returned it to live show business. Today, following an extensive 1999 restoration and pristinization, performances run the gamut from headliners like B. B. King or the Dixie Chicks, to shows like Comic Relief, to the annual Christmas Spectacular starring Radio City's own Rockettes and a nativity cast that includes live animals (picture camels and reindeer sauntering in through the Sixth Ave. entrance). Pricey hour-long guided tours are

available daily on the hour from 11am to 3pm. Call
ⓒ **212/247-4777** for general information, or 212/307-
7171 for tickets (Ticketmaster). You may buy tickets in the
gift shop to the left of the entrance.

Radio City Music Hall anchors the northwest corner of:

7. **Rockefeller Center,** one of the most handsome urban
complexes in New York, extending from 47th to 52nd
streets between Fifth and Sixth avenues. It encompasses
24 acres and 19 skyscrapers, and remains the largest private building project in U.S. history. People scoffed at
John D. Rockefeller in 1929 when he unveiled plans to
build this "city within a city," because it was so far
removed from what was then the commercial heart of
New York. But Rockefeller proved all the critics wrong.
His complex remade the map, drawing business uptown
and setting the standard for future civic projects by incorporating public art and open spaces.

To get a bird's-eye perspective, turn east on 50th
Street. Halfway between Sixth Avenue and Rockefeller
Plaza you'll see the entrance for **Top of the Rock** (ⓒ **212/
698-2000;** www.topoftherocknyc.com). After a 2-decade
hiatus, the observation deck at the top of the G.E.
Building at 30 Rockefeller Plaza has been refurbished and
reopened. From an open-air platform 70 stories up, you
can take in a 360-degree Midtown view. Impressive by
day, the scene turns stunning by dusk, with thousands of
lights glittering to all sides, and stretching out 80 miles
across five different states. The nearby Empire State
Building has a more famous observation deck, but Top of
the Rock offers a distinct advantage: You can purchase
your tickets online and avoid the worst of the lines.

Continue east on 50th Street and you'll reach the
intersection of the street called Rockefeller Plaza. Take a
right and peek inside the lobby of **30 Rockefeller Plaza.**
Above the black marble floors and walls are monumental
sepia-toned murals by José Maria Sert. This Art Deco
building was featured in the movie *Quiz Show.*

Continue down Rockefeller Plaza to its intersection
with 49th. You'll see the wraparound corner windows
where early risers peer through the glass and wave in the

hopes of becoming part of the backdrop during the tap-ing of **NBC's** *Today* **show.**

Stroll back beyond Rockefeller Plaza and take a left to admire the **skating rink.** In the summer, this area becomes an outdoor cafe; in cooler months, it's packed with skaters gliding along the ice to music and the twin-kle of tiny lights in the trees. Each holiday season a giant Christmas tree stands here, towering over the promenade. Paul Manship's massive *Prometheus* lounges above the skating rink, beneath a quote from Aeschylus.

Continue west toward Fifth Avenue through the **Channel Gardens,** so named because they separate the French Building from the British Empire Building. The landscaping here changes at least a dozen times a year to reflect the shifting seasons. The fountain sculptures remain constant, whimsical spouting fountainheads rid-den by mermaids and mermen. When you reach Fifth Avenue, take a left and pause to admire the gilded relief at no. 620, above the Cole Haan store. The sculpture, *Industries of the British Commonwealth,* was completed in 1933 by Carl Paul Jennewein.

Cross Fifth Avenue, where at no. 611 you'll find **Saks Fifth Avenue,** one of New York's most famous depart-ment stores. Rising to Saks' north is the unmistakable neo-Gothic bulk of:

8. **St. Patrick's Cathedral,** the seat of the Archdiocese of New York and the largest Catholic cathedral in America. Designed by James Renwick in 1858 and modeled after Cologne's cathedral, this magnificent structure has twin spires rising 330 feet above street level. Construction took 21 years. Zelda and F. Scott Fitzgerald were married here in 1920.

Across the street as you exit, in front of 630 Fifth Ave., crouches Lee Lawrie and René Chambellan's 1936 *Atlas,* one of New York's most famous statues, in 15 feet of bronze.

Turn up Fifth and cross 51st Street, taking a right. You will pass the doorman-attended residential entrance to Olympic Tower, a 1976 mixed-use glass skyscraper devel-oped by Aristotle Onassis's family trust. Just past the doorman on your left is the entryway to the building's atrium, which houses the:

9. **Onassis Cultural Center** (℮ **212/486-4448;** www.onassisusa.org). The free galleries downstairs here display Hellenic art and culture, with exhibits often focused on painting and sculpture, both modern and ancient. The center is open Tuesday through Saturday 10am to 6pm.

   As you pass through the atrium notice the Parthenon marbles mounted on the walls. These casts, made directly from the Greek originals, were acquired by City College in 1852 from the British Museum. On your right is one of several public waterfalls in the area.

   Exit through the back of the atrium, where you'll see a holdover town house overshadowed by the modern architecture. This stucco building with copper and cobalt touches is the home of **La Grenouille Restaurant,** one of the last of a generation of luxurious French restaurants, now all but extinct from this neighborhood. In an *atelier* (artist studio) upstairs, artist Bernard Lamotte and his wife maintained a bohemian circle that included the likes of Greta Garbo, Charlie Chaplin, and Marlene Dietrich.

   Up the block to your right is a striking, jagged high-rise, home of the **Austrian Cultural Forum** (℮ **212/319-5300;** www.acfny.org). I find the building ominous, like a dagger hanging over the sidewalk. The interior, where there are free art exhibitions and other cultural happenings, is sleek and much more forgiving.

   Double back on 52nd Street toward Fifth Avenue. Fifth Avenue is the city's dividing line, where addresses change from east to west. On the far side of the avenue you'll be on:

10. **West 52nd Street,** designated "Swing Street" because this block holds a special place in jazz history. It was lined with a number of illicit speakeasies during Prohibition, and after its repeal, many of the establishments became jazz clubs, nurturing such great talents as Billie Holiday, Fats Waller, Dizzy Gillespie, Charlie Parker, and Sarah Vaughan.

    The **21 Club,** below an iron balcony lined with lawn jockeys at 21 W. 52nd St. (℮ **212/582-7200**), is still a popular restaurant and one of the few establishments to survive from this era. Operating as a speakeasy during Prohibition, it relied on several clever devices to guard against police raids, including a trap door on the bar that sent everyone's cocktails tumbling into the sewer when a button was pressed. A dress code for men remains (jackets for lunch, and jackets with ties for dinner), though the pricey menu means that the exclusivity is primarily economic.

Continue down 52nd Street, take a right on Sixth, and take another right on 53rd Street. This block has regained its status as one of the city's cultural meccas, starting with the:

11. **American Folk Art Museum** (© 212/265-1040; www. folkartmuseum.org), at no. 45. This stylish new structure was the city's first new museum building in 35 years. The oblique angles of the exterior panels make for an interesting departure from the usual continuity of Manhattan street walls. The interior is clean and modern, which is a little jarring given how rustic the art tends to be. The museum is open Tuesday through Sunday from 10:30am to 5:30pm, with hours extended until 7:30pm on Fridays, when the usual admission charge is suspended. The spaces on either side of the Folk Art Museum have been converted for use by the:

12. **Museum of Modern Art** (© 212/708-9400; www. moma.org), which has its main entrance at no. 11. Back from a brief exile to Queens, the MoMA has returned to the block that has been its home since 1939. Yoshio Taniguchi oversaw an elegant $650 million remodeling job that improved access and traffic flow, in addition to restoring the Sculpture Garden to its original size. With an additional 40,000 square feet of gallery space, more of the collection is on view, including all-time favorites like van Gogh's *The Starry Night,* Picasso's *Les Demoiselles d'Avignon,* and Mondrian's *Broadway Boogie-Woogie.* The interior is graceful and understated. The most assertive element is a 110-foot-high atrium built around Barnett Newman's *Broken Obelisk* sculpture on the second floor. You could easily exhaust yourself trying to take it all in (the museum dedicates space to six curatorial departments: painting and sculpture; prints and illustrated books; drawings; architecture and design; photography; and film and media), so this might be better saved for a separate visit. (The MoMA design store across the street

at no. 44 might be a better candidate for a visit, to avoid being overwhelmed.) MoMA is closed Tuesdays; otherwise, the hours are 10:30am to 5:30pm. Friday nights the museum stays open until 8pm and the usual hefty admission charge is waived starting at 4pm.

On the south side of 53rd Street, at no. 20, is the nondescript exterior of the:

13. **Donnell Library Center** (© 212/621-0618; www.nypl. org). Many New Yorkers don't realize that this branch of the New York Public Library is the permanent home of Winnie-the-Pooh. Take the elevator to the Central Children's Room on the third floor and you'll find Winnie himself, along with friends Piglet, Eeyore, Kanga, and Tigger. These are Christopher's actual stuffed animals, instantly recognizable from their portrayals on author A. A. Milne's pages. Though they look a little forlorn for being stuck behind glass, the animals are holding up pretty well for 80-year-olds. Publishing company E. P. Dutton never got around to shipping the animals home after a 1947 publicity tour, and only after 40 years of obscurity were they donated to the library system. The Central Children's Room is open Monday, Wednesday, and Friday from 10am to 6pm; Tuesday and Thursday from 10am to 8pm; Saturday from 10am to 5pm; and Sunday 1 to 5pm.

Back down on 53rd Street, take a right and cross Fifth Avenue. On the far side at the second vest-pocket granite and waterfall park sits a short, graffiti-covered stretch of the Berlin Wall. These five cement sections divided east from west between the years 1961 and 1989.

Continue east to Madison Avenue and take a right. As you pass 51st Street, take a moment to admire the Gothic-style tracery on the backside of St. Paddy's. On your left, the block is filled with the brownstone-gone-amok mass of the:

14. **New York Palace Hotel,** also known as the Villard Houses after the Bavarian immigrant Henry Villard, who published the *New York Evening Post* and founded the Northern Pacific Railroad. The central courtyard, designed like an Italian palazzo by the firm McKim, Mead & White, was unveiled in 1882. The **Municipal Art**

Society and the **Architectural League of New York** both keep galleries here, with rotating exhibits detailing a love of the city. The bookstore belonging to the **Urban Center** (📞 **212/935-3595**) has an unparalleled selection of urban planning and architecture tomes.

Take a left onto 50th Street and walk toward Park Avenue. As you look right down Park Avenue, you'll see the **Helmsley Building,** a lovely structure that sits astride the avenue, crowned with an elaborate cupola. The Helmsley Building is overshadowed by the **MetLife building,** one of New York's greatest architectural travesties (a big wedge of modernism that clogs the end of one of New York's loveliest old-fashioned avenues).

Across Park Avenue, between 50th and 49th streets, stands one of the most famous hotels in the world:

15. **The Waldorf=Astoria.** For over a century, the Waldorf has been synonymous with wealth and luxury, though the hotel's present location only dates from the early 20th century. Cole Porter and his wife lived for many years in one of the permanent apartments in the Waldorf Towers; one of the hotel's dining spots, Peacock Alley, still boasts his piano. Other famous residents have included Gen. Douglas MacArthur, Herbert Hoover, Henry and Clare Booth Luce, and the duke and duchess of Windsor. Gangster Lucky Luciano also lived here under an alias until he was forced to leave the Waldorf for less luxurious digs in the state penitentiary.

Between 50th and 51st streets on Park Avenue lies **St. Bartholomew's** (📞 **212/378-0200;** www.stbarts.org), a domed Episcopal church from 1918, which was begun in Romanesque style and switched to Byzantine halfway through construction. The church sports a three-arched main portal by Stanford White that came from the original St. Bart's once located down the street.

☕ **Take a Break**   St. Bart's may be the only church in New York with its own terrace cafe, **Café St. Bart's** (📞 **212/888-2664**). Under large umbrellas, with the Byzantine building shading you, you can dine alfresco on cafe fare, like the **Penobscot Bay lobster roll,** or the blue-plate special—roasted tomato soup and a grilled grafton cheddar sandwich. Main dishes run from $17 to $24 for lunch and $20 to $38 for dinner. In winter the cafe moves indoors into an uninspired back room of the church's complex.

Walk around the left side of St. Bart's down 51st Street to Lexington Avenue and turn left up the east side of it. The **subway grating** on this block is perhaps the most famous in the world, ever since 1955 when one of its gusts of hot air sent the skirt of **Marilyn Monroe's dress** billowing right into pinup legend in *The Seven Year Itch.*

Continue north up Lexington to 53rd Street, where the corner office building (**no. 599 Lexington**) features Frank Stella's *Salto nel Mio Sacco,* a colorful 1985 work, in the lobby. Across 53rd Street from this building is the austere, glass-and-buffed-aluminum pinnacle of the Citicorp Center. This pillar of international finance incorporates, at the corner of 54th Street, the modern and angular:

16. **St. Peter's Lutheran Church,** built in 1977. This is a singularly hip house of worship. St. Peter's is famous for its Sunday-evening Jazz Vespers, where many of the greatest names in jazz have performed. St. Peter's also regularly displays works by contemporary artists, though its greatest artwork is an environment designed by Louise Nevelson. Enter the building through the 54th Street entrance and take a right and you'll find the Chapel of the Good Shepherd through the doors around the corner. The room is five-sided, with a gold-leaf crucifix in front and intriguing white-wood sculptural elements on the walls.

Just north of St. Peter's, at 55th Street and across Lexington, is the:

17. **Central Synagogue,** one of New York's finest examples of Moorish Revival-style architecture. The oldest synagogue in continuous use in the city, it was dedicated in 1870. It was recently renovated after a fire in 1998 left it scarred. The results of the renovation are breathtaking, reflecting the synagogue's original design, and adding new ornamental towers and crenellation on the outside, and over 5,000 vividly colored wall stencils inside. Tours are available at 12:45 on Wednesday.

Turn left on 55th Street and right on Park Avenue. On your left, you'll pass a **Mercedes showroom;** the curvilinear interior was designed by Frank Lloyd Wright long before he conceived of his more famous New York landmark, the Guggenheim. Across 56th Street is gourmet superstar store Fauchon, where you can browse the selection of caviar.

The longtime home to many of the city's top art galleries and upscale boutiques, 57th Street recently has been filling with theme restaurants and overblown chain retail stores. From Park Avenue, turn left along 57th Street, and you'll come to the beautiful black-and-white, Art Deco:

18. **Fuller Building** at the northeast corner of Madison Avenue and 57th Street. Look at the bronze doors, marble fixtures, and mosaic floors and plan to spend some time browsing in the many art galleries housed here. Though a changeover from old-guard galleries has occurred in recent years, the remaining galleries usually have one or two interesting shows each year.

Across 57th Street at no. 32 is:

19. **PaceWildenstein Gallery** (© 212/421-3292), a major art gallery with specialty dealers spread out on several floors. The main gallery is devoted to 20th-century painting, drawing, and sculpture. It shows blue-chip artists such as Georg Baselitz, Alexander Calder, Chuck Close, Jim Dine, Jean Dubuffet, Agnes Martin, Louise Nevelson, Isamu Noguchi, Pablo Picasso, Mark Rothko, Julian Schnabel, and Richard Serra. On the seventh floor is **Pace Primitive** and on the third floor is **Pace Master Prints** (prints and drawings by old masters such as Dürer, Goya, Matisse, Picasso, Piranesi, Rembrandt, and Whistler). On the ninth floor is **Pace/MacGill,** which specializes in photography.

Continue along 57th Street to Fifth Avenue. The Niketown New York store at no. 6 has five levels of sporting goods in a theme-park environment. The building is designed to resemble a city school (on the facade, the P.S. 6453 corresponds with n-i-k-e on a telephone). Just ahead on your left stretches the bejeweled:

20. **Tiffany & Co.,** with its windows full of amazing gems. (**Note:** Contrary to popular belief, it's not a good place to try and rustle up some breakfast, even if you are Audrey Hepburn.)

    Cross Fifth Avenue and continue along West 57th Street. Halfway down the next block on your left at no. 40 (an office atrium entrance hallway down the right side of the passage) is the:

21. **Marlborough Gallery** (second floor; ℂ 212/541-4900; www.marlboroughgallery.com), one of the most reputable galleries in the world. Big stars here include the late Francis Bacon (Britain's de Kooning), Fernando Botero, Red Grooms, Richard Estes, Alex Katz, Antonio Lopez Garcia, Tom Otterness, Arnoldo Pomodoro, Larry Rivers, and Jacques Lipchitz.

    Return to Fifth Avenue, cross it again, and turn left (uptown) onto it, passing some of the city's most glamorous shops. On the east (right) side of the street, on the fourth floor of no. 745, you'll find:

22. **Mary Boone Gallery** (ℂ 212/752-2929; www.mary boonegallery.com), a world-class gallery of contemporary art by Richard Artschwager, Ross Bleckner, Eric Fischl, Sean Scully, and Tim Rollins. Also in this building is the **McKee Gallery,** which shows Philip Guston, a major abstract expressionist, as well as Jake Berthot, David Humphrey, Martin Puryear, and Jeanne Silverthrone.

    Continue up Fifth Avenue. Just north of 58th Street is the toy store of every child's dreams and a New York institution since 1870:

23. **F.A.O. Schwarz** (ℂ 212/644-9400; www.fao.com). You may remember Tom Hanks's famous dance interpretation of "Heart and Soul," performed here on a giant piano keyboard in the movie *Big.* The store is a wonderland of toys, with a menagerie of stuffed animals; fantastic, mobile Lego creations; squadrons of Barbie dolls; a candy shop; and command centers of video games where anybody can play.

    Across from F.A.O. Schwarz stands the landmark:

24. **The Plaza Hotel,** built in 1907, when suites rented for $25 a night. Zelda Fitzgerald turned heads here by making a splash (literally) in the fountain in front of the hotel. The

Fitzgeralds stayed here in September 1922 while looking for a home, and F. Scott used the Plaza as the backdrop for a crucial scene in his masterpiece, *The Great Gatsby.* Another famous guest, Frank Lloyd Wright, stayed in a suite overlooking the park while he designed the Guggenheim Museum. In 2004, the hotel was sold for a reported $675 million. The original plan was to convert all 805 rooms into condominium apartments, but the public and the hotel's union bucked. Construction is now under-way for a mixed-use structure, with both permanent resi-dents and hotel guests.

Head back downtown on Fifth Avenue. Detour left at 56th Street to the:

25. **Sony Wonder Tech Lab** (© 212/833-5414; www.sony wondertechlab.com), a blatantly commercial, but undeni-ably fun, high-tech, hands-on "museum" of sorts for Sony products. You can loop your own voice into famous movie scenes on a mixing board, play with special-effects tricks on blue screens, and learn to operate robots. Oh, and indulge in the free movie screenings and the coolest setups for playing the latest PlayStation games. It's open Tuesday to Saturday 10am to 5pm, Sunday noon to 5pm. Admission is free, but tickets are required. Same-day tick-ets are made available, but to ensure that you're not shut out you might want to make an advance reservation (accepted from 1 week to 3 months in advance).

Winding Down There's no better place to stop for an afternoon cocktail than the bar where the Bloody Mary was invented: the **King Cole Bar in the St. Regis Hotel,** 2 E. 55th St. (© 212/753-4500), adorned with a wonderful mural of the merry old monarch him-self. An elegant afternoon tea is served in the Astor Court, a plush venue with a vaulted ceiling, trompe l'oeil cloud murals, and 22-karat gold leaf on the delicate stuccowork. Note that the management recently started enforcing a "no sneakers" policy after 5pm in the bar.

The hotel itself is a landmark, built in 1904 by John Jacob Astor. Ernest Hemingway, Alfred Hitchcock, and Salvador Dalí all stayed at the St. Regis, and John Lennon and Yoko Ono occupied suites here in the early 1970s.

Central Park

Start: Grand Army Plaza, at 59th Street and Fifth Avenue.

Subway: Take the N, R, or W to Fifth Avenue.

Finish: The Vanderbilt Gate, which is the entrance to the Conservatory Garden, at 105th Street and Fifth Avenue.

Time: Approximately 5 hours, including lunch. If you want to explore the park more fully (stopping to visit the zoo for an hour or 2, for instance), consider breaking this tour up into a 2-day-long excursion.

Best Time: Weekends, weather permitting, when the park hums with activity.

Landscape architects par excellence Frederick Law Olmsted and Calvert Vaux designed Central Park in the late 1850s, when the park's land was still on the outskirts of the city. Its creation ensured that New Yorkers would always have access to pastoral tranquillity. One of the world's most beautiful urban parks, Central Park is a recreational greenbelt of woodlands (26,000 trees), wisteria-shaded arbors, duck- and swan-filled lakes and lagoons, meadows, rambling lanes, gardens, fountains, pavilions, and picturesque bridges.

Central Park

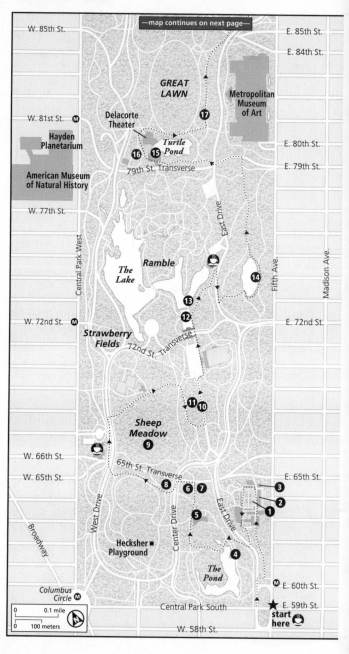

—map continues on next page—

W. 85th St.
E. 85th St.
E. 84th St.

GREAT LAWN

Metropolitan Museum of Art

W. 81st St.

Hayden Planetarium

Delacorte Theater

Turtle Pond

E. 80th St.

American Museum of Natural History

79th St. Transverse

E. 79th St.

W. 77th St.

East Drive

The Lake

Ramble

Central Park West

Fifth Ave.

Madison Ave.

W. 72nd St.
E. 72nd St.

Strawberry Fields

72nd St. Transverse

Sheep Meadow

W. 66th St.

65th St. Transverse

W. 65th St.
E. 65th St.

West Drive

Center Drive

East Drive

Heckscher Playground

The Pond

E. 60th St.

Broadway

Columbus Circle

Central Park South
E. 59th St.
start here

0   0.1 mile
0   100 meters

W. 58th St.

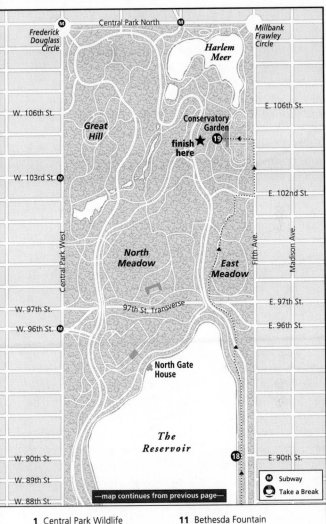

Central Park North

Frederick
Douglass
Circle

Millbank
Frawley
Circle

*Harlem
Meer*

W. 106th St.

E. 106th St.

*Great
Hill*

Conservatory
Garden

★ finish
here

⑲

W. 103rd St.

E. 102nd St.

*North
Meadow*

*East
Meadow*

W. 97th St.

97th St. Transverse

E. 97th St.

W. 96th St.

E. 96th St.

North Gate
House

*The
Reservoir*

W. 90th St.

E. 90th St.

⑱

W. 89th St.

Ⓜ Subway

☕ Take a Break

W. 88th St.

—map continues from previous page—

Central Park West   Fifth Ave.   Madison Ave.

1 Central Park Wildlife Conservation Center	**11** Bethesda Fountain
2 The Arsenal	**12** The Dead Road
3 Delacorte Clock	**13** The Lake
4 The Pond	**14** Conservatory Water
5 Wollman Rink	**15** Belvedere Castle
6 Chess and Checkers House	**16** Shakespeare Garden
7 The Dairy	**17** The Obelisk (Cleopatra's Needle)
8 The Carousel	**18** The Reservoir
9 Sheep Meadow	**19** Conservatory Garden
10 The Mall	

Encompassing 843 acres enclosed by stone walls, the park is 2½ miles long (extending from 59th–110th sts.) and a half mile wide (from Fifth Ave. to Central Park West), encompassing 6% of Manhattan's total acreage. It's the setting for numerous concerts, theatrical productions, and events ranging from marathons to bird-watching walks. There are playing fields for sports, bridle trails, 58 miles of walking and biking paths, boating lakes, a lovely zoo, gardens, playgrounds, and dozens of statues dotting the park; and, of course, it has its own website now: www.centralparknyc.org.

On weekends especially, musicians, acrobats, puppeteers, and other enterprising performers offer a wealth of free entertainment. The Central Park Conservancy and the NYC Parks Department have renovated more than a third of Central Park over the past decade, and the park today is safe, clean, and beautiful.

If you're getting an early start, the plush luxury hotels near the entrance point offer breakfasts, but to dine in such opulent settings does come with a price. At the Café Pierre at the Pierre, or the Atelier at the Ritz-Carlton, continental breakfasts start around $25, and full American breakfasts around $35. Much less pricey (but still very nice) is the Leaping Frog Café, just inside the park. The menu dovetails with the zoo's conservationist bent, utilizing sustainable and organic ingredients. Terrace seating is available, under a wisteria arbor. The cafe is open, as is the zoo, from 10am daily.

An advance note on meals: Although Central Park offers a few restaurants, which I'll point out as we go along, they are a bit pricey. One cheaper alternative is noshing on street food from a hot-dog stand, or bringing along the makings of a picnic.

• • • • • • • • • • • • • • • •

Start at the southeastern corner of the park at Grand Army Plaza (see walking tour 11, stop 1). Cross 60th Street and take the wide, bench-lined path paralleling Fifth Avenue. Fork to the right through the brick gate and onto the path leading past the:

1. **Central Park Wildlife Center,** better known as **The Central Park Zoo** (℗ 212/439-6500; www.nyzoosand aquarium.com). In spite of opposition by both Olmsted

and Vaux, who feared losing natural scenery to gaudy attractions, some sort of zoo has been in the park since 1864. No other American city had a zoo in the mid-19th century, and the zoo's founders viewed the concept as a cultural coup for New York. Originally just a diverse collection of donated animals (Olmsted mockingly opined that they were mostly "pets of children who had died"), early zoo denizens included three African Cape buffaloes acquired by General Sherman during his Georgia siege, and circus animals quartered at the zoo in winter by P. T. Barnum. Eight monkeys (purchased rather than donated) were described in the *New York Times* in July 1871 as "comical 'Darwinian links.'" (Monkeys were of special interest in those early days of Darwinian theory.) The zoo became a more formal establishment in 1934 when a quadrangle of redbrick animal houses was constructed.

In 1988, a renovated 5½-acre zoo opened its doors, replacing confining cages with natural-habitat enclosures and exhibiting a cross-section of international wildlife that comprises about 450 animals. Three major ecological areas are arranged around a formal English-style Central Garden that centers on a sea-lion pool. The dense, junglelike Tropic Zone, a rainforest environment with streams and waterfalls, houses an aviary of brightly hued birds, along with monkeys, alligators, reptiles, and amphibians. In the Temperate Territory, Japanese snow monkeys live on an island in a lake inhabited by Arctic whooper swans; this area also has an outdoor pavilion for viewing red pandas. The Polar Circle is home to penguins, polar bears, harbor seals, and Arctic foxes. If you do go in, make sure to visit the soothingly quiet Intelligence Garden, with wrought-iron chairs under a rustic wooden vine-covered pagoda. The zoo is open 365 days a year, during the summer from 10am to 5pm on weekdays, and until 5:30pm on weekends and holidays. In winter the zoo is open daily from 10am to 4:30pm. Admission is charged.

Across from the entrance to the zoo, up against Fifth Avenue, is:

2. **The Arsenal,** a fortresslike Gothic Revival building complete with octagonal turrets. Built in the late 1840s (predating the park), it housed troops during the Civil War

Kid-Friendly Experiences

- Paying a visit to the animals at the Central Park Wildlife Center (stop 1)
- Watching the Delacorte Clock performances (stop 3)
- Skating in winter or enjoying amusement park rides in summer at Wollman Rink (stop 5)
- Riding on the Carousel (stop 8)
- Boating on the Lake (stop 13)
- Visiting the Alice in Wonderland statue group (stop 14)

and was the first home of the American Museum of Natural History from 1869 to 1877. Originally, its exterior brick was covered with stucco. Today, the brick is ivied, and the Arsenal houses park headquarters, zoo administration offices, and a third-floor art gallery. Walk around to the front entrance and note the stair railing made of rifles and the weapon-related embellishments on the facade. Inside, the 1935 WPA mural by Allen Saalburg merits a look if you're here on a weekday when the building is open. It depicts maps of New York parks, idyllic 19th-century Central Park scenes, and military themes.

Walk all the way around the Arsenal to continue up the zoo pathway, where you will see the:

3. **Delacorte Clock.** Atop an arched brick gate, this whimsical animated clock has been enchanting park visitors since the mid-1960s. Designed by Andrea Spadini, it features six dancing animals: a tambourine-playing bear, a kangaroo on horn, a hippo violinist, a Pan-like pipe-playing goat, a penguin drummer, and an elephant squeezing an accordion. The soundtracks vary with the season, spring featuring tunes like "Raindrops Keep Falling on my Head," while "Silent Night" and "Deck the Halls" are reserved for winter. Schedules vary, but performances are generally on the hour and the half-hour from 8am to 10:30pm.

To get to the next stop, you'll have to double back past the Leaping Frog Café and make the first right after exiting the gate, where a sign indicates the way to Wollman Rink.

Bear left, cross and turn onto East Drive, and then veer left down the first sloped path you come to. Cross Gapstow Bridge over:

4. **The Pond,** originally the site of DeVoor's Mill Stream. On your left is a fenced-in bird refuge, the Hallett Nature Sanctuary. Make a right where the sanctuary fence ends and walk north around:

5. **Wollman Rink.** This popular skating rink, built into the northern bay of The Pond in 1951, provides skatable ice throughout the winter. The rink's refrigerating system broke down in 1980, and the ice rink remained out of operation until Donald Trump came to the rescue in 1986, bringing in his own construction specialists to re-open it. Today, cold weather brings thousands of daily visitors to the rink. During warmer months, skating gives way to Victorian Gardens, a small amusement park with spinning teacups, a whimsical train, and other child-friendly rides.

   Make the first right after the end of the rink, and then take the first left (an uphill slope) to the:

6. **Chess and Checkers House.** A gift from Bernard Baruch in 1952, this octagonal hilltop facility has 10 tables indoors and 24 outside for playing chess and checkers. The outdoor tables are under a rustic wooden arbor covered with vines. If you neglected to bring your own chess or checkers, you can borrow a set, just ahead on the path and to the right, at:

7. **The Dairy.** This Gothic Revival storybook stone cottage, designed by Vaux in 1870, originally served fresh milk and snacks to children. Cows were stabled in a nearby building. Today, the Dairy serves as a park information center, which is open Tuesday to Sunday 10am to 5pm, and houses exhibits on the design and history of the park. You can pick up an events calendar and informative brochures here and check out video information terminals.

   Double back, going around the right (west) side of the Chess and Checkers House. Duck through the tunnel (Playmates Arch) under Center Drive to:

8. **The Carousel.** This charming Victorian merry-go-round, which was originally turned by a blind mule and a horse, is one of the oldest concessions in the park. Its calliope has been playing old-fashioned tunes since 1872. The colorful whirling steeds are among the largest carousel horses in the world. Go ahead: Take the $1.25 ride.

Continuing west (take the path left of the carousel), you'll be walking past the Heckscher ballfields. When you come to West Drive, turn right (north) and walk a short way. Tavern on the Green is across the street, behind the trees.

Take a Break **Tavern on the Green** is located inside the park at West 67th Street (℃ **212/873-3200;** www.tavernonthegreen.com). The original Victorian building was erected in 1870 to house the 200 sheep that grazed on the Sheep Meadow (see stop 9). The dazzling dining room, which Mayor Fiorello LaGuardia opened with a brass key, dates from 1934. In 1976, Hollywood mogul Werner LeRoy sank $20 million in renovating the Tavern as a setting for celebrity-studded parties, film premieres, and political functions. The food is nothing spectacular, but the sylvan setting makes for a memorable lunch atmosphere. It offers patio seating under the trees in a magnificent flower garden where 40,000 bulbs blossom year-round. The lavish, glass-enclosed Crystal Room offers indoor dining with verdant park views.

Make a right on the first path you come to after Tavern on the Green as you make your way north on West Drive. The path borders the:

9. **Sheep Meadow.** Originally mandated as a military parade ground, about which Olmsted was less than enthusiastic, Sheep Meadow took on a more peaceful incarnation in 1878. Until 1934, a flock of Southdown sheep grazed here, tended by a shepherd. Though undoubtedly picturesque, the sheep became deformed from inbreeding and were banished (though only to Prospect Park in Brooklyn) by parks commissioner Robert Moses; the shepherd was reassigned to the lion house in the zoo. During the 1960s, Sheep Meadow was a hippie haven and the setting for antiwar protests, love-ins,

be-ins, and, after the 1969 Stonewall riots that launched
the gay pride movement, a gay-in. Today the lush, green
Sheep Meadow is a popular spot for kite flyers, sun-
bathers, and Frisbee players—a tranquil oasis where loud
radios are off-limits.

Follow the fence on your right, and make a right where
it turns onto the gravel path of Lilac Walk. After you pass
the volleyball court area, cross the road and look for the
bronze *Indian Hunter* statue (1869) by 19th-century
American artist John Quincy Adams Ward. Straight ahead
(look for a group of statues), turn left and go up:

10. **The Mall.** Designed as a Versailles-like grand promenade, this shaded formal walkway, about a quarter-mile in
length, is bordered by a double row of American elms that
form a cathedral arch overhead. Dutch Elm disease's rav-
aging of America's elm population has resulted in this
stately grove being one of the last of its kind. At its
entrance are statues of Columbus (created in 1892 to
mark the 400th anniversary of his voyage), Shakespeare
(like the *Indian Hunter,* by J. Q. A. Ward; Shakespearean
actor Edwin Booth laid its cornerstone), Robert Burns,
Sir Walter Scott, and American poet Fitz-Greene Halleck.

Just west of the Mall is one of my favorite New York
spectacles. Follow the sound of music to:

11. **The Dead Road.** The glam New York of the '70s and
'80s has mostly vanished, but a trace can be found at the
outdoor roller-disco that forms on the weekends along this
asphalt stretch. The music selection can be every bit as
entertaining as watching the rollerbladers and skaters roll
through their paces, especially now that the city has relent-
ed on its anti-beat campaign. (In 1995 music was banned
from the park, so skaters wore Walkmen all tuned to the
same radio station, creating a surreal silent choreography.)

Turn back toward the end of the Mall, where you'll
find the Naumburg Bandshell. (Free concerts are held
here, and occasionally you'll hear a local amateur step up
on stage and belt out some light opera.) To your left,
across East 72nd Street, you'll find a broad stairway with
a massive sandstone balustrade ornately decorated with
birds, flowers, and fruit. On the other side is one of the
park's most stunning vistas:

12. **Bethesda Fountain.** Emma Stebbins's biblically inspired, neoclassical, winged Bethesda (the "angel of the waters") tops a vast, triple-tiered stone fountain with the lake forming a scenic backdrop. Its setting is Vaux's part-Gothic, part-Romanesque terrace, which is the heart of the park and one of its most popular venues. Like Sheep Meadow, Bethesda Fountain was a hippie hub in the 1960s, filled with counterculture types demonstrating against the Vietnam War, smoking pot, and strumming guitars. A *Newsweek* article of that era called it the "craziest, gayest gathering place in the city." The scene is gone and the plaza here is one of New York's most idyllic settings.

Go down the steps (look at the balustrade's bas-reliefs of the Seasons), and make a right on the path closest to:

13. **The Lake.** Its perimeter pathway lined with weeping willows and Japanese cherry trees, the 22½-acre lake was created from Sawkill Creek, which entered the Park near West 79th Street. The neo-Victorian Loeb Boathouse at the east end of the Lake rents rowboats and bicycles; evenings, you can arrange gondola rides. Along the path to the Lake, you'll usually see handwriting analysts, masseurs, reflexologists, and other purveyors of New Age services.

Take a Break The Boathouse Café (© 212/517-2233; www.thecentralparkboathouse.com) at the eastern end of the Lake offers alfresco lakeside seating on a wooden deck under a white canopy. Overhead heaters extend the cafe's season, although after October dinner is suspended (early nights deter many diners from trekking into the park) until April. The menu is contemporary American, biased toward seafood, in keeping with the lakeside location. Entrees are in the $23 to $31 range, with monkfish, wild Atlantic salmon, and sole among the catch. As at Tavern on the Green, the setting is much more of a draw than the food. Lunch is served weekdays from noon to 4pm, and dinners are from 5:30 to 9:30pm. On the weekends, brunch runs 9:30am to 4pm, and dinner 6 to 9:30pm.

If you want something simpler and less expensive, the Boathouse complex houses an express cafeteria with both indoor and outdoor seating. It serves breakfast and light-fare items year-round, and prices are reasonable.

Hours are 8 to 11am for breakfast, and then 11am until 5pm for lunch, 7 days a week.

From the south end of the Boathouse, cross East Drive and follow the path to the:

14. **Conservatory Water.** The above-mentioned Pond and Lake are free-form bodies of water. The Conservatory Water, scene of model-boat races (there's even a model boathouse on the Fifth Ave. side where miniature boats are stored), is of formal design. Originally planned as the setting for a conservatory garden (built later and located farther uptown; see stop 19), it is the site of José de Creeft's *Alice in Wonderland* statues (Alice, the Mad Hatter, March Hare, Dormouse, and Cheshire Cat), which were inspired by the John Tenniel illustrations in the original 1865 edition of the book. Overlooking the water is George Lober's Hans Christian Andersen Memorial Statue, complete with an Ugly Duckling. This gift from Denmark is the setting for storytelling sessions every Saturday 11am to noon from June through September. Circle the pond (*Catcher in the Rye* fans will remember it as the spot where Holden Caulfield came to commiserate with the ducks) and peek into the model boathouse if it's open.

Exit the Conservatory Water on the northwest path (past Alice) and continue through Glade Arch, turning left after the 79th Street Transverse and following the path under Greywacke Arch. Ahead on the right, atop the aptly named Vista Rock, is:

15. **Belvedere Castle.** Built by Vaux in 1869, this fanciful medieval-style fortress-in-miniature sits at the highest point in the park and offers sweeping views across Manhattan's verdant playground. To the south, toward the Lake, stretches a wild-by-design tangle of forested trails known as the Ramble, which is fun for exploring by daylight, but dangerous and seedy after dark. The many birds that call this area home led to the creation of a bird-watching and educational center in the Castle's ranger station.

From Belvedere's balcony, look north over the Delacorte Theater, which in July and August is the setting for the popular **Shakespeare in the Park** series (www. publictheater.org). The series presents a pair of plays in the outdoor theater each summer, performed by both headliner stars (Denzel Washington, Christopher Walken) and eminent Shakespearean thespians (Patrick Stewart did a *Tempest* turn in 1995). Shows start at 8pm, but tickets are free, so it's wise to show up early in the morning and wait until the Delacorte box office opens at 1pm to snag a pair (you can also get tickets at the Public Theater, on 425 Lafayette St., at 1pm). Beyond the Delacorte stretches the Great Lawn, host to some of New York's most famous blowout events, including Paul Simon's gratis concert in the park.

Just past the Castle and before the **Swedish Cottage Marionette Theater** (℗ **212/988-9093;** puppet shows year-round, usually every day but Mon, although the schedule varies by month) you'll find the:

16. **Shakespeare Garden,** where the only flowers and plants in evidence are those mentioned in the Bard's plays.

Double back along the 79th Street Transverse to turn left (north) up East Drive (just before Greywacke Arch). Up ahead, across from the backside of the Metropolitan Museums, rises:

17. **The Obelisk (Cleopatra's Needle).** This 3,500-year-old, 77-foot-high, Egyptian pink granite obelisk was a gift to New York City from the khedive of Egypt in 1881 to thank the United States for its help in building the Suez Canal.

Dating from the reign of King Thutmose III in 1600 B.C., the obelisk stood in front of the Temple of the Sun in Heliopolis, Egypt, until the Romans removed it in 12 B.C. and placed it at the approach of a temple built by Cleopatra (hence its nickname). Its hieroglyphics (which are translated here, a gift of Cecil B. DeMille) tell of the deeds of Thutmose III, Ramses II, and Osarkon I. The four bronze crabs peeking out from each corner of the base are 19th-century replicas of the originals, which it is believed were placed there by the Romans as a decorative means of support.

Follow the path behind (west of) the obelisk. When it ends, bear right and follow East Drive, keeping to the left. Soon you'll come to steps and a cast-iron bridge leading to the South Gate House. Make a right onto the jogging path of the:

18. **Reservoir,** created in 1862 to supply New York City's water system. Occupying 106 acres and extending the width of the park, it is surrounded by bridle and jogging paths. The reservoir holds a billion gallons of water, is 40 feet at its greatest depth, and now serves only as an emergency backup water supply. The path around it is 1½ miles long. Walk or jog along the eastern border of the reservoir, getting off at 96th Street (a playground is diagonally across).

    Continue north on East Drive to 102nd Street, exit the park, and walk north along Fifth Avenue to the Vanderbilt Gate. This ornate portal, designed in Paris in 1894, formerly graced the Fifth Avenue mansion of Cornelius Vanderbilt II. Fittingly adorned with plant motifs, it is the entrance to the:

19. **Conservatory Garden.** This formal garden was commissioned as a WPA project in 1936. As you enter from Fifth Avenue, you'll be facing the elegant Italian garden, a green centered on a classical fountain. It is ringed with yew hedges and bordered by alleys of Siberian crabapple trees. In spring, the crabapples bloom with pink and white flowers, and narcissus grows in the ivy beneath them.

    Walk through the crabapple alley on the left to the lovely mazelike English garden. You'll find a bronze statue of the children from the novel *The Secret Garden* standing in a reflecting pool. In summer, water lilies and a wide variety of flowering plants and shrubs fill the garden. Now walk through the Wisteria Pergola (at the back of the Italian garden). This flower-bedecked, wrought-iron arbor, especially magnificent in late May, connects the English and French gardens.

    Enter the French garden via rose-covered arched trellises. Two levels of flower beds encircle the Untermeyer Fountain, which centers on an enchanting sculpture of dancing maidens by Walter Schott. Here, 20,000 tulips bloom in spring, and 5,000 chrysanthemums bloom in fall.

The Upper West Side

Start: 86th Street and Broadway.

Subway: Take the 1 to 86th Street.

Finish: Lincoln Center.

Time: 3½ hours (allow more time for shopping, refreshment stops, and museum visits).

Best Time: Weekday afternoons, when shops and museums are open but crowds are at a minimum.

The Upper West Side has undergone a decidedly upwardly mobile transformation in the last few decades. Though some magnificent luxury apartment buildings have stood here since the days of gaslights and horse-drawn carriages, they were surrounded by an otherwise unremarkable, largely working-class neighborhood for the first half of the 20th century. Then came Lincoln Center.

A massive urban renewal effort centered around the construction of this performing arts complex in the early 1960s.

The Upper West Side

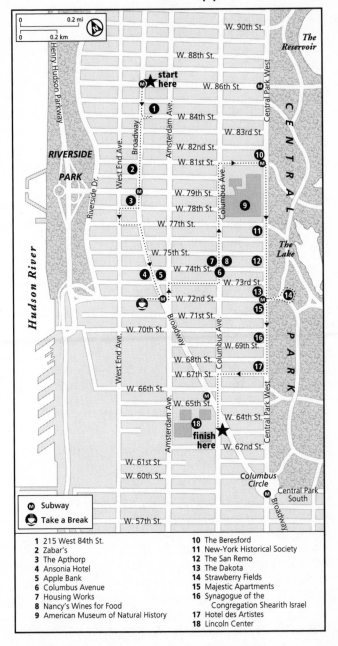

0.2 mi
0.2 km

W. 90th St.
W. 88th St.
The Reservoir
start here
W. 86th St.
W. 84th St.
W. 83rd St.
W. 82nd St.
W. 81st St.
W. 79th St.
W. 78th St.
W. 77th St.
W. 75th St.
W. 74th St.
W. 73rd St.
W. 72nd St.
W. 71st St.
W. 70th St.
W. 69th St.
W. 68th St.
W. 67th St.
W. 66th St.
W. 65th St.
W. 64th St.
W. 62nd St.
W. 61st St.
W. 60th St.
W. 57th St.

Henry Hudson Parkway

RIVERSIDE PARK

Hudson River

Riverside Dr.

West End Ave.

Broadway

Amsterdam Ave.

Columbus Ave.

Central Park West

CENTRAL PARK

The Lake

Strawberry Fields area

finish here

Columbus Circle

Central Park South

Broadway

Ⓜ **Subway**
☕ **Take a Break**

1 215 West 84th St.
2 Zabar's
3 The Apthorp
4 Ansonia Hotel
5 Apple Bank
6 Columbus Avenue
7 Housing Works
8 Nancy's Wines for Food
9 American Museum of Natural History
10 The Beresford
11 New-York Historical Society
12 The San Remo
13 The Dakota
14 Strawberry Fields
15 Majestic Apartments
16 Synagogue of the Congregation Shearith Israel
17 Hotel des Artistes
18 Lincoln Center

Blocks of dilapidated housing and bodegas gave way to pricey boutiques and exclusive residential buildings.

Gentrification transformed the West Side in the decades that followed, but this is still the neighborhood of *Seinfeld*. Mom-and-pop Chinese restaurants, dry-cleaners, and shoe-repair shops help to retain local flavor. Farther uptown, you'll see old-time barber shops thriving next door to trendy new hair salons, or blocks where all the signs are in Spanish and salsa blasts from the windows.

More democratic and informal than the stuffy Upper East Side, the Upper West Side has lately become a magnet for families. Strollers clog the graceful, broad avenues, beside world-class food shopping at Fairway and Zabar's, and coffee table art books stacked on the tables of sidewalk entrepreneurs. Between the cuisine and the culture, Upper West Siders take a justified pride in their neighborhood's enviable quality of life.

• • • • • • • • • • • • • • • •

From the 86th Street subway station, walk south down the east side of Broadway to 84th Street ("Edgar Allan Poe St."). Just off Broadway to your left is:

1. **215 W. 84th St.** As recently as the 1840s, this area was still undeveloped rural countryside. Edgar Allan Poe lived briefly with his wife in a farmhouse that stood here on a rocky knoll. He completed his poem "The Raven" here in the summer of 1844.

   Go back to Broadway and cross the street; turn left, heading downtown. At the northwest corner of 80th Street and Broadway stands:

2. **Zabar's** (© 212/787-2000), a West Side retail institution. The faint of heart should beware: Zabar's is sheer bedlam, and its crowd of serious shoppers will shove you right out of the way for the perfect wheel of Brie. But plunge into the crowds and wander through the aisles for a mind-boggling selection of imported cheeses, breads, cold cuts, salads, and appetizers. At the fish counter, you can get anything from smoked salmon to caviar. If you're taking this tour on a beautiful spring day, you'll find the fixings here for a memorable picnic feast in Central Park.

In inclement weather, Zabar's busy ground-floor cafe is an entertaining place to pause for some freshly ground coffee.

H&H Bagels, just across 80th Street, is a front-runner for the coveted title of Best Bagels in New York; they're so fresh that they're still warm from the oven.

Just south of here rises the magnificent 1908 limestone facade of:

3. **The Apthorp,** which commands an entire square block bounded by 78th and 79th streets, Broadway, and West End Avenue. Admire the 1908 building from the Broadway side, standing in front of the stately iron gates that lead into a landscaped central courtyard with a pair of fountains, marble benches, and statuary. You may recognize it from a conga line of New York–based films in which the Apthorp was featured, including *The Cotton Club, Heartburn, The Money Pit,* and *Network.*

   Continue down Broadway, where you'll see **Citarella** (*©* **212/874-0383**), another excellent gourmet food shop that gives Zabar's a run for its money. At 74th Street, you'll pass Fairway, West Siders' favorite produce store. A block farther south, you'll see on the right the splendid Beaux Arts–style:

4. **Ansonia Hotel,** between 73rd and 74th streets, was built as a luxury residential hotel in 1904. Its architect, W. E. D. Stokes, bought this parcel of land, then surrounded by single-family homes, and decided to raise eyebrows by building a 17-story "tenement" in flamboyant French style. Resembling a lacy, opulent wedding cake, the Ansonia sports a three-story mansard roof and rounded corner towers with high domes.

   The Ansonia contained a grand ballroom, a swimming pool, a trellised roof garden (Stokes kept a small pet bear, goats, and chickens in the roof garden; he sold the eggs to tenants at a discount), a theater, a barber shop, a pharmacist, a florist, and a laundry. Live seals splashed about in the lobby's fountain.

   The Ansonia has always been a favorite address for musicians, among them Stravinsky, Toscanini, and Caruso. (The apartments here are virtually soundproof, so musicians can practice without fear of disturbing other tenants.)

The golden age of the Ansonia ended with the Great Depression, and the building has slid into a decline marked by legal battles between tenants and owners. (You may recognize it as the setting for the thriller *Single White Female*.)

Take a Break Tucked away in a basement on the downtown side of 72nd Street between Broadway and West End Avenue is a dive bar that hosts a crowd of neighborhood regulars. The **All State Cafe,** 250 W. 72nd St. (✆ **212/874-1883**), serves typical bar food, such as fried calamari, spicy chicken wings, and bowls of chili, plus surprisingly good daily specials. The thick, juicy burgers are among the best in town. If you're there on a chilly winter day, you'll appreciate the fire crackling in the hearth beside the bar. And the jukebox has a great selection of classic rock, jazz, oldies, and swing tunes. The All State is open daily from 11:30am to 1am (later on weekends).

In the early 1970s, this joint was H. M. Tweed's singles bar. On New Year's Day 1973, schoolteacher Roseanne Quinn picked up a guy named John Wayne Wilson and figured he'd make a good 1-night stand. After he strangled and stabbed her, he was arrested, confessed, and committed suicide while awaiting trial. The book and movie inspired by the murder, *Looking for Mr. Goodbar*, became an anthem against the casual-sex culture of the '70s.

Go back to Broadway and 73rd Street; now take 73rd Street east and cross Broadway. Between 73rd and 74th streets is the:

5. **Apple Bank,** designed by York and Sawyer in the 1920s and boasting a massive limestone facade and stunning ironwork doors (lately hidden under scaffolding during a complete restoration). The structure's trapezoid shape allows it to fill out the plot of land created where Broadway cuts diagonally across Amsterdam Avenue, and its heavy, monumental style is perfectly suited to a bank building. (Be sure to look back across the street at the Ansonia from here.)

Continue south on Broadway to the corner of 71st, admiring the architectural excesses of the **Dorilton.** This Beaux Arts apartment house was built in 1902 and features lovely details, like the two sculpted women adorning a bay window on the Broadway facade. On the 71st Street side, take note of the courtyard with its soaring arched entryway. Walk east on 71st Street to:

6. **Columbus Avenue,** one of New York's trendiest promenades, lined with boutiques, coffee bars, and restaurants. Stores spring up like weeds on Columbus—and they disappear as fast as yesterday's news. Take this part of the stroll to stop and browse in any place that catches your eye. Try **Kenneth Cole** (no. 353) or **Eileen Fisher** (no. 341) for fashion, or Boyd's (no. 309) for a department store in miniature. My favorite shop on this stretch is:

7. **Housing Works,** at no. 306 (✆ **212/579-7566;** www. housingworks.org). "Upscale thrift shop" may be an oxymoron, but this store takes pride in the excellent taste of its contributors. Proceeds benefit Housing Works, an AIDS advocacy organization. The store is open Monday through Friday, 11am to 7pm, Saturday 10am to 6pm, and Sundays from noon to 5pm.

Another good spot for browsing is:

8. **Nancy's Wines for Food,** at no. 313 (✆ **212/877-4040;** www.nancyswines.com). Nancy's usually has more than 100 labels of wine in stock under $10, and those that are pricier are generally worth it. Each wine is marked with an index card describing its qualities and what foods it best accompanies. There's no enological snobbery here, just good, plain-spoken advice and excellent wines. Nancy's is open Monday to Saturday 10am to 9pm, and Sunday noon to 6pm.

Continue your stroll up Columbus, taking your time to allow for optimum people-watching. At **77th Street,** take a right down a block so admired by Tom Wolfe that he called it "the most beautiful in town" in his book *The Bonfire of the Vanities.* Halfway down it is the entrance to the:

9. **American Museum of Natural History** (✆ **212/769-5100;** www.amnh.org), home to the world's greatest natural-science collection, some 36 million artifacts strong. The building's cornerstone was laid in 1874, but construction was piecemeal, resulting in this mix of architecture styles—Gothic superseded by Romanesque Revival and later American Renaissance. The campus holds 4 square

blocks of towers and turrets, pink granite and red brick. The famous Hall of Dinosaurs has been brought into the 21st century, with high-tech displays accompanying the ancient skeletons. In the astounding minerals and gems section you can see the largest meteorite ever retrieved, in addition to the world's largest sapphire, the 563-carat Star of India. Ethnographic exhibits, dimly lit and wood-paneled, present aboriginal dioramas amid canoes and masks.

The suggested admission is worth it; the museum's hours are daily 10am to 5:45pm (the Rose Center only is also open Fri 10am–8:45pm).

Head back to Columbus Avenue and continue north to **81st Street.** On the back of the AMNH lot you'll see the totally rebuilt, $210 million **Rose Center for Earth and Space.** This amazing museum within a museum tells the history of the universe. The floating sphere across the lawn holds the Hayden Planetarium. The planetarium weighs 2,000 tons, and it's housed within a box made of a literal acre of glass.

Make a right and head toward Central Park West. Further ahead on your left, crowning the northwest corner of the intersection, is:

10. **The Beresford,** the first in a long line of architectural gems you'll pass on Central Park West, is an adaptation of an Italian Renaissance palazzo. Its architect, Emery Roth, arrived in this country flat broke as a teenager. He taught himself design and, through sheer determination, became one of the city's most noted architects.

Apartments at the Beresford start in the millions of dollars. In 2002, a four-story, 15-room, five-bedroom penthouse was going for a cool $14,950,000. Gangster Meyer Lansky lived here in the 1940s, and actor Rock Hudson lived here until his death from AIDS in 1985. Other famous residents have included Margaret Mead, Tony Randall, Peter Jennings, his colleague Diane Sawyer, and writer and *Cosmo* Editor-in-Chief Helen Gurley Brown.

Turn right and head down Central Park West. (Turn back and look up at the Beresford after a half block or so for a better perspective.) Along here is another entrance to the Museum of Natural History, marked by an equestrian statue of Theodore Roosevelt. At the southwest corner of 77th Street and Central Park West, you'll see the:

11. **New-York Historical Society** (☎ 212/873-3400; www. nyhistory.org), a rich repository of artifacts, artworks, and documents that chronicle the city's history. Established in 1804, it is New York's oldest museum. In addition to its research library, the museum's highlights include John James Audubon's original Birds of America watercolor series, more than 150 Tiffany lamps, and an extensive collection of early American art. The museum charges admission, and hours are Tuesday to Sunday 10am to 6pm, with extended hours until 8pm on Friday nights.

From here, cross Central Park West and walk down the park side to better view the buildings we're about to pass. Between 74th and 75th streets stands:

12. **The San Remo,** 145–146 Central Park West. Once home to Jack Dempsey and Rita Hayworth, the San Remo is another grand apartment building by Emery Roth. The two towers rising at each end are crowned with columned temples. After struggling through the Depression, the owners sold the San Remo and the Beresford together in 1940 for the shocking sum of $25,000 over the combined mortgages. More recent residents have included Dustin Hoffman, Mary Tyler Moore, Bruce Willis and Demi Moore, Diane Keaton, Steve Martin, and Barry Manilow.

At Central Park West and 72nd Street is a world-famous architectural masterpiece:

13. **The Dakota,** one of the first luxury apartment buildings in New York, built from 1880 to 1884. Architect Henry J. Hardenbergh, who also designed New York's landmark Plaza Hotel, created a brooding, Germanic structure accented with gables, dormers, and oriel windows, surrounded by a "dry moat." The fortresslike building served as the backdrop to the horror movie *Rosemary's Baby.*

The list of tenants at this prestigious address has included Lauren Bacall, Leonard Bernstein, Connie Chung, John Madden, Roberta Flack, and Boris Karloff (whose ghost reputedly haunts the halls). But the Dakota will forever be associated with its most famous resident,

John Lennon, who was gunned down just outside the building.

Lennon was returning home to the Dakota after a recording session on December 8, 1980, when he was shot by Mark David Chapman, a lone psychopath who had asked for the former Beatle's autograph only hours earlier. Lennon's widow, Yoko Ono, still lives in the Dakota.

Just inside the north side of the 72nd Street entrance to Central Park lies:

14. **Strawberry Fields,** a memorial to Lennon built and maintained by his widow, Yoko Ono. The 3-acre teardrop-shaped "international garden of peace" is adorned with more than 150 species of plants (gifts from as many nations) and 2,500 strawberry plants. Near the entrance, a circular black-and-white tile mosaic, a gift from Naples, Italy, spells out the word *Imagine.* Unfortunately, to protect the tiles the city has taken to blocking off the mosaic with unsightly metal gates.

As you exit the park to continue on your route downtown, you'll be right across the street from the:

15. **Majestic Apartments,** 115 Central Park West, another of the grand apartment houses that define the Central Park West skyline. Until the 12-story Hotel Majestic was built in the 1890s, this site was occupied by wooden shacks and grazing goats. However, it became a sumptuous venue that hosted the likes of Sarah Bernhardt, Edna Ferber, Gustav Mahler, and Vaslav Nijinsky. In 1929, developer Irwin Chanin initiated plans to build a single-tower, 45-story structure. The months that followed, however, saw the stock market crash, so Chanin altered his plans and came up with the 29-story, twin-towered structure you see today between 71st and 72nd streets. He also broke with tradition by scorning the classical European models used for most large residential buildings in New York; instead he chose an adaptation of Art Deco style that he called Modern American. The building was ready for tenants in 1931, but the Depression grew so severe that Chanin had defaulted on his mortgage by 1933.

Famous residents included Fred Astaire, Isadora Duncan, and Milton Berle. Bruno Richard Hauptmann, who was prosecuted for kidnapping the Lindbergh baby, was working as a carpenter here when the crime was committed. A gangland hit took place in the lobby in 1957, when mobster Frank Costello was shot in the head. Fellow gangsters Lucky Luciano and Meyer Lansky also called the Majestic home for a while.

Farther down Central Park West, at the southwest corner of 70th Street, you'll see the neoclassical:

16. **Synagogue of the Congregation Shearith Israel,** which dates from 1897. It's home to the oldest Jewish congregation in the United States, which was founded in 1654 by Sephardic Jews and Spanish and Portuguese immigrants who came to New York via Brazil.

Turn right onto 67th Street, where several buildings contain double-height studio apartments. At no. 1 is the Gothic-style:

17. **Hotel des Artistes,** full of enchanting touches, such as the row of gargoyles below the third-floor windows. Most of the units in the Hotel des Artistes are duplexes and double-height studios. One particularly noteworthy apartment, designed for philanthropist Aaron Naumburg and completed in 1921, has 18-foot ceilings, a wood-balustraded balcony, and lavishly carved woodwork. Naumberg's home was graced with tapestries, fine carpets, antique Italian furniture, paintings, carved figures, and stained-glass windows; it was so spectacular that all the furnishings and artwork were taken as a group to the Fogg Museum in Cambridge and the apartment was re-created as an annex to the museum after Naumberg's death.

The Hotel des Artistes has attracted an astounding number of famous residents, including Rudolph Valentino, Noël Coward, Isadora Duncan, Alexander Woollcott, Edna Ferber, former mayor John Lindsay, former governor Hugh Carey, Norman Rockwell, and Emil Fuchs, portraitist to Queen Victoria. Fuchs, dying of cancer, committed suicide in the Hotel des Artistes in 1929 by shooting himself with a pearl-handled revolver inscribed by Edward VII. More grisliness ensued on December 10, 1929, when bohemian poet Harry Crosby killed both his girlfriend and himself in a ninth-floor apartment.

The ground floor houses the elegant and romantic **Café des Artistes;** peek in the window to see the restaurant's famous wood-nymph murals by Howard Chandler Christy, a longtime tenant in the building. (Some of the models used for the nymphs have returned to dine in the cafe over the years.) Christy's murals and his other depictions of lovely ladies in magazine and book illustrations earned him an invitation to be the sole judge at the first Miss America contest in 1921.

Continue west on 67th Street to Columbus Avenue and make a left. Between 65th and 66th streets stands the **American Folk Art Museum Eva and Morris Feld Gallery** (© 212/595-9533; www.folkartmuseum.org) and its gift shop, stocked with books, jewelry, hand-painted pitchers and vases, prints, and one-of-a-kind greeting cards. Across Broadway, you can't miss:

18. **Lincoln Center** (© 212/875-5000; www.lincolncenter. org), the city's premier venue for the performing arts. In 1956, a committee headed by John D. Rockefeller III selected the site for Lincoln Center in what was then a rundown residential area. *West Side Story* was filmed in these streets before an astounding 188 buildings were demolished to clear the area; 1,600 people had to be relocated to make way for the project.

The committee commissioned a group of architects headed by Wallace K. Harrison; each building they created has classical lines and is covered in Italian travertine. The centerpiece of the complex is an outdoor plaza graced with a cafe terrace and a splashing fountain. Aging now, the area can have a vaguely totalitarian feel. Plans are underway for a major revamping, but in the meantime New Yorkers enjoy free entertainment here under the stars in summer, and one of the city's most beautiful Christmas trees in December.

Left of the plaza is **Avery Fisher Hall** (© 212/875-5030), with a peristyle of 44 columns soaring seven stories high. It's home to the New York Philharmonic (© 212/875-5900; www.newyorkphilharmonic.org), which has counted among its musical directors such luminaries as Zubin Mehta, Arturo Toscanini, Leopold

Stokowski, and Leonard Bernstein. On the right side of the fountain is the **New York State Theater** (© 212/870-5570), designed by architect Philip Johnson, which hosts performances by the New York City Opera and the New York City Ballet (www.nycballet.com), founded by George Balanchine.

Forming the background of the plaza is the **Metropolitan Opera House** (© 212/362-6000; www.metopera.org), which boasts a 10-story marble colonnade. Inside the glass facade, you can see two enormous murals by Marc Chagall. This building is the home of the renowned Metropolitan Opera, one of the most prestigious companies in the world for more than a century; acclaimed stars such as Placido Domingo, Luciano Pavarotti, Jose Carreras, Kathleen Battle, and Marilyn Horne have graced the stage here. You can take a backstage tour (© 212/769-7020; fee charged) through the artisans' shops, the rehearsal rooms, and the auditorium. In early summer, the Met (as the opera house is commonly known) also hosts the American Ballet Theatre's season. The Met's interior houses seven rehearsal halls and space to store scenery for as many as 15 operas.

The remainder of the complex at Lincoln Center includes the **Guggenheim Bandshell,** used for free outdoor concerts; the **Vivian Beaumont and Mitzi Newhouse Theaters** (© 212/362-7600); the **Juilliard School** (© 212/799-5000; www.juilliard.edu), the country's premier academy for the performing arts; and **Alice Tully Hall,** home to the Chamber Music Society (© 212/875-5788; www.chambermusicsociety.org). Also at Lincoln Center is a branch of the **New York Public Library** (© 212/870-1630; www.nypl.org), which serves as both a library and a museum of the performing arts. The library hosts an impressive array of free films and concerts.

One-hour tours of Lincoln Center are available; call © 212/875-5350 to check on the day's tour schedule and to make advance reservations (a fee is charged). Calendars of upcoming events, including free concerts, are also available at Lincoln Center and online (see address above).

The Upper East Side

Start: The southeast corner of Central Park, at 59th Street and Fifth Avenue.

Subway: Take the N, R, or W to Fifth Avenue.

Finish: 92nd Street and Fifth Avenue.

Time: Approximately 3 hours.

Best Time: Weekday afternoons, when museums and restaurants are open but not as crowded as on Saturdays.

Worst Time: Sundays, when stores keep shorter hours, galleries are closed, and the streets seem deserted.

Over a century ago, society watchers predicted that the wealthy and fashionable would settle permanently on the avenues bordering Central Park. Time has proven them right. Fifth Avenue north of Grand Army Plaza, which lies at the southeast corner of the park, is officially called Museum Mile. In the first few decades of the 20th century, it also earned the title Millionaires' Row, with a procession of magnificent private mansions built by the nation's

The Upper East Side

Legend	
Ⓜ	Subway
☕	Take a Break

The Reservoir

CENTRAL PARK

The Reservoir

E. 92nd St.
★ **finish here**

E. 90th St.

E. 88th St.

E. 86th St.

YORKVILLE

E. 84th St.

E. 82nd St.

E. 79th St.

E. 77th St.

E. 75th St.

E. 74th St.

E. 72nd St.

E. 70th St.

E. 68th St.

E. 66th St.

E. 64th St.

E. 62nd St.

E. 60th St.

E. 59th St.

★ **start here**

Grand Army Plaza

Metropolitan Museum of Art

Gracie Mansion

CARL SCHURZ PARK

Queensboro Bridge

East River

FDR Drive

Madison Ave., Park Ave., Lexington Ave., Third Ave., Second Ave., First Ave., York Ave., Fifth Ave.

1 Grand Army Plaza
2 The Pierre
3 Knickerbocker Club
4 820 Fifth Ave.
5 The Arsenal
6 3 East 64th St.
7 Home of President Ulysses S. Grant
8 58 East 68th St.
9 680 Park Ave.
10 Union Club
11 East 70th Street
12 Asia Society
13 Hirschl and Adler/
   Knoedler and Company
14 Frick Collection
15 Polo/Ralph Lauren
16 11 East 73rd St.
17 Whitney Museum of American Art
18 972 Fifth Ave.
19 Metropolitan Museum of Art
20 Former Home of Jacqueline
   Kennedy Onassis
21 Neue Gallerie New York
22 Guggenheim Museum
23 Cooper-Hewitt National
   Design Museum
24 Convent of the Sacred Heart
25 The Jewish Museum

wealthiest industrial tycoons. Today, patrician mansions still stand along the avenue, though others have ceded their coveted real estate to large apartment houses. But the age of imperial living isn't over by any means. Some of the buildings on Fifth Avenue (as well as on Park Ave. and elsewhere on the East Side) contain apartments every bit as palatial and sumptuous as the vanished mansions. Even New Yorkers are surprised to hear of apartments with 20, 30, or even 40 rooms, but they do exist in this neighborhood.

• • • • • • • • • • • • • • • •

Start your tour where Fifth Avenue and 59th Street meet at:

1. **Grand Army Plaza,** which is adorned with a brilliant gold statue of William Tecumseh Sherman, the ruthless but effective Civil War general who devastated the Southern countryside and brought the civilian population to its knees with the Union army's scorched-earth March to the Sea. "War is cruelty, and you cannot refine it," Sherman once observed, but sculptor Augustus Saint-Gaudens has tried. He's created a classical equestrian statue of the crusty general with a female Winged Victory striding along in front of the horse. A popular story goes that a proper Southern lady, upon being told whom the statue represented and the identity of the winged maiden, harrumphed, "Ain't that just like a Yankee, to make the lady walk." The statue was unveiled on Memorial Day 1903, with bands playing "Marching Through Georgia" and a military parade. (Some of Sherman's men were among the marchers.) If you need sustenance before setting out on

Kid-Friendly Experiences

This walk isn't really cut out for kids, though they might enjoy the chocolate at Godiva, or playing with the gadgets at The Sharper Image. The sometimes oddball art at the modern museums might appeal to some kids, and the Metropolitan (stop 19) has plenty to amuse just about everyone. The Guggenheim (stop 22) and the Whitney Museum (stop 17) may also interest art-loving kids.

your tour, you can hit one of the hot-dog carts in the area for a traditional New York lunch on the go.

Now stroll up Fifth Avenue, staying on the park side of the street for the best view of the buildings as you pass. In good weather, bookstalls from The Strand line the sidewalk, full of used volumes at a fraction of the cover price. On the east (right) side of Fifth Avenue, at 61st Street, is:

2. **The Pierre,** one of Manhattan's priciest and most exclusive hotels since its opening in 1930. In 1932, mystery writer Dashiell Hammett stayed here while working on *The Thin Man,* though, unfortunately, he couldn't pay the bill that he had run up during his stay. He allegedly donned a disguise to sneak out without settling his tab.

   If you're starting out early in the morning, breakfast at the Pierre makes for a pricey but elegant beginning to your tour.

   At the southeast corner of 62nd Street stands the third home of the:

3. **Knickerbocker Club,** which looks a lot like the big private houses that once characterized the avenue. The Georgian brick Knickerbocker, completed in 1915, was the work of a firm called Delano and Aldrich, a favorite of high society in the early 20th century. It retains a pedigreed look. Ernest Hemingway, looking for peace and quiet, rented an apartment here in 1959 and stayed for about a year.

   The next block up is 63rd Street, and on the east corner you'll see:

4. **820 Fifth Ave.,** one of the earliest apartment houses built hereabouts and still one of the best. Built in 1916, it has only one apartment on each floor, with five fireplaces and seven bathrooms in each one.

   Continue northward on Fifth Avenue to 64th Street. Walk just inside Central Park for a look at:

5. **The Arsenal,** built in 1848 when this neighborhood was distant and deserted. Now housing zoo administration offices, the structure was once a bunkhouse and weapons depot for Civil War troops. (Notice the railing made of rifles; also see walking tour 9, stop 2.) The Central Park Zoo is right behind the building.

Head back onto Fifth Avenue. Opposite the park at the southeast corner of 64th Street (**828 Fifth Ave.**) is the former mansion of coal magnate Edward Berwind.

Head east (away from the park) on 64th Street toward Madison Avenue. This particularly handsome East Side block is lined with architectural extravaganzas. Note in particular:

6. **3 E. 64th St.,** an opulent Beaux Arts mansion built in 1903 for the daughter of Mrs. William B. Astor. The house was designed by Warren and Wetmore, the firm responsible for Grand Central Terminal, and it now houses the Consulate General of India. Also worthy of admiration on this block are nos. 16, 19 (now home to a Wildenstein Gallery, open Mon–Fri 10am–5pm), and 20.

At Madison Avenue, turn left and saunter 2 blocks north to 66th Street. Note the rather fantastic apartment house built in 1900 on the **northeast corner of 66th and Madison,** and then turn left (west) off Madison onto 66th Street, heading back toward Fifth Avenue.

Among the many notable houses on this block is the magnificent French Renaissance–style house at **5 E. 66th St.,** with its wooden doors, elegant stonework detail, and opulent arched entryway. Built in 1900, it's now home to the Lotos Club, which is dedicated to literature and the fine arts.

Next door, at 3 E. 66th St., is the former:

7. **Home of President Ulysses S. Grant,** where he lived from 1881 until his death in 1885. The former Civil War hero purchased a brownstone once located on this spot and set to work penning his memoirs, which no less an authority than Mark Twain termed a "literary masterpiece."

Double back to Madison Avenue, turn left, and continue north for 2 more blocks, stopping to browse in any of the **boutiques** that catch your eye. There's Nicole Miller; La Perla for lovely lingerie; Emanuel Ungaro; Godiva, where you can treat yourself to some coffee and a decadent truffle; and Frette for fine Italian linens. At 68th Street, turn right (east) toward Park Avenue. One of the best houses on this block is:

8. **58 E. 68th St.,** on the southwest corner of the intersection with Park Avenue. The house was built in 1919 for Harold J. Pratt, son of Rockefeller partner Charles Pratt.

   Walk to the north side of 68th Street to:

9. **680 Park Ave.,** a neo-Federal town house, built from 1909 to 1911 for banker Percy Rivington Pyne and designed by McKim, Mead, and White. Its style and architecture were copied all along this Park Avenue block. When, from 1948 to 1963, it housed the Soviet Mission to the United Nations, Premier Nikita Khrushchev waved to curious crowds from the balcony during his famous shoe-banging visit to the U.N.

   The Marquesa de Cuevas bought 680 Park Ave. in 1965, staving off a slated demolition by presenting it to the **Americas Society** (www.americas-society.org). The society is the only national not-for-profit institution devoted to educating U.S. citizens about their Western Hemisphere neighbors. The society sponsors concerts, video screenings, and other cultural programs on Latin American and Canadian affairs. The art gallery (open Wed–Sat noon–6pm; free admission) here has exhibited everything from Pre-Columbian to colonial to contemporary art. The other buildings on this block house the Spanish Institute and the Italian Institute, which also have full calendars of cultural events.

   Head north on Park Avenue to 69th Street. On the northeast corner stands the:

10. **Union Club,** designed in 1932 to house New York's oldest club. On the other side of 69th Street is Hunter College. Turn right onto 69th Street and continue east toward Lexington Avenue, noting en route **117 E. 69th St.,** a prototypical, not-so-small, private East Side house with beautiful stained-glass panels around the door.

    When you arrive at Lexington Avenue, detour right a few steps to a still-operating branch of **Shakespeare and Co.** (no. 939; ✆ **212/570-0201;** www.shakeandco.com), Manhattan's famously literary bookseller whose West Side main branch was put out of business in 1996 when Barnes & Noble strategically built two megastores within walking distance. Double back up Lexington 1½ blocks uptown to 70th Street. Turn left and head back toward Park Avenue along:

11. **70th Street,** which presents a succession of elegant houses, each more beautiful than the next. Note in particular no. 125, a post–World War II mansion built for Paul Mellon in a French provincial style, which is only slightly marred by the bulbous security camera affixed to the fourth floor. Some consider this the finest street in New York. The continuity of the Park Avenue end of the block is interrupted by a clumsy glass atrium belonging to the Garden Court Café of the:

12. **Asia Society** (© 212/288-6400 or 212/517-ASIA; www. asiasociety.org). John D. Rockefeller III founded the Asia Society in the mid-50s to encourage cultural exchanges and understanding between Asians and Americans. This newly renovated headquarters building has beautiful galleries, showing off parts of Rockefeller's collection in addition to rotating exhibits of Asian art both ancient and modern. The interior architecture is impressive. The glass atrium that looks so out of place on 70th Street is neatly integrated with the sleek ground floor, and the stairs between the galleries are engineered like the skeleton of a snake. The exhibits are open Tuesday through Sunday from 11am to 6pm, with hours extended until 9pm on Friday between Labor Day and July 4th. An admission fee is charged, except for Friday nights between 6pm and closing. Entrance to the society's gift shop is free, and with the latest in Asian design among the items on display, AsiaStore is a browser's delight.

Cross Park Avenue and note **720 Park Ave.** on the northwest corner of the intersection. This building is a prime example of the sort of swanky, enormous apartment building that lured former mansion dwellers away from their private houses. The upper stories of buildings like no. 720 often contain apartments with three or four floors and dozens of rooms.

Continue on East 70th Street, crossing Madison, toward Fifth Avenue. Two of the Upper East Side's premier art galleries are along 70th Street.

13. **Hirschl and Adler** (*C* 212/535-8810; www.hirschland adler.com), at no. 21, shows quality American and European art, from 18th-century to current-day master-pieces, in many media. Over five floors, various galleries cover everything from American decorative arts to mod-ern art (including Southern black folk artist Forrest Bess, Cy Twombly, Joseph Beuys, performance artist team Gilbert and George, John Moore, and Fairfield Porter), to the big old guns, from John Singleton Copley, Winslow Homer, Edward Hopper, and Georgia O'Keeffe to Mary Cassatt, Picasso, Matisse, and Renoir.

Next door, at no. 19, is **Knoedler and Company** (*C* 212/794-0550; www.knoedlergallery.com), a major gallery for established American artists such as Helen Frankenthaler, Adolph Gottlieb, Nancy Graves, Frank Stella, and John Walker.

Nearing Fifth Avenue, you'll pass a lovely courtyard and lily pond, surrounded by stately black iron gates, before reaching the entrance to an often-overlooked classic New York museum, the:

14. **Frick Collection** (*C* 212/288-0700; www.frick.org), housed in the Gilded Age mansion of steel magnate Henry Clay Frick, completed in 1914 for the princely sum of $5 million. The beautiful formal garden overlooking 70th Street was built in 1977. Frick always intended that his art collection be opened to the public after his death. The works are arrayed in rooms, many with Frick's original fur-nishings, centered around a small, plant-filled atrium with classical styling, a vaulted skylight, and a softly splashing fountain. If you have time for only one museum on this tour, the modestly sized but rich Frick Collection may be your best choice.

The collections range from Italian medieval (a panel from Duccio's *Maestà*) and the Renaissance (Piero della Francesca, Bellini, Bronzino, Titian, and El Greco), to later French, Spanish, Flemish, German, and American masterpieces from the likes of Rembrandt, Ingres, Gainsborough, Boucher, Goya, Whistler, Degas, and Monet. Fragonard's racy rococo *The Progress of Love* series is installed in a vestibule. Also, don't miss Hans Holbein the Younger's pair of incisive portraits of rivals Thomas Cromwell and Sir Thomas More.

The Frick Collection is open Tuesday to Saturday 10am to 6pm, and Sunday 1 to 6pm. Admission is charged, and no children under 10 are admitted (children ages 10–16 must be accompanied by an adult).

Turn right at the corner of Fifth Avenue, passing a beautiful colonnade on the side of the Frick building. Continue 2 blocks north, and turn right onto 72nd Street, heading toward Madison Avenue. On your left, at no. 9, is the **Lycée Français** (a French primary and secondary school), housed in an elaborate 1894 building of the late French Renaissance style. At the southeast corner of 72nd Street and Madison is:

15. **Polo/Ralph Lauren.** This showcase store, housed in a renovated mansion that dates from 1895, looks for all the world like an English country mansion inside, complete with working fireplaces, Persian rugs, antiques, and a grand baronial staircase. The store is open 7 days a week, as is the less elaborate Polo store directly across the street.

Take Madison Avenue up a block to 73rd Street, passing **The Sharper Image** (no. 900), the catalog store for the gadget-hound in all of us. Detour to your left on 73rd Street to see:

16. **11 E. 73rd St.,** a particularly sumptuous house built in 1903 by McKim, Mead, and White for Joseph Pulitzer, the Hungarian-born publisher of a once-famous but long-vanished newspaper called the *New York World.* Pulitzer rarely lived in this house because of his extreme sensitivity to sound. At one time, it contained a special sound-proofed room (mounted on ball bearings, no less) to prevent vibrations. When he died in 1911, Pulitzer bequeathed $2 million to the Columbia Graduate School of Journalism, whose trustees bestow the Pulitzer Prize awards for outstanding achievement in journalism, literature, drama, and musical composition.

Retrace your steps back to Madison Avenue and turn left. At the southeast corner of 75th and Madison you'll see the:

17. **Whitney Museum of American Art** (℃ 212/570-
3676; www.whitney.org), housed in a 1966 architectural
masterpiece by Marcel Breuer. The Whitney contains an
impressive collection of 20th-century American art, with
paintings that reflect trends from naturalism to pop art and
abstract expressionism. Roy Lichtenstein, Georgia
O'Keeffe, Edward Hopper, and Jasper Johns are just a few
of the artists represented in the permanent collection. As far
as the 21st century goes, the temporary exhibits here favor
up-and-coming artists, as seen in the Whitney Biannual, a
survey show that's one of the major events in the New York
art world. Hours are 11am to 6pm on Wednesday,
Thursday, Saturday, and Sunday; Friday the museum is
open from 1 to 9pm. An admission fee is charged, although
Friday from 6 to 9pm it's pay-what-you-wish to get in.

Take a Break In the museum's basement,
Sarabeth's at the Whitney (℃ 212/570-3670) is
much more than your average museum cafeteria—and
more expensive, with dishes starting at $14 and brunches
starting at $6.75. You can't go wrong with Sarabeth's
delightful velvety cream-of-tomato soup. Sarabeth's is also
famous for its scrumptious desserts. It's open Tuesday to
Thursday 11am to 4:30pm, Friday 11am to 3:45pm, and
Saturday and Sunday 10am to 4:30pm.

Though it's housed in the museum, you don't have to
pay to reach the cafe; just pick up a free pass at the main
ticket desk. (You can bypass the museum admissions line.)

Leave the museum and continue uptown on Madison
Avenue. Past 76th Street, you'll pass one of New York's
grand old hotels, **The Carlyle,** which has counted two
presidents (Harry Truman and John F. Kennedy) among
its famous guests. The west side of Madison Avenue from
76th to 77th streets is lined with a procession of intriguing contemporary art galleries, including the **Gagosian
Gallery** (www.gagosian.com) in the penthouse of no. 980
(20th-century artists, including Frank Stella, Richard
Serra, Andy Warhol, Mark di Suervo, Chris Burden, and
Walter de Maria) and **David Findlay** (www.davidfindlay
galleries.com) at no. 984 (American and French figurative
art, with an emphasis on the use of color).

Turn left when you reach 79th Street and return to Fifth Avenue. The impressive row of buildings includes everything from French château-style structures to neo-Georgian town houses. When you reach the corner of Fifth Avenue, turn left for a look at:

18. **972 Fifth Ave.,** between 78th and 79th streets. It is now the French Embassy's Cultural Services Office, but it was built in 1906 as a wedding present for Payne Whitney by his doting (and childless) rich uncle, Oliver Payne, a Civil War officer and one of the benefactors who helped to found Cornell's Medical College. This McKim, Mead, and White opus cost $1 million and was the talk of the town in its day. The town house was put back on the map when an NYU professor at a reception noticed a broken statue on a pedestal in the entryway. The statue was pegged as a long-lost work by Renaissance master Michelangelo. After years of service as a fountain spout, the suddenly famous Cupid (or, depending on whom you ask, young Apollo or a young archer) sculpture was spirited away for a world tour while the controversy over its attribution raged. Some say Michelangelo's teacher Bertoldo sculpted it; others claim that it's a 19th-century fake.

Next door, on **the corner of 78th Street,** is the French-style mansion of tobacco millionaire James B. Duke (as in Duke University). His daughter Doris occupied the house intermittently until 1957, when she donated it to New York University. The building now houses NYU's Institute of Fine Arts.

Now turn around and walk north on Fifth Avenue. On your left at 82nd Street is the grand entrance to the:

19. **Metropolitan Museum of Art** (© 212/535-7710; www.metmuseum.org), one of the world's greatest cultural institutions. The block of 82nd Street that faces the museum's mammoth staircase acts as a sort of formal court. The Met's collection is enormous—the largest in the Western Hemisphere—and includes an Egyptian wing that boasts tens of thousands of objects. Its Temple of Dendur, around 15 B.C., from Lower Nubia, was shipped piece by piece to the Met and painstakingly reconstructed. It would take a lifetime to see all of the

Met's treasures, so it might be best to save it for another day and admire the exterior for now.

Museum hours are Sunday and Tuesday to Thursday 9:30am to 5:15pm, Friday and Saturday 9:30am to 8:45pm. There's a hefty suggested admission price.

Continue uptown past 85th Street. The building at 1040 Fifth Ave. was for many years the:

20. **Home of Jacqueline Kennedy Onassis.** After her first husband's assassination, she moved here so that Caroline could attend school at nearby Sacred Heart. The former first lady adored New York and was often spotted strolling nearby in her beloved Central Park. After her death from cancer in 1994, hundreds of mourners gathered outside this building, many leaving flowers on the sidewalk in her memory.

On the southeast corner of Fifth Avenue and 86th Street you'll find the:

21. **Neue Galerie New York** (© 212/628-6200; www.neue galerie.org). This 1914 brick and limestone mansion was originally built for industrialist William Starr Miller, who employed the firm Carrère & Hastings, better known for their work on the New York Public Library. Grace Vanderbilt, once the queen of America's high society, moved here in 1944 following the death of her husband Cornelius. After Vanderbilt's death in 1953, the mansion housed the YIVO Institute for Jewish Research. Ronald Lauder, a billionaire son of Estée Lauder (nee Josephine Esther Mentzer of Corona, Queens), bought the building from YIVO in 1994. With Serge Sabarsky, an art dealer and curator, Lauder began a meticulous process of transforming the mansion into a museum dedicated to 20th-century German and Austrian art and design. The original marble and oak paneling of the interior have been perfectly restored, augmented with subtle modern touches and one of the city's best museum cafes. **Café Sabarsky** (© 212/288-0665) recreates a *fin de siecle kaffeehaus,* complete with sausages, wursts, and goulashes (in addition to exquisite tarts and strudels). Upstairs in the two floors of galleries you'll find works by Gustav Klimt, Egon Schiele, Paul Klee, Adolf Loos, and Max Beckman. The space is intimate—only 375 visitors can be accommodated at one

time—so you may see lines to get in. The museum is open Friday through Monday from 11am to 6pm, with closing extended until 9pm on Friday. Admission is charged, and children under 12 are not admitted.

Two blocks farther up Fifth Avenue is the unmistakable:

22. **Guggenheim Museum** (② 212/423-3500; www. guggenheim.org), between 88th and 89th streets, whose building piques just as much interest as the collection of 19th- and 20th-century masterpieces it houses. Designed by Frank Lloyd Wright in 1959, it set off a storm of architectural controversy when it was built. Nowadays, the building is a treasured landmark for New Yorkers. The interior has an effect like a nautilus shell; visitors generally take an elevator to the top floor, and then walk down the ramp, viewing the works of art hung along the curved walls. Special exhibitions occupy the central spire, while a separate square-walled tower holds a permanent collection that includes Brancusi, Alexander Calder, Marc Chagall, Kandinsky, Joan Miró, Mondrian, Picasso, and van Gogh.

The Guggenheim's hours are Saturday to Wednesday 10am to 5:45pm and Friday 10am to 8pm. Admission is charged, although on Friday night from 6pm you may pay as much or as little as you like. Check out the museum store's T-shirts, gifts, prints, and books.

Uptown from the Guggenheim, between 90th and 91st streets, is another major sight, the:

23. **Cooper-Hewitt National Design Museum** (② 212/ 849-8400; www.si.edu/ndm). Under the auspices of the Smithsonian Institution, this museum is housed in the former Andrew Carnegie mansion. Built in 1901, this Georgianesque palace originally shared the neighborhood with squatters' shanties and roaming pigs. By the time the squatters were gone and the streets were built up with fine houses, Carnegie was dead. His widow lived in the house until 1949. The museum, with its changing design exhibits, is open Tuesday to Thursday 10am to 5pm, Friday 10am to 9pm, Saturday 10am to 6pm, and Sunday noon to 6pm; admission is charged.

Across 91st Street from the main entrance to the Cooper-Hewitt is the:

24. **Convent of the Sacred Heart Girls' School,** occupying what was once the largest private house ever built in Manhattan. Financier Otto Kahn bought the property from Andrew Carnegie in 1913, and construction of his mansion, which was modeled on the papal chancellery in Rome, was completed in 1918. Other houses on this 91st Street block, notably nos. 7 and 9, are almost as grand. C. P. H. Gilbert co-designed the Kahn mansion, a few years after he constructed the ornate mansion just across 92nd Street. That building now houses:

25. **The Jewish Museum** (*(C)* 212/423-3200; www.the jewishmuseum.org). The original mansion was built in 1909 as the home of Felix and Frieda Schiff Warburg. In 1944 the widowed Frieda donated the structure for use as a museum. Built along the lines of a French Gothic château, the building has lovely proportions. The 1993 expansion that doubled the exhibition space was neatly integrated with the original lines. The museum's collection of nearly 30,000 objects delves into Jewish identity from Torahs to television. A two-floor permanent exhibit, *Culture and Continuity: The Jewish Journey,* anchors the museum and provides an informative overview. The museum's hours are Sunday through Wednesday 11am to 5:45pm; Thursday 11am to 8pm; and Friday 11am to 3pm. There is an admission charge, but like many of the other Museum Mile venues, there is a pay-what-you-wish policy in effect 1 night of the week (Thurs 5–8pm).

    Take 91st Street east to Madison Avenue and turn right (downtown) if you'd like to end the tour with a pick-me-up.

    Winding Down At the southwest corner of Madison Avenue and 91st Street is **Jackson Hole** (*(C)* 212/427-2820). Many New Yorkers argue that Jackson Hole flips the best burgers in the city, and you certainly get a lot for your money (burgers start at $5.25). In addition to juicy burgers, Jackson Hole offers omelets, honey-dipped fried chicken, sandwiches, salads, and great desserts. Open daily.

Morningside Heights & Harlem

Start: 110th Street and Broadway.

Subway: 1 to Cathedral Parkway (110th St.).

Finish: 125th Street.

Time: Approximately 4 hours.

Best Time: Wednesdays (for Amateur Night at the Apollo Theater).

Harlem's not just a neighborhood; it's a whole separate city. No, seriously. The Dutch founded two cities on this isle between the East River and the Hudson River. The first of those early Dutch colonies was Nieuw Amsterdam, down in the tip of Manhattan and bounded by the wall of Wall Street, with farmland north of the city walls. ("Farm" in Dutch is *bouwerie,* and the Bowery district was once just that.)

In 1658, way up the East River, where the island of Manhattan started narrowing and an Indian village once lay, the Dutch founded a separate town called Nieuw Haarlem. It took quite a while for New York and New Harlem to grow together and fuse into one city. In 1837, the railroad brought development to this sleepy town of just over 200 residents, but it also created the squalor of a factory-and-warehouse neighborhood. The farms disappeared, and Irish immigrants arrived in droves looking for places to squat for free.

East Harlem, its landscape slashed by more railroad lines in the 1880s, never grew out of its working-class roots, as successive waves of the most downtrodden citizens called it home: Russians, Italians, Irish, Hungarians, Scandinavians, Spaniards, Jews, and eventually Puerto Ricans.

The core of Harlem slowly became middle-class. A largely German population built the brownstones and row houses that line many of Harlem's streets to this day. When the IRT subway line extended up here in 1901, immigrants from the crowded Lower East Side poured in for lower rents and more space, and by 1917 Harlem had some 170,000 Jewish residents. This crashed the housing market, and when the Jews moved on, the black community saw a great opportunity to secure excellent housing at low cost and moved in.

This change in the neighborhood's makeup dovetailed with the opening up of the country after the Civil War. More and more black sharecroppers left the South and workers sailed up from the Caribbean, all looking for a better life. When you wanted to find those streets paved with gold, New York City was the place to go—and the place to live, if you were black, was Harlem.

From 1920 to 1930, Harlem's black population swelled from 83,000 to almost 204,000, giving rise to the Harlem Renaissance. W. E. B. Du Bois encouraged his African brothers and sisters to explore their own culture and expand their intellect. Harlem's creative geniuses responded in force. Langston Hughes penned poetry and Eubie Blake and Noble Sissle wrote plays (in which Florence Mills acted). William H. Johnson and Aaron Douglas painted while Cab Calloway and Duke Ellington headlined at the (whites-only) Cotton Club. Marcus Garvey started telling blacks it was okay to be proud of their heritage.

The stock market crash of 1929 and the ensuing Great Depression snuffed out the Harlem Renaissance. Theaters, concert halls, and other venues were almost entirely white-owned. Black Harlem may have created its own renaissance, but it was the whites who profited from it. As poet Langston Hughes put it: "The ordinary negro hadn't heard of the Negro Renaissance. And if they had, it hadn't raised their wages any."

Tensions in the city were running high after the Depression, and race riots began in 1935. After World War II, African-American culture turned its eyes once again to Harlem as Malcolm X and other Muslim ministers began preaching in the mosques that were popping up there. Tensions increased, and riots plagued Harlem throughout the 1960s.

Things didn't really get better for Harlem with the Civil Rights movement of the late 1960s. The neighborhood got poorer and poorer, the landlords more corrupt, the people more dispirited, the gangs rougher. In some parts, Harlem looked like a Third World shantytown. So much was abandoned, boarded up, burned out, squatted in, and half-ruined, and so many landlords were caught as tax cheats, that by the end of the 1970s the city took ownership of 65% of the neighborhood. And, shame on them, it took them almost 30 years to turn the area around.

By the mid-1990s, Harlem was still in a pitiful state. When compared to the rest of NYC, it had nearly twice the unemployment and a 20% lower median income. A combination of poor sanitation, lack of health care, gang violence, and disease epidemics such as AIDS gave Harlem a death rate *five times* the city's average—and those are 1997 figures!

But 1997 was perhaps the nadir of Harlem's troubles. In the years since, it has started on a remarkable turnaround. Millions in investments and seed money have been poured into the area to jump-start local businesses. Housing plans have rehabilitated row houses and created lower-income co-ops and apartments (replacing those awful projects). New shopping centers are opening up every year, cultural institutions are mushrooming across the landscape, and galleries are popping up. What's more, middle-class folks from outside the neighborhood have already begun shopping for bargains on homes that would cost three to five times as much if they were just a dozen or two blocks farther south (though not for long).

This is a neighborhood of gorgeous (if often decaying) brownstones and row houses; busy barbershops and nail salons where old friends pass the day; street markets and wide, slightly desolate boulevards; tiny crowded restaurants; and churches, temples, mosques, and other houses of worship.

Walking around Harlem also affords the chance to sit down and dig into a plate piled high with soul food—succulent fried chicken, sticky-fingers barbecue, slightly spiced mac and cheese, mashed potatoes with gravy, black-eyed peas, collard greens, grits, hush puppies, sweet-potato pie, and spoon bread.

Many people associate Harlem with African Americans, but the whole of East Harlem — "Spanish Harlem"—is one of the largest Latino neighborhoods in the city. And Italian Harlem still exists around 116th Street and Pleasant Avenue. There's even a sliver of Harlem that's traditionally Irish Catholic. (I've never found it, but George Carlin claims to have grown up there.) The recent influx of bargain-hunting Downtowners and cash-strapped Columbia grads have brought more white faces to the urban mix. These days, Harlem is seeing a degree of racial integration that surely would bring a smile to Dr. King's face.

That said, for a century, the bulk of Harlem has been black, its overarching identity African American, and it's that culture and history that make this walk interesting.

Fair warning: After we leave Morningside Heights and cross into Harlem proper, this will not always be the prettiest of walks. Much of the neighborhood is still struggling out of its old urban slum identity. There are plenty of "development corporations" and offices devoted to helping out new businesses, but alas, they are outnumbered by the boarded-up brownstones, abandoned apartment buildings, and derelict storefronts. The neighborhood still has a long way to go.

Harlem is a neighborhood in flux, undergoing its biggest change since the civil rights era. However, this only makes it all the more exciting to wander, explore, dig into the soul food, and witness firsthand this second Harlem Renaissance.

Our walk starts in Morningside Heights, a cliff between Harlem and the Hudson. The land was too steep and rocky and isolated to be developed and long remained largely drowsy farmland (along with the usual insane asylum and orphanage). Then 1880 brought Riverside Drive, the Eighth Avenue El, and the developers. Still, it remains a somewhat more stately and wide-open area of Manhattan, defined by institutes of higher learning (Columbia University, Barnard College, the Union and Jewish Theological seminaries, Teacher's College) and gargantuan houses of worship (St. John the Divine and Riverside Church).

Note: You could very easily make this into two shorter walks, one of Morningside Heights, the other of Harlem. (Just grab the 2 or 3 subway to 116th St. and Amy Ruth's for the Harlem section of the tour.)

• • • • • • • • • • • • • • • •

From the 110th Street subway stop, walk east on Cathedral Parkway (aka 110th St.), noting the funky gargoylish stone braces under the lower-level windows of no. 527 on the left. Turn left up Amsterdam Avenue to our first stop and a nip of bracing brew.

Starting Out **Hungarian Pastry Shop,** 1030 Amsterdam Ave. (© **212/866-4230**), is popular with Columbia students for its scrumptious Eastern European pastries, Vienna-style coffee, and lethal rum balls. This simple, delightfully dingy cafe also has some tables out on the sidewalk looking across the street to our first stop, the:

1. **Peace Fountain,** built in 1985 by Greg Wyatt, the fountain is a pile of swirling bronze with Michael the archangel sticking it to Satan atop a double-helix pedestal of DNA. Weird. Much more charming is the ring encircling the fountain, a series of animals dancing along the rail to meet at a large Noah's Ark, all of them molded by middle- and high-schoolers. Surrounding the fountain are booklike plaques of educators, writers, musicians, philosophers, and other cultural heroes, while beyond, in the park, a 40-foot-high, neo-Gothic, 1916-vintage **Outdoor Pulpit** stands forlornly with only a wandering, bedraggled, and much-photographed peacock to keep it company.

Next door is the unmistakable bulk of:

2. **The Cathedral of St. John the Divine** (© 212/316-7540; www.stjohndivine.org). For those of you doing the

Morningside Heights & Harlem

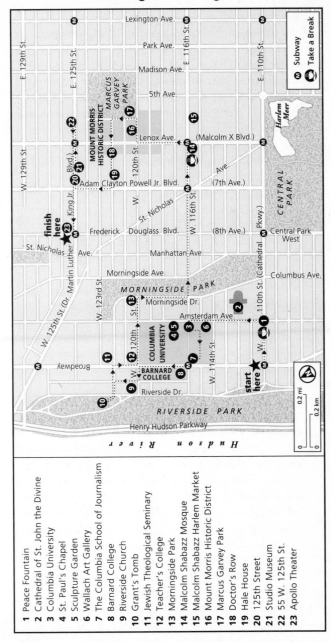

1 Peace Fountain
2 Cathedral of St. John the Divine
3 Columbia University
4 St. Paul's Chapel
5 Sculpture Garden
6 Wallach Art Gallery
7 The Columbia School of Journalism
8 Barnard College
9 Riverside Church
10 Grant's Tomb
11 Jewish Theological Seminary
12 Teacher's College
13 Morningside Park
14 Malcolm Shabazz Mosque
15 Malcolm Shabazz Harlem Market
16 Mount Morris Historic District
17 Marcus Garvey Park
18 Doctor's Row
19 Hale House
20 125th Street
21 Studio Museum
22 55 W. 125th St.
23 Apollo Theater

math on your fingers and wondering how NYC can have two cathedrals (St. Patrick's and St. John's) the answer is: Episcopalians. St. Paddy's is Catholic. St. John's has the better organ. Oh, and at 121,000 square feet, it's also the largest cathedral in the entire world (take *that,* Europe). At 146 feet wide, it's twice as broad as Westminster, the roof towers 177 feet above the ground, and its record-breaking length of 601 feet led to the quip that it would fit "two football fields, end to end, with room left for the football."

It actually wasn't supposed to be Gothic at all. The original architects drew up plans for a structure in the then-fashionable neo-Romanesque style, but between the 1887 purchase of the land, the 1892 ceremonial laying of the cornerstone, and 1911 when the choir was finally put in place, the old plan was chucked and Ralph Adams Cram came in with his own grandly Gothic ideas. The cathedral had its formal debutante party on November 30, 1941. One week later, the Japanese bombed Pearl Harbor and World War II put a halt to construction, which continued fitfully thereafter.

By 1967, the church started pouring funds into the community, and in 1978 they started raising the cash to continue the masonry. By 1992, with just 50 feet of the first tower completed, work halted, with most of the building funds going to preserving the raw, half-finished structure (though they did continue to carve the statuary around the main door, completed in 1997). Many despair that, in this secular age, it will never be completed, but as Ed Koch pointed out way back in 1979, "I am told that some of the great cathedrals took over 500 years to build. But I would like to remind you that we are only in our first hundred years." So New York's well ahead of the scheduling curve on cathedral building, although a damaging fire in the north transept in late 2001 has further pushed back the completion date.

The church houses some fantastic artistic treasures among its thematic chapels (dedicated to sports, poetry, patriotism, law, medicine, firefighting, conservation, and more). There are two sets of Renaissance-era tapestries. The Mortlake Tapestries in the chapels were woven in 1623 on English looms, but the design—the acts of the Apostles—

was actually a commission from Pope Leo X to Renaissance titan Raphael, who drew up the original sketches. The Barberini Tapestries are also from the 17th century, this time depicting scenes from the Life of Christ and woven in Cardinal Barberini's papal tapestry factory. Sadly, two of the tapestries were badly damaged in the 2001 fire.

The rose window, 50 feet across if it's an inch, is composed of 10,000 pieces of colored glass, and that Christ figure in the center is life-sized (assuming Jesus was tall for his era, at 5 ft., 7 in.). The 61 silver trumpets ranked below it belong to the Ernest M. Skinner organ, 8,035 pipes put together in 1910. The pipe chambers filled with soot during the fire, and the organ is currently awaiting restoration.

Head into the ambulatory (the hallway that wraps around the choir and back behind the altar) from the left aisle. The third chapel (St. Columba) and the fourth, or central chapel (St. Savior's) are both prefaced by arched statues carved by Gutzon Borglum, who did a pretty good job considering this is relatively teensy compared to the scale he was used to (he's the guy who used blasting caps to sculpt Mt. Rushmore's giant presidential noggins).

Inside the Savior's Chapel is a 600-pound bronze altarpiece coated in white gold leaf and depicting the *Life of Christ* (1990) finished by Keith Haring 1 month before he succumbed to AIDS. In the sixth chapel (St. Ambrose's) is a statue of St. Anthony by the Italian Renaissance master of glazed terra cottas, Luca della Robbia.

St. John the Divine is open Monday to Saturday 7am to 6pm, and Sunday 7am to 7pm. There are $5 tours ($4 for students and seniors) Tuesday to Saturday at 11am, Sunday at 1pm.

Exit the cathedral from the front door and continue north on Amsterdam Avenue. On your right as you continue walking is the expansive bulk of **St. Luke's Hospital,** bits of the original (1890s) Beaux Arts architecture by Ernest Flagg still visible amid the modern accretions. At 116th Street, turn left onto the campus of:

3. **Columbia University** (© 212/854-1754; www. columbia.edu), an illustrious member of the Ivy League. Columbia's profs and alums have earned 64 Nobel Prizes in various disciplines, and it, along with sister institution

Barnard College, has matriculated the likes of Enrico Fermi, Allen Ginsburg, Jack Kerouac (okay, so he dropped out), Art Garfunkel, Langston Hughes, Lauryn Hill (another dropout), Martha Stewart (hey, I only specified "famous"), and Paul Robeson, with a faculty ranging from John Dewey to Franz Boas. One past university president, Dwight D. Eisenhower, only left his tenure (1948–53) in order to pursue the White House.

Columbia's sprawling city campus—covering 7 blocks, from 114th to 120th streets, between Amsterdam and Broadway—is the world's largest collection of McKim, Mead, and White buildings. Charles Follen McKim designed the lot in Italianate style but on the plan of Athens's Agora, where strolling philosophers once taught young toga-clad apprentice thinkers. This wasn't the school's first home, however.

King George II granted New York City a royal charter for a school in 1754. At that time the college was called, naturally, "King's College." The school changed its name to "Columbia" in 1784, after the American Revolution. As King's College, the school matriculated the likes of Alexander Hamilton and John Jay, the first Supreme Court Chief Justice (they've since churned out six more), and in 1767 the very first medical doctors were granted degrees in America.

In 1814, the state gave the college a lot of useless, weed-ridden, rock-filled land way up north of the city, around Fifth Avenue in the unpopular zone between 47th and 51st streets. In 1857 the college moved uptown to a 49th Street address before making the final move here to Morningside Heights in 1897 to occupy the former site of an insane asylum. In the meantime, Columbia held on to that worthless plot of midtown land, leasing it out in 1928 to a developer named John D. Rockefeller Jr. In 1985, the university finally sold the land to its tenant, Rockefeller Center, for $400 million in the single biggest real estate deal in New York history.

From the group of eight young men first taught by Samuel Johnson in July 1754 in the schoolhouse at Trinity Church downtown, the school has grown to an enrollment of 23,813, of which only around 7,200 are undergrads—the bulk of enrollment is in the graduate and professional colleges of journalism, medicine, architecture, nursing, law, engineering, social work, and business. Of course the habit of teaching only "young men" took a while to kick—try 1983, when the first women were admitted, making Columbia the last Ivy League school to pull its head out of the sand on this issue by a good number of years.

The pedestrianized bit of 116th Street that you're walking on is called College Walk. Saunter up to its center; to your left (south), across a lawn below you, stretches the facade of Butler Hall, one of the largest libraries in America boasting more than 5 million volumes (there's a rare book and manuscript section up on the sixth floor that hosts regular exhibits). To your right, dominating the campus, is the impressive rotunda of **Low Memorial Library,** modeled vaguely after Rome's Pantheon and named to honor the father of one of Columbia's greatest presidents, Seth Low (the guy who moved the college up here before becoming an NYC mayor). Walk up the steps, around the right side of Low, and on your right you'll see:

4. **St. Paul's Chapel,** cute as a button and at least twice as majestic, a vaguely neo-Byzantine "churchlet" built of brick (laid in a quirky herringbone pattern) and bricklike tiles in the dome, all the brainchild of Howells & Stokes from 1904 to 1907. The chapel sponsors a free classical concert series Tuesdays at 6pm and Saturdays at 7 or 8pm (© **212/854-6242;** www.columbia.edu/cu/earl/music_ schedule.htm).

Upon exiting the chapel from the front door, turn left and then left again to walk down the chapel's right side, past a small grove of chestnut trees on your right where a cast of Rodin's *Thinker* ponders the passing students. Continue up a small pedestrian bridge into a neat little:

5. **Sculpture Garden** on a brick terrace suspended above Amsterdam Avenue. Among the modern works poised on pedestals are Henry Moore's globular 1967 *Three Way Piece: Points,* Gertrude Schweitzer's balancing act of bodies called *Flight* (1981), and a massive, typically lumpy Lipchitz work glowering atop the entrance to the modern

Law School called *Bellerophon Taming Pegasus*. It was
installed in 1977, is 30 by 28 feet, and weighs 23 tons
(looks it, too).

Double back over the pedestrian bridge and past the
chapel to turn right, past Avery Hall to Schermerhorn
Hall, which houses the:

6. **Wallach Art Gallery** (℃ 212/854-7288; www.columbia.
edu/cu/wallach), founded in 1986 and presenting a rotating series of exhibitions of contemporary art throughout
the academic year. It's open Wednesday to Saturday 1
to 5pm.

Exiting Schermerhorn, go back toward Avery Hall but
veer right, past the double-loop sculpture *Curl* (1968, by
Clement Meadmore), then left to walk down the far side
of Low and back onto College Walk. Turn right onto it;
then divert left to walk around to the entrance to:

7. **The Columbia School of Journalism** (℃ 212/854-
3828; www.jrn.columbia.edu), one of the top two journalism schools in the country (the other is in Columbia,
Missouri), founded in 1912 by publishing mogul Joseph
Pulitzer. The school is in charge of awarding the annual
prestigious Pulitzer Prize for journalism. A 1914 statue of
Thomas Jefferson by alumnus William Ordway Partridge
frowns from the top of the steps to the school.

Continue along College Walk to pop off campus onto
Broadway and turn right. On your left, you're passing the
closed campus of:

8. **Barnard College** (℃ 212/854-5262; www.barnard.
edu), a women's college and one of the prestigious "seven
sisters" schools. Columbia University's rather enlightened
10th president, Frederick Barnard, who spent his tenure
from 1864 to 1883 convincing the trustees to set up a
course for women, established Barnard. Of course, because
women weren't allowed on campus, and professors weren't
allowed to talk to them in any event, the course didn't really take off, but by 1889 they'd worked out the kinks by
founding a whole college just for the ladies across the street
and naming it Barnard after the crusading Columbia president. Though students at both Columbia and Barnard

can take classes at each other's schools, Barnard remains a separate and proud institution.

Turn left on 120th Street, then right on Claremont Avenue, passing the **Union Theological Seminary** (turning out liberal Protestant ministers since 1836), to the unassuming main entrance on your left into:

9. **Riverside Church** (© 212/870-6700; www.theriverside churchny.org), just about the grandest Baptist church I've ever seen, built with John D. Rockefeller, Jr.'s, money. Rockefeller was born a Baptist, but was a big believer in healing the rifts in Christianity, a philosophy called the Interfaith movement, and the church to this day remains as much community center as house of worship, and its Interfaith Center offices host Christians, Jews, and Muslims.

Though the structure bears a passing resemblance to the French cathedral at Chartres and is festooned with Gothic frippery, this one's all modern, sporting a skeleton of steel girders that lets its tower soar to an incredible 392 feet. It's a big church, too: 265 feet long and 100 feet wide, with seating for 2,500, but the overall effect is light and airy, with some stellar stained-glass windows, quality stone carvings, and one whopper of a sound system.

Riverside's famed carillon was first installed in 1925, its 53 bells making it the largest carillon in the nation. It kept that title (enlarged to 72 bells in 1931 with two more added in 1956) until 1960 when it slipped to second place (though it's still the heaviest set in the USA). It's played Sundays at 10:30am, and 12:30 and 3pm (sometimes 2:30pm). The church is open daily 9am to 5pm.

Continue north on Claremont Avenue, to 122nd Street, where you turn left to cross Riverside Drive and pay your respects at:

10. **Grant's Tomb** (© 212/666-1640; www.nps.gov/gegr). You'll never guess who's buried here! (Actually, Grant's wife is also interred here, so a lot of people get the answer to that famed nonriddle only half right.) The tomb of the only president buried in NYC is as bullet-headed as the man it honors, a giant round-peg-in-a-square-hole game with a colonnaded rotunda perched atop a square

Classical temple, all topped off at 150 feet by a flattened cone for a roof. It's the largest tomb in America.

The 8,000 tons of marble are meant to resemble the Mausoleum at Halicarnassus. Inside, the associations continue with a design modeled after Napoleon's tomb in Paris, the white Carrara marble brightened with mosaics depicting the high points of Grant's military career, including the Surrender of Robert E. Lee at Appomattox (it's the one in which the two generals seem to be shaking hands amiably).

The hero of the Civil War and post-bellum President was still a very popular guy by the time he died in 1885, and 90,000 people contributed the $600,000 (and that's in 1890s dollars) to build this tomb. Ulysses and his wife, Julia Dent, are buried in the basement tomb. Above the entrance are Grant's famous words—all the more moving coming from a man of war—"Let us have peace." The tomb is open 9am to 5pm, with tours hourly until 4pm.

Cross back across Riverside Drive and down 122nd Street to Broadway. Across at the northeast corner (at no. 3080), you'll see the:

11. **Jewish Theological Seminary** (✆ 212/678-8000; www.jtsa.edu). A neo-Georgian building houses this seminary, founded in the rather enlightened year of 1886 to train up passels of American rabbis. The library of 300,000 volumes comprises the largest collection of Judaica in the Western Hemisphere.

Turn right down Broadway. Between 121st and 120th streets, you'll pass the facade of the:

12. **Teacher's College** (✆ 212/678-3000; www.tc. columbia.edu). In 1889, with all the future religious and secular leaders graduating from Columbia and neighboring seminaries, Nicholas Murray Butler decided New York could do with some quality educators to do the teaching. So he took the Kitchen Garden Club based at St-Mark's-in-the-Bowery (which was busy mucking about the public school system with a wonderfully ill-conceived program to train working-class girls on how to keep, if you'll pardon the expression, better homes and gardens), attached it to Columbia, and slowly evolved the operation into one of the nation's most progressive educational

think-tanks, producing such luminaries as John Dewey.

Turn right on 120th Street to walk down the long side of the college all the way to Morningside Drive and:

13. **Morningside Park** (© 212/937-3883; www.morning sidepark.org). This is not so much a park by design as by force of nature: It's the schist cliff that separates lofty Morningside Heights from the lowlands of Harlem, part of the ridge of solid rock that rides along the spine of Manhattan island. Even New Yorkers didn't know how to make good real estate use of a cliff back in the middle of the 19th century, so master landscapists Frederick Law Olmsted and Calvert Vaux, of Central Park fame, were called in to beautify this strip of schist and trees.

The two loved the views from this natural balcony, and laid out their plans to make best use of it, but a guy named Jacob Mould butted in, started building bastions of masonry against the cliff, and threatened to ruin the whole setting. Luckily, after he kicked off, the Dream Team of park planners were brought back, and Vaux started doing what he could with what was left, planting small gardens, leaving craggy rock faces bare, fitting in stands of trees, and lacing it with a zigzag of pathways that lets you gently waft your way down from the Heights into Harlem.

Before plunging in, turn right down Morningside Drive to skirt the park for a bit, enjoying the sweeping views across Harlem, which you're about to plunge into. At 116th Street—where on the right at no. 60 you'll see the lovely 1912 McKim, Mead, and White–designed house of Columbia University's president—turn into the park itself and pick a path down the bluff to get to the Harlem side of 116th Street.

The change in neighborhoods is dramatic, from elegant academia to dingy-but-vibrant urban. Take a few blocks to adjust as you continue east on 116th Street. Just before Lenox Avenue at no. 113, you'll find one of the best purveyors of soul food in New York.

Take a Break Amy Ruth's (© 212/280-8779). Growing up, owner Carl Redding and his siblings spent summers on the farm in Alabama. While his brothers did farm chores, Carl stuck by the side of his grandmother, Amy Ruth, learning timeless soul-food recipes from the world's leading expert: a black, Southern, country grandma.

If you try nothing else, make sure someone orders their signature dish of fried chicken and waffles. Oh, and the bourbon-glazed Virginia ham. But then you also can't miss the smothered pork chops. And what about the fried catfish with sweet-potato fries you can get on Fridays? Look, either bring a lot of friends or, better yet, make plans to come back a few times so you can work your way through the menu properly.

Amy Ruth's is open Sunday through Thursday 7:30am to 11pm, staying open 24 hours Friday and Saturday nights, and the upstairs back room hosts a variety of events, including comedy performances, concerts, open-mic nights, and more.

Across the street, at the southwest corner of the intersection of 116th Street and Lenox Avenue, sit the boxy yellow walls of the:

14. **Masjid Malcolm Shabazz Mosque** (✆ 212/662-2200), a giant, green onion dome perched atop a squat shape that harks back to its origins as the Lenox Casino. Elijah Muhammad turned it into the Temple of Islam in 1965, and Malcolm X was a resident preacher until his break with the movement.

Cross Lenox Avenue and walk down the south side of 116th Street half a block to the:

15. **Malcolm Shabazz Harlem Market** (✆ 212/987-8131), a colorful outdoor bazaar of tiny shops and stalls hawking West African crafts and Harlem souvenirs.

Double back to Lenox Avenue and turn right (north) up it, past (at no. 130) the recently finished (it opened in 2000) *The Renaissance,* a low-income co-op of 241 apartments, with parking, ringed on the ground level by 60,000 square feet of retail space, all part of the neighborhood's recent revival efforts. At 120th Street, where the **Mount Olivet Baptist Church** (built in 1907 as a Jewish Temple) rises on the corner, turn right to enter the core of the:

16. **Mount Morris Historic District,** a clutch of 19th-century brownstones between 119th and 123rd and one of

the first New York neighborhoods to be declared a Historic District (in 1971). The area is slowly being rehabilitated and renovated to its former glory. The street spills into the southwest corner of:

17. **Marcus Garvey Park** ((C) **212/860-1373;** http://itsmy park.org/brochures/marcus_garvey.html). This gnarly outcropping of Manhattan mica-schist was just too darn hard to level for development, plus it made a handy lookout point. Were you to scrape away Manhattan's skyscrapers and other buildings, the pinnacle of this park would be one of the highest points on the island, used as a lookout point by everyone from Indian tribes to the 19th-century fire department. In fact, their iron watchtower from 1865 still perches atop the highest point, 10,000-pound bell and all, the only such tower to remain in the city (great views from the top).

The park was renamed in 1973 to honor the famed local black activist Marcus Garvey.

Walk north along Mount Morris Park West and turn left at 122nd Street. Cross Lenox Avenue and continue west on 122nd Street onto:

18. **Doctor's Row,** a lovely stretch of row homes (though a few brownstones are still boarded up) from the late 1800s. The best are nos. 133 to 143, a lovely row of ornate brick homes built by Francis H. Kimball from 1885 to 1887, the best Queen Anne–style homes surviving in all of Manhattan, a brick festival of gables, dormers, decoration, and stained glass.

At the far end of the block on the south side, at no. 152–154, is the:

19. **Hale House** ((C) **212/663-0700;** www.halehouse.org), established in 1969 by Mother Clara Hale to provide aid for drug-addicted (and now also HIV-infected) infants and their mothers. In 1996, 4 years after Hale's death, sculptor Robert Berks memorialized Mother Hale in a sculpture surrounded by etched bronze plaques of children.

Turn right up Adam Clayton Powell Jr. Boulevard to head north. Turn right onto:

20. **125th Street,** the bustling, vibrant heart of the new Harlem Renaissance, the epicenter of a development boom in the past few years. These 3 blocks are home to the Studio Museum, the Apollo Theater, the National Black Theatre, the Harlem USA shopping complex, and a multiplex cinema owned by Magic Johnson. Is it any wonder Bill Clinton chose this hip-hop-happening spot for his post-presidential offices in New York?

    Turn right and walk down about a quarter of the block to the:

21. **Studio Museum,** 144 W. 125th St. (© **212/864-4500; www.studiomuseum.org**), a vast gallery space that since 1968 has been devoted to collecting, preserving, and promoting contemporary African-American art, from Harlem, across the USA, and around the world. The bulk of its display space is taken up with rotating exhibits, though they also have a fine and growing collection. The gift shop is also quite excellent. The gallery hours are Sunday and Wednesday to Friday noon to 6pm, Saturday 10am to 6pm. Admission is $5, but free on the first Saturday of the month.

    Continue toward the end of the block at Lenox Avenue. Across the street, along with a Chase bank, you'll see the 14-story office building of:

22. **55 W. 125th St.,** which became famous in 2001 when a new resident moved in and the top floor became the offices of former president Bill Clinton. After flirting with pricey Midtown digs, Clinton chose to put his money where his mouth was and move into the heart of Harlem, one of the Federal Empowerment Zones (a program that provides federal aid for economically depressed areas) that he himself created as president.

    After all, Toni Morrison once called him "our first black president," pointing out the similarities between his upbringing (raised by a single mother, as a Baptist, on Southern soul food and at the edge of poverty) and the experience of many in the black community. Not everyone buys that, but the fact is, the man does seem to be fitting in nicely enough.

    Turn around to double back up 125th Street, cross Adam Clayton Powell Jr. Boulevard, cross to the north side of the street, and finish this tour with perhaps the best-known stop in Harlem. Folks, it's show time at the:

23. **Apollo Theater,** 253 W. 125th St. (📞 **212/531-5300;** www.apollotheater.com). The Apollo, like most old Harlem entertainment venues, including the vanished Cotton Club, began life as a burlesque house open to whites only: Hurtig and Seamon's Music Hall, established in 1913. But in 1934, new owners Frank Schiffman and Leo Brecher threw open the doors to the local black community and a legend was born.

How do you even begin to pare down the list of musicians and entertainers who have graced the Apollo's stage? Bessie Smith, Count Basie, Billie Holiday, Louis Armstrong, Dizzy Gillespie, Duke Ellington, Charlie "Bird" Parker, Nat "King" Cole, Marvin Gaye, Bo Diddley, Gladys Knight (I assume with the Pips in tow), Aretha Franklin, Stevie Wonder, George Clinton, B. B. King, Prince . . . Look, just go to the R&B section of your local record store and read off the names; it might be quicker. When the Beatles invaded America in 1964, there was only one thing they wanted to see in New York City: the Apollo Theater. And I haven't even started in on the entertainers who didn't sing their way to fame (Redd Foxx, Whoopi Goldberg, Bill Cosby . . .).

The famous, and famously tough, Amateur Night at the Apollo (Wed at 7:30pm; tickets start at $16) has kick-started many careers, among them Ella Fitzgerald, James Brown, Lauryn Hill, Sarah Vaughn, and a little Motown group called the Jackson 5.

When a show is not on, you often can't enter the theater, but from the doorway you can see the stump of the Tree of Hope, which once grew outside the Lafayette Theater. Performers would kiss that tree (and, later, its replacement donated by Mr. Bojangles himself, the dancer Bill Robinson), and latter-day hopefuls always touch it for good luck before taking the stage.

Our walk officially ends here. Harlem continues all the way to 168th Street, but truth be told, the rest of Harlem doesn't lend itself well to walking. It tends to have points of touristic interest only every 10 blocks or so, with the interim spaces often depressed areas. However, I highly recommend you hop on the subway here at 125th Street and ride it one stop north to 135th Street to fit in a few more must-see Harlem stops.

Here you can visit a branch of the New York Public Library that has become the excellent **Schomburg Center for Research in Black Culture** (© 212/491-2200; www.nypl.org/research/sc) at 515 Lenox Ave. The **Abyssinian Baptist Church** (© 212/862-7474; www.abyssinian.org) on 138th Street is famous for its Sunday-morning gospel service and as the place where Adam Clayton Powell, Jr. got his start, preaching in the pulpit here from 1938 before moving on to organize black boycotts of exclusionary businesses, hold a post on the city council, and eventually take a seat in the U.S. Congress.

Make sure you also stroll down 139th Street between Frederick Douglass Boulevard and Adam Clayton Powell Jr. Boulevard, a lovely stretch of row houses in dark brick Italianate style on the north side and in yellow brick colonial revival style on the south side. It's officially part of the St. Nicholas Historic District, but is much better known as **Striver's Row** after the upwardly mobile blacks and others who once made these blocks their home, including Memphis-born father of the blues W. C. Handy (232 W. 139th St.) and—appropriately enough, given the gorgeous surroundings—Vertner Tandy, the first black architect registered in New York State (221 W. 139th St.).

As long as you're up here, you can fit in some more soul food at **Miss Maude's Spoonbread Too** (© 212/690-3100; www.spoonbreadinc.com) at 547 Lenox Ave. between 137th and 138th streets. Every meal begins with a basket of warm cornbread brought to your table, and the kitchen serves up a full menu of Southern standards: fried chicken, Carolina-style barbecued ribs, golden fried shrimp, smothered pork chops, Louisiana catfish, collard greens, potato salad, candied yams, banana pudding, peach cobbler, sweet-potato pie . . . Mmm . . . soul food.

Essentials

This chapter includes all the information you'll need to get your bearings in New York City.

ORIENTATION

Laid out on a grid system (except for the Village), Manhattan is the easiest of the boroughs to negotiate. Avenues run north (uptown) and south (downtown), and the streets run east to west (crosstown). Broadway runs southeast to northwest diagonally across the grid.

Both avenues and streets are numbered consecutively: Streets are numbered from south to north (1st St. is downtown just above Houston St.), and avenues are numbered from east to west (with Fifth Ave. in the center), from First Avenue near the East River to Twelfth Avenue near the Hudson River. The only major exceptions are the three named avenues on the East Side: Madison (east of Fifth Ave.), Park (which would be Fourth Ave.), and Lexington (west of Third Ave.). Sixth Avenue is also now called the Avenue of the Americas, though die-hard New Yorkers refuse to call it that.

Fifth Avenue is the dividing line between the East Side and the West Side, so an address on West 43rd Street will be west of Fifth Avenue. All east-west street addresses are counted from Fifth Avenue, starting at no. 1 on either side of Fifth and increasing in number as they move away from Fifth Avenue. In other words, at the corner of Fifth Avenue and 35th Street, you'll find 1 E. 35th St. to the east and 1 W. 35th St. to the west. Street addresses increase by about 50 per block starting at Fifth Avenue. For example, nos. 1 to 50 East are just about between Fifth and Madison avenues, while nos. 1 to 50 West are just about between Fifth and Sixth avenues. Therefore 28 W. 23rd St. is a short walk west of Fifth Avenue; 325 E. 35th St. would be a few blocks east of Fifth.

A few avenues acquire new names as they move uptown: Eighth Avenue becomes Central Park West above 59th Street, Ninth Avenue becomes Columbus Avenue above 69th Street, and Tenth Avenue becomes Amsterdam above 72nd Street. **Beware:** Avenue addresses are irregular. For example, 994 Second Ave. is at East 51st Street, but so is 320 Park Ave. Thus, it's important to know a building's cross street to find it easily.

The handy grid pattern wasn't imposed on the older downtown sections below 14th Street on the West Side or below Houston Street on the East Side. Downtown streets have names rather than numbers, and in the oldest sections, roads follow the old street plans of "Nieuw Amsterdam" and the surrounding small villages and farms that long ago joined together to become New York City.

VISITOR INFORMATION

Before You Go

For information before you leave home, a great source is **NYC & Company,** the organization that fronts the New York Convention & Visitors Bureau (NYCVB), 810 Seventh Ave., New York, NY 10019. You can call ✆ **800/NYC-VISIT** or 212/397-8222 to order the **Official NYC Visitor Kit,** which contains the *Official NYC Guide* detailing hotels, restaurants, theaters, attractions, events, and more; a foldout map; a decent newsletter on the latest goings-on in the city; and brochures on attractions and services. It costs $5.95 to receive the packet (payable by credit card) in 7 to 10 days, $9.95 for rush delivery (3–4 business days) or international orders. (**Note:** We have received complaints that packages don't always strictly adhere to these time frames.)

You can also find a wealth of free information on the bureau's website, **www.nycvisit.com.** To speak with a travel counselor who can answer specific questions, call ✆ **212/484-1222,** which is staffed daily weekdays from 8:30am to 6pm

Eastern Standard Time, weekends from 9am to 5pm Eastern Standard Time.

For British visitors, the **NYCVB Visitor Information Center** is at 36 Southwark Bridge Rd., London SE1 9EU (℡ **020/7202 6368**). You can order the Official NYC Visitor Kit by sending an A5-size self-addressed envelope and 72p postage to the above address.

When You Arrive

The **Times Square Visitors Center,** 1560 Broadway, between 46th and 47th streets (where Broadway meets Seventh Ave.), across from the TKTS booth on the east side of the street (℡ **212/768-1560;** www.timessquarenyc.org), is the city's top info stop. This pleasant and attractive center features a helpful info desk offering loads of citywide information. There's also a tour desk selling tickets for Gray Line bus tours and Circle Line boat tours; a Metropolitan Transportation Authority (MTA) desk staffed to sell MetroCard fare cards, provide public transit maps, and answer all of your questions on the transit system; a Broadway Ticket Center providing show information and selling full-price show tickets; ATMs and currency-exchange machines; and computer terminals with free Internet access courtesy of Yahoo! It's open daily from 8am to 8pm.

The New York Convention and Visitors Bureau runs the **NYCVB Visitor Information Center** at 810 Seventh Ave., between 52nd and 53rd streets. In addition to loads of information on citywide attractions and a multilingual counselor on hand to answer questions, the center also has interactive terminals that provide free touch-screen access to visitor information via Citysearch and sells advance tickets to major attractions, which can save you from standing in long ticket lines once you arrive. There's also an ATM, a gift shop, and phones that connect you directly with American Express card member services. The center is open Monday through Friday from 8:30am to 6pm, Saturday and Sunday from 8:30am to 5pm. For over-the-phone assistance, call ℡ **212/484-1222.**

For comprehensive listings of films, concerts, performances, sporting events, museum and gallery exhibits, street fairs, and special events, the following are your best bets:

• The *New York Times* (**www.nytimes.com** or www.ny today.com) features terrific arts and entertainment coverage, particularly in the two-part Friday "Weekend" section and the Sunday "Arts & Leisure" section. Both days boast full guides to the latest happenings in Broadway and Off-Broadway theater, classical music, dance, pop and jazz, film, and the art world. Friday is particularly good for cabaret, family fun, and general-interest recreational and sightseeing events.

- *Time Out New York* (**www.timeoutny.com**) is a comprehensive weekly magazine. Attractive, well organized, and easy to use, it also tends to be heavy on hype. *TONY* covers all categories, from live music, theater, and clubs (gay and straight) to museum shows, dance events, book and poetry readings, and kids' stuff. The regular "Check Out" section will fill you in on upcoming sample and closeout sales, crafts and antiques shows, and other shopping-related scoops. A new issue hits newsstands every Thursday.

- The free weekly *Village Voice* (**www.villagevoice.com**), the city's legendary alterna-paper, is available late Tuesday downtown and early Wednesday in the rest of the city. From classical music to clubs, the arts and entertainment coverage couldn't be more extensive, and just about every live music venue advertises its shows here.

GETTING AROUND

By Subway

Run by the **Metropolitan Transportation Authority (MTA),** the much-maligned subway system is actually the fastest way to travel around New York, especially during rush hours. Some 3.5 million people a day seem to agree, as it's their primary mode of transportation. The subway is quick, inexpensive, relatively safe, and pretty efficient, as well as being a genuine New York experience.

The subway runs 24 hours a day, 7 days a week. The rush-hour crushes are roughly from 8 to 9:30am and from 5 to 6:30pm on weekdays; the rest of the time the trains are relatively uncrowded.

For transit information, call the Metropolitan Transportation Authority's **MTA/New York City Transit's Travel Information Center** at © 718/330-1234. For online information that's always up-to-the-minute, visit **www.mta.nyc.ny.us**.

Paying Your Way The subway fare is $2 (half price for seniors and those with disabilities), and children under 44 inches tall ride free (up to three per adult).

The iconic token has been phased out, rendered obsolete by the **MetroCard,** a magnetically encoded card that debits the fare when swiped through the turnstile (or the fare box on any city bus). Once you're in the system, you can transfer freely to any subway line that you can reach without exiting your station. MetroCards also allow you **free transfers** between the bus and subway within a 2-hour period.

MetroCards can be purchased from each station's staffed token booth, where you can only pay with cash; at the ATM-style vending machines in just about every subway station in the city, which accept cash, credit cards, and debit cards; from a MetroCard merchant, such as most Rite Aid drugstores or Hudson News at Penn Station and Grand Central Terminal; or at the MTA information desk at the Times Square Visitor Center, 1560 Broadway, between 46th and 47th streets.

MetroCards come in a few different configurations:

Pay-Per-Ride MetroCards, which can be used for up to four people by swiping up to four times (bring the whole family). You can put any amount from $4 (two rides) to $80 on your card. Every time you put $10 on your Pay-Per-Ride MetroCard, it's automatically credited 20%—that's one free ride for every $10. You can refill your Pay-Per-Ride card at any time until the expiration date on the card, usually about a year from the date of purchase, at any subway station.

Unlimited-Ride MetroCards, which can't be used for more than one person at a time or more frequently than 18-minute intervals, are available in four values: the **daily Fun Pass,** which allows you a day's worth of unlimited subway and bus rides for $7 (reduced-fare discounts not available); the **7-Day MetroCard,** for $24; and the **30-Day MetroCard,** for $76, which are insured against loss if purchased with plastic. Note that Fun Passes cannot be purchased at token booths—you can buy them only at a MetroCard vending machine; from a MetroCard merchant; at the MTA information desk at the Times Square Visitor Center; or from www.mta.nyc.ny.us/metrocard. Unlimited-Ride MetroCards go into effect not at the time you buy them but the first time you use them—so if you buy a card on Monday and don't begin to use it until

Wednesday, Wednesday is when the clock starts ticking on your MetroCard. A Fun Pass is good from the first time you use it until 3am the next day, while 7- and 30-day MetroCards run out at midnight on the last day. These MetroCards cannot be refilled; throw them out once they've been used up and buy a new one.

If you're not sure how much money you have left on your MetroCard, or what day it expires, use the station's MetroCard Reader, usually located near the station entrance or the token booth (on buses, the fare box will also provide you with this information).

To locate the nearest MetroCard merchant, or for any other MetroCard questions, call © **800/METROCARD** or 212/METROCARD (212/638-7622) Monday through Friday between 7am and 11pm, Saturday and Sunday from 9am to 5pm. Or go online to **www.mta.nyc.ny.us/metrocard**, which can give you a full rundown of MetroCard merchants in the tri-state area.

See the full-color subway map on the back inside cover of this book to figure out your route.

By Bus

Less expensive than taxis and more pleasant than subways (they provide a mobile sightseeing window on Manhattan), MTA buses are a good transportation option. Their very big drawback: They can get stuck in traffic, sometimes making it quicker to walk. They also stop every couple of blocks, rather than the 8 or 9 blocks that local subways traverse between stops. So for long distances, the subway is your best bet; but for short distances or traveling crosstown, try the bus.

Paying Your Way   Like the subway fare, **bus fare** is $2, half price for seniors and riders with disabilities, free for children under 44 inches (up to three per adult). The fare is payable with a **MetroCard** or **exact change.** Bus drivers don't make change, and fare boxes don't accept dollar bills or pennies. You can't purchase MetroCards or tokens on the bus, so you'll have to have them before you board; for details on where to get them, see "Paying Your Way" under "By Subway," above.

If you pay with a MetroCard, you can transfer to another bus or to the subway for free within 2 hours. If you use coins, you must request a **free transfer** slip that allows you to change to an intersecting bus route only (legal transfer points are listed on the transfer paper) within 1 hour of issue. Transfer slips cannot be used to enter the subway.

Using The System

You can't flag down a city bus—you have to meet it at a bus stop. **Bus stops** are located every 2 or 3 blocks on the right-side corner of the street (facing the direction of traffic flow). They're marked by a curb painted yellow and a blue-and-white sign with a bus emblem and the route number or numbers. Guide-A-Ride boxes at most stops display a route map and a hysterically optimistic schedule.

Almost every major avenue has its own **bus route.** They run either north or south: downtown on Fifth, uptown on Madison, downtown on Lexington, uptown on Third, and so on. There are **crosstown buses** at strategic locations all around town: 8th Street (eastbound); 9th (westbound); 14th, 23rd, 34th, and 42nd (east- and westbound); 49th (eastbound); 50th (westbound); 57th (east- and westbound); 65th (eastbound across the West Side, through the park, and then north on Madison, continuing east on 68th to York Ave.); 67th (westbound on the East Side to Fifth Ave. and then south on Fifth, continuing west on 66th St. through the park and across the West Side to West End Ave.); and 79th, 86th, 96th, 116th, and 125th (east- and westbound).

Most routes operate 24 hours a day, but service is infrequent at night. During rush hour, main routes have "limited" buses, identifiable by the red card in the front window; they stop only at major cross streets.

To make sure the bus you're boarding goes where you're going, check the maps on the sign that's at every bus stop, get your hands on a route and subway map, or just ask.

Signal for a stop by pressing the tape strip above and beside the windows and along the metal straps, about 2 blocks before you want to stop. Exit through the pneumatic back doors (not the front door) by pushing on the yellow tape strip; the doors open automatically. Most city buses are equipped with wheelchair lifts, making buses the preferable mode of public transportation for wheelchair-bound travelers. Buses also "kneel," lowering down to the curb to make boarding easier.

Index

FROMMER'S® DAY BY DAY GUIDES

Amsterdam	London	Rome
Chicago	New York City	San Francisco
Florence & Tuscany	Paris	Venice

FROMMER'S® NATIONAL PARK GUIDES

Algonquin Provincial Park	National Parks of the American West	Yosemite and Sequoia & Kings
Banff & Jasper	Rocky Mountain	Canyon
Grand Canyon	Yellowstone & Grand Teton	Zion & Bryce Canyon

FROMMER'S® MEMORABLE WALKS

Chicago	New York	Rome
London	Paris	San Francisco

FROMMER'S® WITH KIDS GUIDES

Chicago	National Parks	Toronto
Hawaii	New York City	Walt Disney World® & Orlando
Las Vegas	San Francisco	Washington, D.C.
London		

SUZY GERSHMAN'S BORN TO SHOP GUIDES

Born to Shop: France	Born to Shop: Italy	Born to Shop: New York
Born to Shop: Hong Kong, Shanghai	Born to Shop: London	Born to Shop: Paris
& Beijing		

FROMMER'S® IRREVERENT GUIDES

Amsterdam	Los Angeles	Rome
Boston	Manhattan	San Francisco
Chicago	New Orleans	Walt Disney World®
Las Vegas	Paris	Washington, D.C.
London		

FROMMER'S® BEST-LOVED DRIVING TOURS

Austria	Germany	Northern Italy
Britain	Ireland	Scotland
California	Italy	Spain
France	New England	Tuscany & Umbria

THE UNOFFICIAL GUIDES®

Adventure Travel in Alaska	Hawaii	Paris
Beyond Disney	Ireland	San Francisco
California with Kids	Las Vegas	South Florida including Miami &
Central Italy	London	the Keys
Chicago	Maui	Walt Disney World®
Cruises	Mexico's Best Beach Resorts	Walt Disney World® for
Disneyland®	Mini Las Vegas	Grown-ups
England	Mini Mickey	Walt Disney World® with Kids
Florida	New Orleans	Washington, D.C.
Florida with Kids	New York City	

SPECIAL-INTEREST TITLES

Athens Past & Present	Frommer's Exploring America by RV
Cities Ranked & Rated	Frommer's NYC Free & Dirt Cheap
Frommer's Best Day Trips from London	Frommer's Road Atlas Europe
Frommer's Best RV & Tent Campgrounds	Frommer's Road Atlas Ireland
in the U.S.A.	Retirement Places Rated

FROMMER'S® PHRASEFINDER DICTIONARY GUIDES

French	Italian	Spanish